The Beginner's Observing Guide

*An Introduction
to the Night Sky
for the Novice Stargazer*

The Beginner's Observing Guide

*An Introduction
to the Night Sky
for the Novice Stargazer*

Revised, Fifth Edition
Leo Enright

with Foreword by David H. Levy

The Royal Astronomical Society of Canada
136 Dupont Street, Toronto ON M5R 1V2

An Invitation to Membership in
The Royal Astronomical Society of Canada

The Royal Astronomical Society of Canada is the oldest and largest association of astronomers in Canada. Its history goes back to the middle of the nineteenth century. The Society was incorporated in 1890 and received its Royal Charter in 1903. Its membership includes professional astronomers, but it is largely an amateur organization with members of all ages, from all walks of life, and also from many countries around the world. In Canada there are 27 branches or "Centres of the Society" in the major cities across the country. Current membership is more than 4500. The common bond among the members is an interest in and a desire to promote the study of astronomy and the related sciences.

Serious users of this observing guide would benefit from membership in the Society. Members receive the publications of the Society and are entitled to other benefits. Information about joining the Society may be obtained from the secretary of the nearest Centre or from the National Office of the Society. A special discount rate is offered to youth members. More information about the Society, including the addresses of all of the 27 Centres, is given in Chapter 23 of this book (pages 163 - 164). The address of the National Office of the Society, from which this and other publications may be ordered, is 136 Dupont Street, Toronto ON Canada M5R 1V2.

Canadian Cataloguing in Publication Data

The National Library of Canada has catalogued this publication as follows:

The Beginner's observing guide.

Enright, Leo, 1943-
"An introduction to the night sky for the novice stargazer."
ISSN 1188-1798
ISBN 0-9689141-5-2 (revised, 5th edition)

  I. Enright, Leo II. Royal Astronomical Society of Canada

QB63.B42 1992-   520   C92-031664-6

Acknowledgements

The idea of producing an introductory guide to the night sky began to be considered by the Royal Astronomical Society of Canada in about 1982. Eventually the National Council of the Society established what was known as "The Mini-Handbook Committee," and more serious discussions ensued about undertaking a new Society publication. At the time of the 1990 General Assembly, I was asked to be in charge of the project. Since then four previous editions have appeared, the most recent in 1999.

I want to thank the members of committees, such as the Publications Committee, who supported the previous editions, in particular Dr. John Percy, who endorsed the concept for many years before it was realized. I am grateful to the chairman, Mr. Peter Jedicke, and the other members of the current Publications Committee, who show support for this worthwhile project. The star maps which are an important part of this book are adapted from those designed and drafted by Dr. Roy Bishop, Past-President of the Society and a former editor of the *Observer's Handbook*. My diagrams showing four variable stars, new to this edition, are based on the corresponding star maps, which have appeared in the *Observer's Handbook* over the past forty years, and which were originally designed by the A.A.V.S.O. Dr. David Levy, a long-time friend and someone who is known throughout the astronomical world for both his writing and his 21 comet discoveries, contributed to the section on meteor showers. Helpful suggestions are acknowledged from Mr. Dieter Brueckner of the Kingston Centre and Mr. David Garner of the Kitchener-Waterloo Centre. In addition, numerous ideas from many readers have been gratefully received, and, in most cases, have been incorporated. Appreciation is extended, also, to my many Astronomy classes at Algonquin College in Perth, Ontario, particularly those classes of the past two years whose students, while using the previous edition of *The Beginner's Observing Guide* as their primary text, "field tested" most of the materials that are new to this edition.

I appreciate the encouragement and assistance of the Society's National President, Dr. Rajiv Gupta, and the support of the National Council. A particular debt of gratitude goes to Mr. Mark Howes for his untiring, and extremely successful, efforts at enhancing the publication's graphics, and to Ms. Valerie Jarus at the School of Policy Studies, Queen's University, for countless hours spent, in many ways, in assisting the publication of this book.

June Solstice, 2003   *Leo Enright*
Oso Observatory,
Box 196, Sharbot Lake, ON K0H 2P0

Introduction

This book is intended as an introduction to the night sky and to the joy of observing it carefully.

It is for those who have no previous background in astronomy, and may be totally unacquainted with any of the stars and constellations that fill our nighttime sky. Perhaps it will be especially useful for young people who, at a summer camp or on a family holiday, are taking serious note of the night sky for the first time.

At most libraries and book stores the novice observer can find several introductory guides to astronomy, many of them more thorough in their approach than this one. They can be used profitably, and perhaps one of them should be used, as a resource and further reference, if the reader thinks it is necessary to have such additional assistance. The best resource books and guides are listed in Chapter 23, beginning on page 165.

What is presented here are simple guidelines and observing exercises to be used in conjunction with the star maps that form the core of the text. If used as suggested, these guidelines will assist the novice observer in becoming familiar with the night sky, and they will do it in a way that avoids technical jargon and mathematical detail.

Enjoy the adventure!

Foreword

A Key to the Heavens

You hold in your hands a key to a house full of wonders, a ticket to a vast and exciting journey. If you are just beginning to explore the sky, I envy you. Back on September 1, 1960, I started that same journey with Echo, a diminutive 3 ½ inch (90 mm) diameter reflector. I had no guide like this book, just the unopened pages of the sky above me. I pointed the telescope to the brightest thing, and when I focussed the eyepiece, I found Jupiter. I even saw two dark bands across its face, and a line of Moons nearby. That was my first night of discovery, and I haven't stopped since.

As you begin your own journey into the night, however, you have Leo Enright's *Beginner's Observing Guide*, in this latest edition, to help find your way. You will explore the basic motions of the sky caused because the Earth rotates, and revolves along with the other planets. You will understand how to find directions using the stars. You will appreciate the world of "shooting stars," really just specks of dust heated to incandescence and called "meteors." You will learn to use binoculars and a telescope to expand your journey even further. You will enjoy stars that change their brightness. And finally, what I think is the most important part of all, you will learn to record what you see. If I didn't do that, I would never remember what night, month, or year I really did look through Echo for the first time, nor would I remember when I saw my first meteor shower, or discovered my first comet.

Your guide on this journey is Leo Enright, one of the most enthusiastic observers I have ever met. For many years he taught at Sharbot Lake High School north of Kingston. There he developed his penchant for detail and accuracy that is a hallmark of this book, and near there he continues to observe under the pristine, dark night skies of his Oso Observatory. As you go through these pages, it will be as though Leo is taking you on a personal tour of the sky he loves so much.

I hope you enjoy this book, and especially the night sky that is its subject. May your journey be a happy one.

Summer Solstice (June 21), 2003   *David H. Levy*

Cover Photo

The cover photograph of Comet Hyakutake was taken by the author on the night of Saturday-Sunday, March 23-24, 1996. It was a 10-minute exposure beginning at 5:23:30 UT on March 24, using a 135 mm f/2.5 camera lens guided on the telescope at Oso Observatory using Kodak Ektachrome 1600 Professional film commercially processed in the usual manner.

"After I returned home from the day-long March National Council Meeting in Toronto, I was eager to open the roof of my observatory because, with Moonset only a short while away, I would soon be able to appreciate the full impact of a very bright comet under dark, rural skies. Comet Hyakutake, discovered just two months previously, had brightened amazingly as it raced through the inner Solar System, and within the next day or so, it would, except for Comet Lexell, be closer to Earth than any comet in recorded history. (At 0h UT on March 25, less than 24 hours hence, it would be 0.102 AU, or only 15 million kilometres, from our planet!) For almost three hours, from 4:20 to 7:10 UT, I observed a number of objects, but I was distracted from everything else by the overwhelming presence above me of something totally awesome. At magnitude 0, the coma was large and pure white in colour, and the incredible tail, stretching many degrees to the south, had hints of twisting blue strings, as the photograph shows. Faint patterns were discernible in a tail that stretched down past the star Epsilon Virginis, 35 degrees to the south. For a brief while, the inner core of the ion tail passed over the bright star Gamma Bootis, as the photo shows, but within 20 to 30 minutes, I could detect that the tail had moved past that star. Before my eyes, the comet was clearly moving northward, as the Earth's rotation carried it closer to the zenith. My thought was that, if only I could stretch a little higher than the observatory's roof, I could touch this amazing object. Trying not to be too distracted from the photographic task at hand, I kept coming back to thoughts of a pagan classical writer who had used a metaphor to described a bright comet: 'It was the flaming sword of an avenging god.' I now understood what he had meant."

Table of Contents

A Centenary of our Society's Name

Just days before "going to press" with this fifth edition of *The Beginner's Observing Guide*, I received important news from the Society's annual General Assembly which was being held in Vancouver. At the meeting of the National Council on June 29, 2003, approval was given to a motion to make this fifth edition of *The Beginner's Observing Guide* a special commemorative edition to mark the centenary of the Royal Charter of the Royal Astronomical Society of Canada.

What happened in 1903 was a significant and culminating step in the evolution of our Society's name. In the middle of the nineteenth century when our organization was based in Toronto, it had been known as the Toronto Astronomy Club, until the name was changed to the Toronto Astronomical Society in 1868 (though for a period of time beginning in 1884, it was known also as The Astronomical and Physical Society of Toronto, the name used at the time of incorporation in the Province of Ontario in 1890). In a petition to the Governor-General of Canada, signed by our then president R.F. Stupart and Secretary J.R. Collins, and dated January 7, 1903, the Society, which had recently changed its name to The Astronomical Society of Canada to reflect the inclusion of other Centres of astronomical activity, requested permission to prefix the term "Royal" to the new name. The monarch of the British Empire, Edward VII, willingly granted the request, and the reply to the Society came in a letter dated February 27, 1903 from Joseph Pope, Canada's Under-Secretary of State, who was himself a member of the Society. The letter stated that the monarch had been pleased to grant the requested name change to 'The Royal Astronomical Society of Canada.' Final recognition for the name change occurred when the Province of Ontario granted its approval, in a letter dated March 3, 1903.

This book's current edition recognizes the centenary of these important events in the long history of our Society.

L.E.

Welcome to Astronomy and to the Night Sky

Welcome to a new and exciting adventure! It is called astronomy, and it is about the stars,[1] constellations and other objects of the night sky. For hundreds of years, our ancestors have looked at the night sky, used their imagination, saw patterns among the many stars, and enjoyed talking about them. They often wondered what might really be out there where the Moon, planets and stars were — far from their Earthly homes. The more we, too, look at the night sky the more we will enjoy it. We will soon notice its changes from month to month. Yet there are also many things that we will see staying the same from year to year.

For many years I have enjoyed looking at the sky and showing it to my friends. As you learn more about what is in the sky, you too will enjoy "sharing" the stars, planets, and constellations with other people. You will want to show your friends which constellations are in the southern or in the western sky on a certain night. In fact, you will probably soon surprise yourself because within a few nights you will be able to recognize a dozen or more constellations.

Recently a well-known astronomer wrote that she was twenty years old before she knew that ordinary people with no expensive equipment could actually see the planets, such as Mars, by just looking up in the sky. She had often read about the planets in science fiction, but thought that they could be seen only by astronomers with telescopes. Soon, of course, she learned that some of the planets are brighter than any of the stars in the sky, and are second in brightness only to the Moon. That person then started to devote her life to sharing the beauty of the night sky with other people, and teaching them the many things that she was learning.

This is an example of what you, too, can do *without* a telescope or without any equipment at all. There will be more information about this topic later, especially in Chapters 10 and 11. In the meantime, *DO NOT* plan to buy a telecope or other equipment. First get to know the stars and constellations as good friends. Only later when you are very familiar with the night sky, should you consider what equipment you need. Even then, using binoculars should be the next step. Using a telescope will come much later.

[1] Whenever you see words highlighted in this way, you are invited to refer to the Glossary (page 180 ff.) for more information on this topic.

Make yourself comfortable under the stars. Enjoy your new-found hobby as you go. Do not become discouraged if you have three or four cloudy nights in a row. Just read a little more of this observing guide and become more familiar with what you will be able to see on the next clear night. The secret to enjoying your observing sessions under the night sky is being prepared for what you will see. Remember the wise old Scouting motto — "Be Prepared." That is why you should get to know where in this guide you will find the maps and the descriptions of what you can see on a certain night.

The Basic Motions of the Sky

Before we start using the star maps, we should understand something about the apparent movement of the stars in the sky.

What we see in the sky changes all the time because, as we know, the Earth is always rotating. Think about what happens during the daytime. The Sun in the morning appears to rise in the east. At noon it appears in the southern part of the sky. In the evening it is seen setting in the west. Similarly, on a clear night, you can see a bright star rise above the eastern horizon in the early part of the night. At about midnight (which means the middle of the night) this same star will be up in the southern part of the sky. When the night ends and morning is coming on, the star will be in the western part of the sky, setting as the Sun does in the evening. This motion of the sky is sometimes called *apparent motion*, because it is really we on the surface of the Earth who are moving. It is like the view seen by passengers on a fast train when they look out the window. The trees seem to be moving quickly past the windows of the train, but we know it is really the passengers and the train that are moving. Studying *Figure 1* will help us to understand the daily motion of the sky. (See Photo 1.)

The stars that we see in the sky also change from season to season. We know that the Earth is in orbit around the Sun. If we look out into the clear night sky at midnight *in January*, we will see many beautiful bright stars. If we look out at midnight on a clear night *in July*, which is half a year later, we will see many stars too, but they will all be different, because we will be looking in a completely different direction. Study *Figure 2*. This diagram will help us to understand why there are different stars to be seen during the different seasons of the year.

We may also notice that for this view of the Sun and the Earth we would have to be very far above the northern hemisphere of the Sun and the Earth. We may also notice, from the diagram, that we are *not exactly* above the North Pole of the Earth. The dot showing the North Pole of the Earth is slightly to the left of centre on each circle representing the Earth. We can see that the North Pole is in the dark half of the Earth during the winter season (at the left of the diagram) and in the Sunlit half of the Earth during the summer season (at the

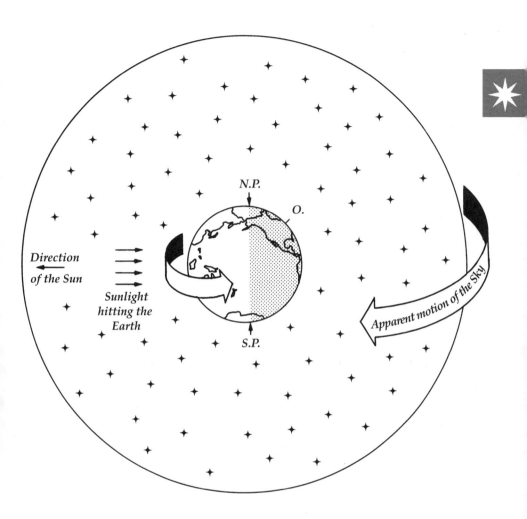

Figure 1

This diagram shows the rotation of the Earth. All the stars are represented as being on a very large sphere surrounding the Earth. N.P. and S.P. represent the Earth's North Pole and South Pole. The observer (O.) is on the "night side" of the Earth. *Because the Earth is turning* and carrying the observer from west to east, the stars *seem* to be moving from east to west, like the trees beside a moving train when a passenger looks out the window. Observers on the other side of the Earth do not see the stars at this moment because the sunlight is too bright. They do see the Sun. The Sun also seems to be moving from east to west because the Earth is turning from west to east.

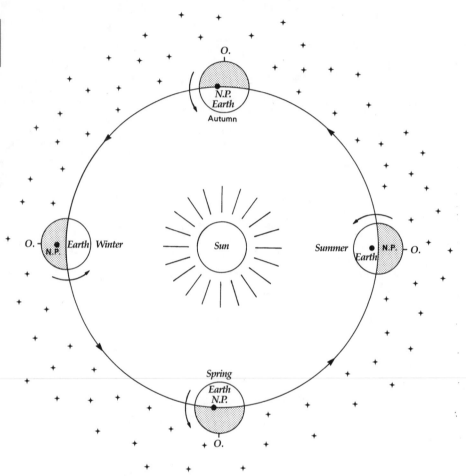

Figure 2

This diagram shows an observer (O.) looking out at the nighttime sky at midnight at four times during the year. Notice that this observer will be looking in a completely different direction each time. Therefore, this observer will see different groups and patterns of stars each time. Notice the arrow beside each drawing of the Earth. This arrow shows the direction that we would see the Earth turning or rotating if we were far, far above the North Pole of the Earth or the North Pole of the Sun and could look down at the Sun and the Earth.

right of the diagram). In fact, the Earth is tilted in this way, and this is what causes the seasons of the year.

Therefore, what is in the sky is always changing for *two* reasons. First, the stars that we see in a certain part of the sky change from hour to hour because the Earth is rotating, *and* secondly, the stars that we see during the night change from season to season because the Earth is in orbit around the Sun.

There is another fact that we should know also. Our position on the planet Earth is also very important because the Earth on which we stand is always hiding half of the sky from us. We have often heard about what is called "the horizon." We can see the sky above it, but all the stars and planets below it are always hidden from us. Refer to *Figure 3*. We can see that if we lived at the North Pole [as shown in *Figure 3(a)*], we would see only the stars that were above the northern half of the Earth; we would never see the entire southern half of the sky. The star above the North Pole of the Earth, called Polaris or the Pole Star, would be directly overhead. Astronomers say that it is in the zenith — meaning straight overhead.

An observer living at the equator of the Earth [as shown in *Figure 3(c)*] might be able to see the Pole Star, but it would be right down at the northern horizon. That same person would also be able to see the stars above the South Pole of the Earth but they would be right down near the southern horizon. The stars above the Earth's equator would be in the zenith.

Observers in the southern part of Canada are located about at Latitude 43 to 55 degrees North, which is about half-way between the Earth's equator and the North Pole. As shown in *Figure 3(b)*, when this observer looks toward the northern horizon, he or she can see the stars above the Earth's North Pole. In fact, the Pole Star that is above the Earth's North Pole would appear to be up in the sky about half way between the northern horizon and the zenith. This observer *is* able to see the stars that are above the Earth's equator, but *is not* able to see the stars that are above the Earth's South Pole.

We can understand now why it is difficult to draw a good single map showing all the stars that anyone could see during a whole night. It is best to draw a map showing the stars that we see at one certain time and from one location on

> ## Our 6 star maps will show us the sky as seen from mid-northern latitudes during different hours of the night through the whole year.

the Earth. In this booklet we will show only the sky that can be seen from the middle-northern latitudes (those of southern Canada), and there will be six

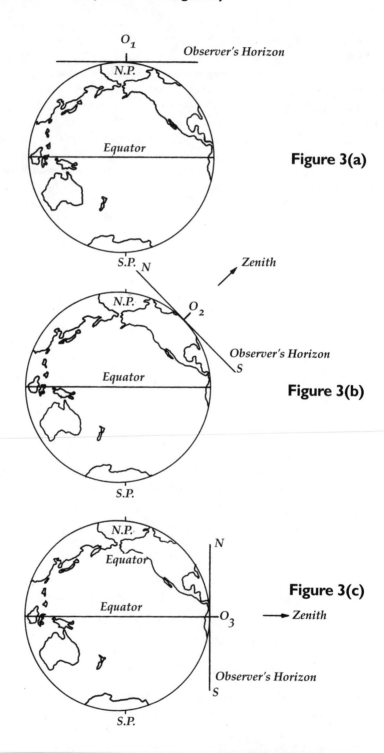

Figure 3(a)

Figure 3(b)

Figure 3(c)

Figures 3(a), 3(b), and 3(c)

These three diagrams show that each observer on the surface of the Earth has a horizon, and the horizon is different depending on where you live on the surface of the Earth. In FIGURE 3(a), the observer is at the North Pole, also called Latitude 90° North. In FIGURE 3(b), the observer is at the mid-northern latitudes (about 45° North). In FIGURE 3(c), the observer is at the Earth's equator (0° in latitude).

For the observer (O_1) at the North Pole in FIGURE 3(a), the North Pole Star is directly overhead at a great distance from the Earth, and the observer can never see any stars above the southern half of the Earth.

For the observer (O_2) at the mid-northern latitudes in FIGURE 3(b), the North Pole Star that is far above the Earth's North Pole will appear above his Northern Horizon and he or she will never see the stars that are far above the South Pole.

For the observer (O_3) at the Earth's equator in FIGURE 3(c), the North Pole Star that is far above the North Pole of the Earth will appear just at the northern horizon or very near the northern horizon. The stars that are far above the South Pole of the Earth will be just at the southern horizon or very near the southern horizon. Because the North Pole Star appears so close to the horizon, this observer will never have a very good view of it. However, this observer (O_3) at the Earth's equator will be able to see many stars that the other two observers will never be able to see because the southern horizon allows him or her to see many stars that are blocked from view for the other observers.

Notice that there is a relationship between where the North Pole Star is seen and the latitude of the observer. The observer at the North Pole (also called Latitude 90 degrees North) sees the North Pole Star directly overhead (also called 90 degrees altitude). The observer at latitude 45 degrees North sees it as half-way up in the sky (also called 45 degrees altitude). Finally the observer at the Earth's equator (also called Latitude 0 degrees) sees the North Pole Star on the horizon or at 0 degrees altitude. It is now easy to see that the observer's latitude on the Earth is the same as the altitude or height in the sky of the North Pole Star.

Notice that the position directly overhead or above each observer is called the Zenith. For the observer at the North Pole, the Pole Star is presently only about one degree from the Zenith. There will be very different stars in the Zenith for Observer (O_2) and Observer (O_3).

different maps to show the sky at different times of the night during different times of the year.

If we combine the diagram in *Figure 3(b)* with part of the diagram in *Figure 1*, we can understand better why some stars appear to rise and set, whereas other stars are above the horizon all the time and do not rise and set. That is what has been done in *Figure 4*. Study it carefully. It shows the horizon all around an observer at about Latitude 43 to 55 degrees North, which is approximately the location of most observers in southern Canada. Imagine that you are the observer [O$_2$] at the centre. Above the northern point on the horizon you can see the North Pole Star. It is up in the sky, about half-way between the horizon and the zenith, which is the point directly overhead. When you look to the east, you see stars that are rising above the horizon as the Earth rotates. When you look to the west, you will see stars that are setting.

Star A appears in the north-eastern part of the sky, to the right of the North Pole Star but not as high up in the sky as the Pole Star. As the Earth rotates, it will later rise higher in the north-eastern sky and will be up near the zenith. Later still it will appear to move down in the north-western sky, but it will not set. It will appear to make a large circle in the northern sky. This is an example of a circumpolar star — one that does not set.

Stars B and C have just risen in the east a little while ago. They will rise higher in the sky later in the night as the Earth rotates. If the observer watches them long enough, he or she will see them setting in the west. Star B rose a little to the north of the east point on the horizon, and later it will be up very high in the sky, and it will later set at a point to the north of the west point on the horizon. Star C rose to the south of the east point on the horizon. It will later be up in the southern part of the sky but will not be up as high as Star B. Star C will later set at a point south of the west point on the horizon.

We can compare Star B and Star C to certain stars on our six main star maps. Star B is like the bright star Regulus on Map 1. It has just risen in the east. A few hours later it will be much higher in the sky as Regulus is on Map 2.

As a second example, Star B and Star C are like the bright stars Deneb and Altair on Map 3. They have just risen in the east. A few hours later they will be higher in the sky, just as Deneb and Altair are on Map 4. Notice that a few hours later they have started to go down in the west (as seen on Map 5). Finally, later, Deneb and Altair are about to set in the west (as seen on Map 6).

As a third example, Star B is like the bright star Aldebaran on Map 5. Notice that later in the night it is higher in the sky as shown on Map 6. Later it is going down in the west as shown on Map 1, and it is just about to set in the west as shown on Map 2.

As a fourth example, Star A is like the star at the end of the handle of the Big Dipper on Map 1. Later in the night, it is higher in the sky as shown on Map 2. Later still, it is in the north-western part of the sky, as shown on Map 3. This star is called a circumpolar star, as are all the stars in the Big Dipper.

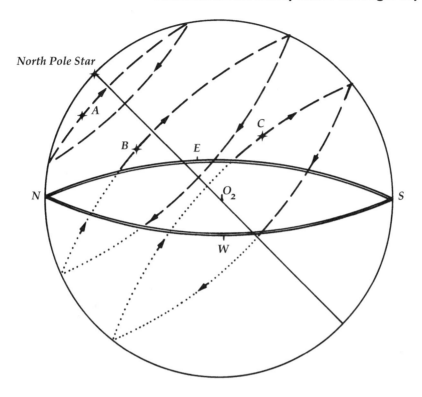

Figure 4

This diagram shows the sky above the Observer (O_2) as seen in FIGURE 3(b) on page 6. This observer is at mid-northern latitudes. Try to put yourself at the centre of the diagram in this observer's position. This diagram has the horizon marked with a double line around the observer, and the four directions (or compass points) are marked: N, E, S, and W. Notice that the North Pole Star is seen by the observer to be above the northern part of the horizon.

Three other stars are marked on this diagram.

Star A is in the northern sky. The dashed line near it shows that, as the Earth rotates, this star will appear to move upward and to the east of the North Pole Star and then later to move downward making a circle in the sky.

Star B is just rising above the north-eastern horizon. As the Earth rotates, it will rise higher and later it will set below the north-western horizon.

Star C has risen a while ago and is in the south-eastern sky. As the Earth rotates, it will rise higher in the sky, and later it will set in the western sky south of the western compass point.

On this diagram the dashed lines show the motions of the three stars while they are above the horizon. Star A is always above the horizon, but, of course, we will not see it when the Sun rises because of the brightness of the sunlight.

Star B and Star C will both appear to rise and set once each day as the Earth turns or rotates, just as the Sun appears to rise and set once each day.

Reading the Star Maps and Seeing the Constellations

Introduction to Our Six Star Maps

Star maps are very useful to those who study the night sky; both beginners and very experienced observers use them all the time.

As we have already seen, the Earth is always moving. The stars and all the objects in the sky always *appear to be moving* from east to west in great giant circles around the Earth.

In this book, there are six maps of the night sky. They have been drawn for a latitude (the measure of distance from the Earth's equator) of about 45 degrees North, which is approximately that for southern Canada and northern United States, though they can be used for the whole mid-Northern area of North America up to the southern parts of the Yukon and Northwest Territories.

In the early evening hours (meaning about dinnertime for most people during the winter months, or just after dinnertime), you will use one of the six maps.

During the later hours of the evening, or the night, when most people do their observing of the night sky, you will turn to another map — the one that is called the *Night Map* for that time of year.

If you continue to observe the sky during the middle of the night, you will turn to another map that can be used for the hours *after midnight*.

Finally, the *early morning* observers will be able to use another map for the sky before dawn.

In other words it may be necessary to use three or four maps to show the night sky during a whole night.

It is important to note that these maps show the stars and constellations *approximately* as they appear. Some stars shown on the maps near the horizon may not be visible to observers in some locations, particularly those who live in more northerly locations, like the cities of Edmonton or Churchill. On the other hand, some observers in some locations may see some stars that are below the horizon lines on some of the maps; this will be true if you observe the sky from a southerly location, such as one you may visit during a winter vacation.

The six star maps of this guide have titles, as listed below.

Map 1 – January and February Night Map
Map 2 – March and April Night Map
Map 3 – May and June Night Map
Map 4 – July and August Night Map
Map 5 – September and October Night Map
Map 6 – November and December Night Map

The following chart indicates the months and hours of the night when each map is to be used.

You will have noticed that on the chart there is no map listed for the evening or early morning hours during the months May through August. The reason is

WHEN TO USE THE SIX STAR MAPS:				
Months	Evening Hours 6 p.m.-8 p.m.	Night 9 p.m.-midnt	After Midnight 1 a.m.-4 a.m.	Early Morning 5 a.m.-7 a.m.
Jan. & Feb.	6	1	2	3
Mar. & Apr.	1	2	3	4
May & Jun.	–	3	4	–
Jul. & Aug.	–	4	5	–
Sep. & Oct.	4	5	6	1
Nov. & Dec.	5	6	1	2

that daylight is much longer during these months, and sunlight or twilight will not allow you to observe the starry sky at these times.

By now you will also have noticed that for any particular night, *as the hours pass* and morning gets closer, you can turn to the *following* map to show the stars and constellations that you will see in the sky.

Map Orientation

At the *centre* of each map is the point that astronomers call the *zenith* which was mentioned already in Chapter 1. Remember that it is the point directly overhead in the sky.

The heavy black circle that forms the outer edge of each map is the horizon, the line where the Earth meets the sky.

Use the maps outdoors where you have a good view of the sky and a good view of the horizon in the directions where you want to look.

When you use one of the maps, be sure you have the correct one, as listed in the chart above, and hold the map out in front of you so that *the direction marked below the horizon (N, E, S, or W) on the map matches the direction in which you are facing (NORTH, EAST, SOUTH, or WEST)*. In other words, if you are facing south, and using Map 1 (January-February Night Map), you should hold it so that the letter "*S*" is at the bottom. If the sky is clear, you should notice the constellations Columba and Lepus above the horizon. Do a quarter-turn to the left. You will now be facing East. You will see the stars of the constellations Canis Major, Hydra, Sextans, and Leo directly in front of you as you turn. Now that you are facing East, you will notice the bright star Regulus, which is part of the constellation Leo, almost in front of you. Practise the same thing turning to the west in order to see other constellations marked on the map.

The Constellation Patterns

As you may already have guessed, constellations are just stars that seem to group themselves into certain patterns or form certain shapes because they appear in the same part of the sky.

In learning to use the star maps, you have already seen several constellations, such as Canis Major, which may or may not appear as a large dog, and Hydra which may or may not appear as a long snake-like monster.

The stars in a particular constellation are not necessarily near or related to each other at all; they just appear to be close to each other. If we were living on a planet in a distant part of the galaxy, the constellation patterns would look completely different from the way they appear to us on the planet Earth.

On the star maps in this book you will notice that many of the bright stars forming the constellation patterns are linked by straight lines. These lines may help you to "see the pattern" in the sky, but *do not worry* if you do not see the pattern that you think you should see. The constellation patterns were designed long ago by people with active imaginations. It is more important to see the stars, or most of them, than to "see the constellation patterns."

The names of the constellations are given on the star maps in upper case (capital) letters. A complete list of all 88 constellations is given in the appendix at the end of the book. Of course, from our northern latitudes on the Earth, we cannot see all 88 constellations, even over the course of a whole year. Just try to see as many as possible of the constellations named on the star maps.

Other Objects Marked on the Star Maps

The brightest and best-known stars are shown in lower case (small) letters.

The size of the dots indicates the brightness of the stars; the largest dots indicate the brightest stars (such as Sirius, on Map 1); the very smallest dots indicate stars that are just visible to the unaided eye (such as the three stars below the bright star Rigel, on Map 1).

Very small circles of dots indicate some of the well-known star clusters, nebulas, and galaxies. Some of these are not visible to the unaided eye, but can be seen with binoculars.

You will notice that there is a blue pathway across all the maps. This pathway shows where the Milky Way is located.

You will notice a *yellow* line with black dashes across each map from E to W. This is the *celestial equator*. For an explanation of the numbers along this line, see the entry "Right Ascension" in the Glossary, page 186. You will also notice a *green* line with black dashes crossing each map and intersecting the celestial equator at either VE (Vernal Equinox) or AE (Autumnal Equinox). This line is the *ecliptic*. For an explanation see the Glossary, page 182. The initials along this line (e.g.: J, F, M, ...) indicate the apparent position of the Sun at the beginning of each month of the year, and the initials "SS" and "WS" indicate *summer solstice* and *winter solstice*. (See "solstice" on page 187.)

On Map 4 (July - August Night Map), the little asterisk marked GC indicates the direction of the centre of our Milky Way Galaxy.

The following objects are *not* marked on the star maps:

- the Moon (See Chapter 13),
- the planets (See Chapter 14), and
- comets, asteroids, and meteors.

The reason is that these objects, within our Solar System and relatively close to us, continually move and are not located at one fixed position in the sky.

3

Finding North in the Night Sky

Locating the Big Dipper and the North Pole Star is the key to finding your directions in the night sky. The Big Dipper is a very large and easily recognized star pattern. Try to introduce yourself to it by facing in a more or less northerly direction. The most easily noticed star pattern in this direction is one that has

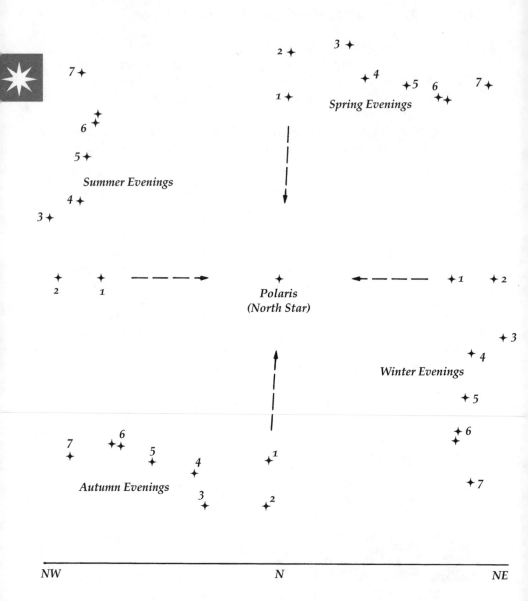

Figure 5

This illustration shows approximately the position in the sky of the Big Dipper in the early evening during the four seasons of the year. Notice that at all times the pointer stars of the Big Dipper point to Polaris (the North Pole Star).

seven very bright stars. These seven stars may seem to form a large dipper standing *on its handle*, or they may seem to make a huge question mark, *if you are looking during a winter evening*. They may seem to form a large dipper standing *on its cup* with the handle pointing upward *if you are looking during a summer evening*. *Figure 5* shows that this pattern of seven stars appears in different positions in the sky depending on the time of year. As you can see, the Big Dipper is standing on its handle *in the winter evenings*; it is standing on the cup *during the summer evenings*; it is high in the sky turned to spill its contents downward *during the spring evenings*, and it is low in the sky turned upward as if sitting on a shelf *during the autumn evenings*. Notice that, no matter what the season is, it is still shaped the same — like a dipper. At certain periods of history, people have also called it The Plough and The Wagon. Whether in your imagination you see a dipper or a plough or a wagon or question mark, or just seven bright stars, does not matter — just as long as you learn to recognize the star pattern.

> ## Finding the Big Dipper will always be helpful in locating True North, since two of the Big Dipper's stars always point to the North Pole Star.

The Big Dipper is not a whole constellation, but is only a part of the constellation that astronomers call Ursa Major. These are Latin words meaning the Bigger, or Larger, Bear. It is clearly marked on all six star maps. Perhaps as you see some of the fainter stars near the cup of the dipper, you will see why people of long ago were reminded of a huge bear, though it is a strange bear, since it is one with a long tail. Most real bears on Earth, of course, do not have long tails, but this is a heavenly bear. If you read the story about how it came to be in the sky, you will find out that a long tail is part of that legend.

Finding the Big Dipper will always be helpful in locating the True North direction. Two of the stars in the cup of the Big Dipper always point to the North Pole Star in the sky. If you are ever lost and need to know directions at night, the two stars in the cup of the dipper that are farthest from the handle are the most important stars in the sky to know. These two stars will easily lead you to the North Pole Star. It is the star that would be almost exactly overhead if you were viewing the sky from the North Pole of the Earth. (See Photo 6.)

[Those two famous stars at the end of the cup of the Big Dipper are known by the Arabic names of Dubhe and Merak (pronounced "Doo - Bay" and "May - Rack"). They are the stars number 1 and 2 in Figure 5.]

Draw an imaginary straight line on the sky from the star Merak to Dubhe and extend it on *five times farther*, as shown in *Figure 5*, until you come to the brightest star in the area. This star is Polaris, which means "the Pole Star." You have now found the most important stars in the sky for people of the Northern Hemisphere who want to find their directions. Whenever you see Polaris, you know you are looking North.

In fact, this is also the only star that does not seem to move slowly from east to west as the Earth rotates hour after hour during the course of a night. It actually does move in a *very* small circle in the course of one day because it is not *exactly* above the Earth's North Pole, but it is so close to the North Pole of the sky that we cannot notice its movement with the unaided eye.

The seven stars of the Big Dipper form one of the most distinctive star patterns in the whole sky and one of the easiest for most people to find and remember, if they live in the Northern Hemisphere of the Earth. From all parts of Canada and the northern United States, it is easy to find the Big Dipper on *any clear night* of the year. That is why we can use it as a starting point for finding all the other constellations in the sky at any time of the night or at any time of the year. (See Photo 6.)

Knowing all the stars of the Big Dipper by name, as well as by number, can be useful when you are talking about them. We can name and number these seven famous stars starting with the star at the end of the cup, going around the cup, and then along the handle. (Refer in *Figure 5* to the numbers near the stars of the Big Dipper as seen in the Spring and Autumn evenings.) The Arabic names that have been used for many years are:

1 – Dubhe	5 – Alioth
2 – Merak	6 – Mizar
3 – Phad or Phecda	7 – Alkaid
4 – Megrez	

The star marked near Mizar has a name also. It is called Alcor. It is so close to Mizar that many people do not see it until someone tells them about it. For many years it has been used as a test of good eyesight. Try to find it yourself and test your own eyesight.

Once you can find North in the night sky, you can easily find all the other directions or compass points. Face directly north, that is, toward Polaris (the North Pole Star), which you have just found. Hold your arms straight out as if you were about to begin doing a cartwheel. Your left hand will point to the west and your right hand to the east. Your back will be toward the south.

You have now learned how to find all the compass directions using only the Big Dipper and the star Polaris.

4

Distance, Position, and Brightness in the Sky

Measuring the Distance Between Objects in the Sky

Many people are confused about how to measure distance from one star to another star. They sometimes say, "I think it is about two metres from that red star to that bright white one." They forget that metres or centimetres are linear measures of distance. Instead, they should be using an *angular* measure of distance, since thay are measuring the distance apart that the two objects appear to be as viewed from their eyes. Any person can use his or her hand held at arm's length as a guide to *approximate angular measurement.* If you hold up your hand at arm's length, you will see that your little fingernail more than covers the Full Moon. This means that your little fingernail is a bit more than a half-degree in width. The Full Moon is about a half-degree in diameter. The width of the first knuckle on your little finger is about one degree. The width of your first three fingers extended side by side is about five degrees. The width of the clenched fist is about ten degrees. The width of the first and little fingers extended wide is about fifteen degrees, and the width of the thumb and little finger extended wide is about twenty degrees.

On a clear night, practise these measurements on the Big Dipper. Here is a list of the approximate distances between Dubhe and five of the other stars in this famous group:

1–Dubhe	to	2–Merak	–	5 degrees
1–Dubhe	to	4–Megrez	–	10 degrees
1–Dubhe	to	5–Alioth	–	15 degrees
1–Dubhe	to	6–Mizar	–	20 degrees
1–Dubhe	to	7–Alkaid	–	25 degrees

PRACTISE YOUR SKILLS

(1) On a clear night, estimate the angular distance between any two stars that are in the same part of the sky.

(2)   On a clear night, estimate the angular distance between Dubhe and Polaris (the North Pole Star). (Then check the answer at the end of this chapter.)

Stating the Location of an Object in the Sky

We are all familiar with the four main points on a compass — North, East, South, and West. These four directions are marked on the horizon on *Figure 4*, and we used them to become familiar with the rising and setting of the stars. We can use these compass directions or *azimuth*, as astronomers call them, to help us state the location of an object in the sky. The horizon around an observer is a large circle of 360 degrees. We start measuring in the north and go around to the east, then south, then west, and finally back to the north where we began. In other words,

North	is	0 degrees.
East	is	90 degrees.
South	is	180 degrees.
West	is	270 degrees.

This means that an object on the horizon in the North-East would be at azimuth 45 degrees, and an object on the horizon in the South-East would be at azimuth 135 degrees. An object at azimuth 158 degrees would be in the South-South-East. An object at azimuth 265 degrees would be almost due West — just 5 degrees south of the West point. An object of azimuth 315 degrees would be in the North-West.

Altitude is measured from any point on the horizon to the zenith, which we know to be the point directly overhead; it is measured in degrees, 0 degrees being exactly on the horizon, and 90 degrees being exactly in the zenith. An object at altitude 45 degrees is half-way between the horizon and the zenith. An object at altitude 30 degrees is exactly one-third of the distance up from the horizon to the zenith, and an object at altitude 60 degrees is exactly two-thirds of the distance up from the horizon to the zenith or one-third of the distance down from the zenith to the horizon.

This system of naming the location of an object in the sky is called the *horizon system* or the *alt-azimuth* system (which is short for *altitude* and *azimuth*). We should know the name to distinguish it from other systems that are used.

Whenever we use this system to state the location of an objects seen in the sky, we must *also* state *the time* when we made our observation.

For example, with the help of Map 1, name the star at azimuth 100 degrees and altitude 25 degrees at 10:00 p.m. local time on February 2. The answer would be Regulus.

PRACTISE YOUR SKILLS

(1) Name the star that is at azimuth 225 degrees and altitude 10 degrees at 10:30 p.m. local time on April 2. (Use Map 2.) (Check the answer at the end of the chapter.)

(2) Name the two stars that are about at azimuth 300 degrees and altitude 15 degrees at 10:00 p.m. local time on June 1. (Use Map 3.) (Check the answer at the end of the chapter.)

(3) On a clear night, choose any three bright stars. Carefully estimate the azimuth and altitude of each one. One hour later, do the same thing. (You may be surprised at the different numbers.)

In this system of naming the location of an object, you should name the azimuth first, then the altitude, and finally the exact time.

Later you will learn other systems of describing the locations of objects in the sky, but this simple system is the one that you should learn first.

Explaining the Brightness of an Object in the Sky

Hundreds of years ago, long before the invention of the telescope, a Greek astronomer invented a system of describing the difference in brightness among the many hundreds of stars in the sky. This man, whose name was Hipparchos, divided the stars that could be seen into six categories. The brightest stars were called category one or *first magnitude*. The faintest stars that a keen-eyed person could see were called category six or *sixth magnitude*. This system is still used today with only a few changes. The higher the number, the fainter the star. Most people with good eyesight can see sixth magnitude stars, if they are out in the country away from the smog and light pollution of a city and if the Moon is not in the sky. In a small town or if a Quarter Moon is in the sky, most people can see stars of third or fourth magnitude. From a city or with a Full Moon in the sky, only first magnitude stars are usually seen, that is, stars such as Deneb, Spica, Altair, and Aldebaran. (These four stars are marked on the star maps.)

One change that has been made in this old system is the addition of numbers lower than one. A few *very* bright stars, like Arcturus, Vega, and Capella, are given magnitude numbers zero (0) and minus one (-1). Sirius, the brightest star of all, is given the magnitude number -1.46. Some of the planets are even brighter than this. Jupiter is often brighter than -2. Sometimes Venus is brighter than -4. On this scale the Full Moon would be brighter than -12, and the Sun brighter than -26.

> ## Sirius, the brightest star of all, has a magnitude of -1.46. Two planets, Jupiter and Venus, are even brighter than that.

At the other end of the scale, very faint objects have higher numbers. The planet Neptune is a magnitude 8 object, and Pluto is about magnitude 14; it is extremely faint.

Here is a list of examples of stars of certain brightnesses:

Magnitude		
	0	– Capella (in Auriga) (Maps 1, 2, 5, and 6) *and* Vega (in Lyra) (Maps 3, 4, 5, and 6)
	1	– Aldebaran (in Taurus) (Map 1, 2, 5, and 6) *and* Spica (in Virgo) (Maps 2, 3, and 4)
	1.5	– Castor (in Gemini) (Maps 1, 2, 3, and 6)
	2	– Polaris (North Pole Star) (All Maps)
	2.5	– Alpha Pegasi (Star in the Square of Pegasus that is farthest from Andromeda) (Maps 1, 4, 5, and 6)
	3	– Megrez (Star Number 4 in Big Dipper) (Figure 5 and All Maps)
	3.5	– Alpha Trianguli (Star in the triangle that is nearest to the constellation Aries) (Maps 1, 5, and 6)
	4	– Mu Andromedae (Star below the galaxy that is below the letter "n" in the word Andromeda on Map 5)
	4.5	– Delta Ursae Minoris (In the handle of the Little Dipper the star that is next to Polaris) (All Maps) *and* Theta Leporis (Star at the end of curving row of stars in upper part of constellation Lepus (Maps 1 and 6)

You will notice that almost all the stars on our star maps are between magnitude 1 and magnitude 4.5. Star atlases, of course, can show you fainter stars. Some atlases show stars as faint as magnitude 6; some show 7 or 8; a few star atlases show stars as faint as magnitude 9 or 10, but when we want to show stars that faint, there are many hundreds of thousands of stars to show.

PRACTISE YOUR SKILLS

(1)   On the next clear night, choose any fairly bright star (other than one of those listed above). Estimate its brightness — by comparison with one or more of the stars on the list above, such as Capella, Polaris, or Phad. (If its brightness is about half-way between that of Polaris and Phad, it is about magnitude 2.5.) (Repeat the exercise several times.)

   If you do this exercise regularly, you will become more aware of the magnitude of stars, and you will be more able to estimate the brightness of *any* star.

(2)   Ready for a challenge? On a clear night observe the seven stars of the Big Dipper. (a) Which is the faintest? (b) Which one is the brightest? (Check answers at the end of the chapter.)

Later you will also learn about stars that vary or change in brightness. There are many such stars, called *variable stars*, which have *noticeable* changes in brightness. Two very good examples are Algol in Perseus (See Maps 1, 2, 5, and 6), and Mira in Cetus (See Maps 1, 5, and 6). Try to find and observe these two stars as often as you can. Algol is easily seen with the unaided eye, and Mira is sometimes seen in this way and sometimes requires binoculars. Before long you may start to notice changes in the brightness of these two famous stars, and maybe even in the brightness of other stars.

   Chapter 16 gives an introduction to observing variable stars. A list of the 30 brightest stars is given on page 193, and a list of 10 variable stars that can be observed "naked-eye" is given on pages 193 and 194.

[Answers to PRACTISE YOUR SKILLS questions:
   Distance: (2)   29 degrees. Saying "30 degrees" is close enough.
   Location: (1)   Sirius
                 (2)   Castor and Pollux
   Brightness: (2)   (a) Megrez is noticeably fainter than Phad.
                       (b) The three brightest are Dubhe, Alioth, and Alkaid.
                            They are almost the same brightness! It was a challenge!]

5

Names of the Stars

Long ago people who watched the night sky gave names to the brightest of the stars. Often they used the names of animals or heroes of their mythology for the stars, just as they did for the constellations. (We have already noted in Chapter 2 some constellation names.) Sometimes stars received their names from the parts of the constellation in which they were found; for example, there are star names which mean "the horse's foot" and "the lion's tail."

In modern times many more stars have been given their own designation, but we still use some of the names that were used hundreds or even thousands of years ago.

The beginner should not worry about having to learn hundreds of star names. It would be wise to become familiar with the twenty or so bright stars that have their own proper names, as shown on the star maps in this book. Most of them are seen in the sky for several months at a time and are found on several of the star maps. The name, and place in the sky, of these stars can be gradually learned as the constellations are recognized, and as you become familiar with the sky in general.

The following information explains how the stars have received their names over the years. Reading it will help you understand the star maps and atlases that you will use in the future.

1. Bright Stars with Proper Names

The very brightest stars have their own proper names, such as Sirius, Capella, Vega, Rigel, and Aldebaran. One modern book lists over 250 stars that have individual names, but only about 50 of these are commonly used.

As noted in Chapter 3, the seven stars of the Big Dipper have Arabic names. Many star names begin with "al," an Arabic word which is like the English word "the." It is found in the names Algol, Altair, Alcor, and many others. Besides Arabic, ancient Greek and Latin names are given to some stars, like Sirius, Capella, Castor, and Pollux.

2. The Bayer System of Star Names

In the year 1603, a German astronomer, Johann Bayer, published a star atlas which used a system of naming stars that is still used today. In the Bayer System, the stars in each constellation are named, usually in order of brightness, with the letters of the Greek alphabet. This alphabet has 24 letters and begins with "alpha," "beta," "gamma," .... The complete alphabet is given in the Appendix on page 194. The full name of a star in this system is the Greek letter followed by the constellation name (in the Latin possessive form). "Alpha Centauri," for example, is the brightest star in the constellation Centaurus. "Beta Cygni" is the second brightest star in Cygnus. "Gamma Cassiopeiae" is the third star designated in Cassiopeia. This system is used to identify several hundreds of the "naked-eye" stars. It is used in all star atlases.

> **For over 400 years Bayer's system of naming stars, and for almost 300 years Flamsteed's system of naming stars, have been used by astronomers around the world.**

3. The Flamsteed Number System

Another very common way to identify stars is to use the Flamsteed Number System. It is named after John Flamsteed, a British astronomer who invented the system in the early 1700s. In this system the stars in each constellation are numbered from west to east. The full name of a star in this system is the number followed by the constellation name (in the Latin possessive form). An example is "61 Cygni," a well-known star in the constellation Cygnus. This system is used to identify several thousand stars, and it also is found in all star atlases.

4. Stars From the Catalogues

For the faint stars that are not named by any of the above systems, astronomers refer to one of several catalogues of stars that list many thousands of stars. Usually, two or more letters are used to identify the catalogue; then the star's number is given according to its listing in the catalogue.

One such catalogue is the Henry Draper Catalogue. An example of a star is HD186882. The position of this star can be found by checking in that catalogue.

Another is the Smithsonian Astrophysical Observatory Star Catalogue. An example of a star from its listings is SAO48796.

Many double stars are listed in Aitken's General Catalogue of Double Stars. An example of a star found in this listing is ADS12880.

These three numbers all identify the same star, which can be found in the constellation Cygnus. Many stars, like this one, are listed in several different catalogues.

5. The Variable Star Identification System

Stars known to be variable, that is, to have changes in their brightness, have a very different system of identification from other stars. Within each constellation variable stars are given a single letter designation such as R, S, or T, or a double letter designation such as RR, RS, or RT. In a few constellations, such as Orion, which has hundreds of variable stars, some of them are designated by a number. In that case the letter "V," meaning "variable," is used, followed by a number. (One such example is the variable star "V351 Orionis," which is found near the belt of Orion.) Whether the variable star has a single letter, a double letter, or a V-plus-number designation, it is followed by the name of the constellation (in the Latin possessive form). Three well-known examples of variable stars are R Leonis, RR Lyrae, and T Tauri; they are found, of course, in the constellations Leo, Lyra, and Taurus. David Levy's book, recommended in Chapter 23 on page 165, gives further details about the naming of variable stars.

The maps in this book use *only* the first method of naming the stars, that is, the proper names for the brightest stars.

The star maps and star atlases, that you will be using in the future, usually identify the bright stars in two or three different ways on the same map. For example, the star Capella is usually named, as in this book, and also identified as "Alpha" (using the Bayer System since it is the brightest star in the constellation Auriga), and also "13" since that is its Flamsteed number. Betelgeuse, found in this book on maps 1, 2, and 6, is identified on most star maps also as "Alpha" (using the Bayer System) and "58" since that is its Flamsteed number.

Beginners should become familiar with the names of the brightest stars shown on the star maps in this book, and should be aware that the above systems are used on other star maps and in star atlases.

As you use star atlases, such as those recommended later in this book, you will gradually become familiar with more star names and with other ways of identifying stars.

6

The Six Star Maps

The January-February Night Sky (Map 1)

Constellations and Naked Eye Objects

The following information is about what you can expect to see in the night sky during January and February and at other times when you use Map 1.

Since you have read Chapter Two, you should already know how to use the star maps.

You are now expected to use Map 1 as your guide in preparing to observe at the times indicated on the star map, and you should take Map 1 (and the other maps in this book too) with you when you go outdoors to observe.

Since you have read Chapter 3 you should now also be able to find the Big Dipper in the northern sky. You will see that it is standing up on its handle. Use it to locate Polaris (the North Pole Star).

Ursa Minor If you are observing under clear dark skies and away from the light pollution of a city, you will be able to see that there is a curving row of stars extending down and bending slightly to the right from the star Polaris, as shown on Map 1. This is called the Little Dipper. You will notice several things about this "dipper": (1) it is smaller than the Big Dipper (that you learned about in Chapter 3), (2) most of the stars are fainter than the stars in the Big Dipper, (3) the two dippers seem to face each other, (4) the handles and cups of the two dippers point in opposite directions, and (5) the handles of the two dippers are bent but they are not bent in the same way. You will notice that, besides Polaris, there is another bright star in the Little Dipper. It is at the end of the dipper's cup, and is known as Kochab (pronounced "coe-cob"). It is the one marked by the large dot below the letter "o" in the words "Ursa Minor" on Map 1.

This dipper is part of the constellation called Ursa Minor (Latin words for Smaller or Little Bear). Here is another bear with a long tail that was put in the sky. It also invites us to learn the story from mythology about why it was put in the sky and why it had this strange feature.

Draco Perhaps you will be able to see some of the stars that form the constellation Draco, the dragon. As Star Map 1 shows, the tail of this huge animal curls between the two dippers that you have just been observing, and its head now points downward toward the northern horizon. You will notice that one of the bright stars in the dragon's tail is about half-way between Kochab in Ursa Minor and Mizar in Ursa Major. This star, which is called Thuban, is famous because about 3000 years ago it was known as the North Pole Star. If you do not have a good view of the head of Draco, wait until later in the year. Then it will be higher in the sky and easier to see.

Cassiopeia   While facing north, trace a line from the star Mizar (in the handle of the Big Dipper) to Polaris and then extend the line the same distance toward the west until you see what looks like a large letter "W" tilted on its right side. These five bright stars that seem to form the letter "W" or "M" are of almost equal brightness. They are the brightest stars of the constellation Cassiopeia. You may also notice that they are within a hazy band of soft light that crosses the sky — the Milky Way. This whole area of the sky contains constellations with the names of characters from Greek mythology, particularly from the story of the hero Perseus. Besides the hero Perseus himself, there is Andromeda, the princess whom he saved from a sea monster, and also her mother, Queen Cassiopeia, and her father, King Cepheus.

Using their imagination, the people of long ago saw not just a letter "W" or "M," but the image of Queen Cassiopeia sitting on her throne in the sky. Most modern observers, however, do not try to see a royal family, but look for simple patterns like letters of the alphabet, or squares, or triangles.

Cepheus Near Cassiopeia (as shown on Star Map 1) and between the "W" and the northern horizon are the stars of the constellation Cepheus. The ancient people may have seen a king sitting on a throne. To us it looks like five bright stars forming a toy house that is tilted to one side, with the peak of its roof pointing toward Polaris. The constellation Cepheus is partly in the Milky Way. (See Photo 11.)

Andromeda The king and the queen were the parents of the Princess Andromeda, the rescued maiden in the story of the hero, Perseus. This famous constellation is easily found by tracing a line from Polaris out to the middle of Cassiopeia's "W" and extending it on further about the same distance. As you can see, this brings you westward to a long, slightly curving line of bright stars. Three of them are very bright and stand up from the horizon. Near them is another curving line of stars that are not nearly as bright and will not be easily seen if you live near a city with bright lights.

The most famous object in this area of the sky is the great Andromeda Galaxy, which is shown on Star Map 1, below the first "A" in the word

"Andromeda." This galaxy is a member of the group of galaxies that our own Milky Way Galaxy belongs to, and it is the nearest spiral galaxy. It is only 2.4 million light-years away from our galaxy! (A light-year is the distance that light travels in one year, moving at a rate of 300 000 kilometres per second.) If observing conditions are good, you can see the Andromeda Galaxy with the unaided eye. It looks like a fuzzy smudge of light or a small fingerprint on the sky. If you are able to see it, remember that you are looking at a galaxy containing several hundred billion stars and some of them are like our own Sun. Remember, too, that the light from all those stars has taken over two million years to reach your eyes.

Pegasus Moving downward from Andromeda's curving line of bright stars, you may see near the western horizon part of the Great Square of Pegasus, a constellation that appeared to the ancient peoples as a huge winged horse that was part of the story told about another one of the heroes of mythology. As you can see from the star maps, one of the stars of Andromeda is also part of the Square of Pegasus, showing that two different constellations can sometimes claim the same star. If your view of the western horizon is not good, because of trees or light from a nearby city, you will not see all of the Square of Pegasus. You will have to wait until later in the year to have a better view of this large constellation.

Perseus As you move your eyes upward along the line of bright stars in Andromeda, you will come to the bright stars of Perseus. You could also find it if you follow along the Milky Way from Cepheus to Cassiopeia and then move further upward. Rather than seeing Perseus as a great strong hero who rescued the Princess Andromeda, most people nowadays see another curving row of bright stars as shown on Map 1, but this row of stars is not as long as the one in Andromeda.

Not far from this row of stars is the famous slightly reddish star called Algol, which is also marked on the star maps. This is one of the very first stars that was noticed to be variable, that is, to change in brightness. It has a regular period of such changes, fading noticeably every 2.9 days, but it is still easily visible to the unaided eye when it is at its minimum brightness. Try to take note of it every night when Perseus is visible and you may soon start to notice the fading or "winking" that occurs every 2.9 days. (See Photo 10.)

From a good observing location, you will be able to observe a cluster of stars located about half-way between Perseus and Cassiopeia and also marked on the star maps. With binoculars you can see that this is really a double cluster — two groups of many beautiful stars.

The Six Stars Maps

Auriga Following further along the Milky Way from Cassiopeia and Perseus, you come to Auriga, high overhead. This constellation has five bright stars. The brightest of them is Capella (meaning "the little goat"). This very bright star, as shown on the star maps, has three fainter stars near it, as though they are kids gathered around a mother goat. In fact, these three stars are often called "The Kids." Amid the five bright stars that form the body of Auriga (a Latin word meaning "the charioteer") you will notice on the star maps that there are three special objects. These are three open clusters of stars, called M36, M37, and M38. They can easily be seen in binoculars.

Orion Moving down from the overhead point toward the *southern* horizon, your eyes will feast upon the largest collection of very bright stars found anywhere in the sky. Midway between the zenith and the horizon is the huge distinctive constellation — Orion, the Hunter. This is a star pattern that really does resemble a mighty giant. Its many bright stars help us, like the people of long ago, to see the image of a great hero charging across the sky. Two bright stars (Betelgeuse and Bellatrix) form his shoulders, and two more (Saiph and Rigel) show his knees. Two of these (Betelgeuse and Rigel) are marked on the maps. The three stars of his belt are in a straight line, and below his belt in the area of his sword, we can see, among the stars, the glowing mass of hydrogen gas that astronomers call M42 and M43. This region has been studied carefully for many years, since it is a very active area where new stars are being born and where variable stars are monitored by keen observers. Take note of "Orion's sword" whenever you get the chance, whether it is with the unaided eye, binoculars, or a small telescope. You will find it a very interesting area of the sky, especially if you are using binoculars.

Canis Major Following the stars of Orion's belt in a straight line toward the left (or the southeast) brings you to the constellation Canis Major (Latin words for the Larger or Bigger Dog), with the steely white star Sirius that some people say forms the eye of the dog. This star is the brightest star in the whole sky and for over a hundred years astronomers have known that it has a companion star, though this companion is too close to the primary star to be easily seen in a small telescope. Sirius is also interesting because it is among the ten closest stars to our Sun. Its distance from us is about 8.6 light-years, meaning that it is closer than any other star that can be seen with the naked eye from the northern latitudes of the Earth.

Besides Sirius, Canis Major has several other stars that are among the brightest 50 stars in the sky. Try to view all the stars of Canis Major that are marked on the star maps and try to arrange them in order of brightness.

It is interesting to know that Sirius was very important to the ancient Egyptians. They looked forward to the rising of Sirius before the Sun each year as a sign of the flooding of the Nile River and growth of crops in the coming season.

Taurus Following the three stars of Orion's belt in a straight line to the right (or to the westward) brings you upward and to a very bright reddish star called Aldebaran. It is part of a grouping of stars called "the Hyades." They seem to form the shape of the letter "V," and to the ancient peoples, this looked like the head of a giant bull from one of the legendary stories. The Hyades are shown on the star map just above the first two letters of the word "Aldebaran," although the word "Hyades" is not there.

Moving on further westward past the Hyades, your eyes will come to the famous cluster of stars called "the Pleiades." They are not named on the star map, but they are shown by a tiny cluster of five dots located under the "s" in the word "Taurus." Under good observing conditions, they are easily visible to the unaided eye. Some people call the Pleiades "the Seven Sisters." Many stories were told about them in ancient times. Some people say they can see six individual stars; other people claim they can see seven stars or even more. Test your own eyesight. Can you see six individual stars?

On the star map you will see that a line is drawn from the star Aldebaran to another star to the east of it and also from another star in the Hyades eastward to one of the five brightest stars in Auriga. Notice that these two lines are like the "horns of the bull," and Aldebaran and the star near it are like the "eyes of the bull." On the star map you will see a tiny pattern of dots near the end of one of the "horns of the bull." This indicates the position of the object that astronomer call M1 or the Crab Nebula. This is the remains of a giant supernova explosion in our galaxy that became visible in the year 1054 A.D. This object can be seen as a small, fuzzy patch of light in binoculars; it cannot be seen with the unaided eye.

Eridanus Below Taurus and to the west of Orion a large area of the sky is filled by the constellation called Eridanus. The ancient peoples saw it as a long, winding river. There are no stars as bright as Aldebaran in this large constellation.

Aries and *Triangulum* In the area between the Pleiades and the western point on the horizon there are two small constellations, both of which have only three bright stars. About half-way between the Pleiades and the western horizon, as Map 1 shows, the stars of Aries form what looks like a letter "L" written backwards. The brightest of the three bright stars is the one at the top; the second brightest is the one forming the angle; the faintest of the three is the one further down and to the left.

The constellation Triangulum is inside the area bounded by the Pleiades, the stars of Aries, and upper star in Andromeda's row of bright stars. Triangulum is really a very simple constellation. The three stars of the triangle are usually easy to see if observing conditions are good. The most interesting object for binocular observers is M33, a spiral galaxy that is a little more distant than M31. M33 is marked on the star map about half-way between the star forming the sharp point in Triangulum and the middle star of the three brightest stars in Andromeda. M33 looks very different from M31; this spiral galaxy in Triangulum is "face on," meaning that it is oriented so that we can see the "full face" of the galaxy. Do not expect it to be very bright even in binoculars. Most observers find that it is much larger and fainter than they expect it to be.

Pisces and *Cetus* Below Taurus, Aries, and Triangulum are two large constellations, both of which may be partly hidden below the horizon. Below Aries and Triangulum you may see the constellation Pisces, which has two rows of fairly faint stars that seem to be trying to form the letter "V" which has been tipped over on its side. The ancient peoples saw this "V" as a string that held two fish, one on each end. Using your star map, you can see where one fish is located — between the constellations Aries and Andromeda. The other fish, at the other end of the string, is hidden below the horizon. You will need to wait until later in the year to see it.

Stretching out between the area of Eridanus and Pisces is the constellation Cetus, which the ancient peoples saw as a sea monster or whale. In fact, it was often seen as the monster from which the hero Perseus saved Andromeda. If you have good observing conditions, you may note, as the star map shows, that there is a four-sided figure between Aries and Eridanus. This figure forms the head of the monster. A row of faint stars reaches downward to a large oval of brighter stars forming the main body of the creature. At this time of year, part of the main body of Cetus is below the horizon. Later in the year, you may see all of this huge constellation.

The most interesting star in this area is the one marked "Mira" on the star maps. This is one of the most famous of the variable stars, and one of the first of them to be discovered. At certain times in its cycle it is as bright as the stars in the belt of Orion; at other times it is so faint that it cannot be seen with the unaided eye and you may have trouble seeing it with binoculars. When it is at the bright part of its cycle, it is easy to find because the stars in the "string of Pisces" point, like an arrow, straight toward it.

Gemini If you now look high toward the zenith, and return to the large constellation Auriga, you will be ready to explore the constellations in the eastern part of the sky. From Capella, the brightest star in Auriga, move across the constellation to the two bright stars on the eastern side of the constellation; then move further eastward about twice that distance. You will immediately see two close, very bright stars called Castor and Pollux, almost equal in brightness, though there is a detectable difference with Pollux being slightly brighter. As you can see from the star map, there is an irregular row of stars extending from each star and toward the constellation Orion. Ancient peoples saw these rows of stars forming the bodies of the twin sons of the god Zeus. They were called Castor and Pollux, the names we give to the two brightest stars in the constellation. Gemini is the Latin word for "the Twins."

Leo From Castor and Pollux, moving eastward toward the horizon, you will notice one star that is much brighter than any other in this area of the sky. This is the star Regulus, the brightest star in the constellation Leo. It is about half-way between Pollux and the eastern horizon. If you have good observing conditions you will also notice extending to its left what looks like stars forming the shape of a sickle or a backwards question mark. Closer to the horizon is a triangle of stars, as shown on Map 1. Together the ancient peoples saw these shapes as forming the body of a huge lion, the one slain by Hercules in one of his twelve labours. The "sickle" formed the head and mane of the lion; the triangle formed its hind quarters.

This area of the sky is famous for having a number of galaxies that may be viewed with a small telescope. One of them is marked near the triangle of stars.

Cancer About half-way between Gemini and the "sickle" of Leo is a group of stars that are known as the constellation Cancer, the Crab. None of the stars in this area is as bright as Castor, Pollux, Regulus, or some of the other stars in Gemini and Leo. You will see from your star map that there are two "deep sky objects" marked in this constellation. They are both star clusters. The larger, brighter one is called M44 or Praesepe or the Beehive Cluster and it can even be detected with the unaided eye. It is marked on the star map just below the "n" in the word "Cancer." To the unaided eye it looks like a fuzzy patch of light. Binoculars will show dozens of individual stars. The other cluster, called M67, requires binoculars just to see it.

Try to see as many stars as you can in this constellation, but do not worry if your conditions do not allow you to see all of those that are marked on the star map.

Hydra In the area between Cancer and the southeastern horizon, there is a long, winding pathway of stars that make up the constellation called Hydra, the sea-serpent. Most of the stars in this constellation are not very bright. One exception is the star named Alphard, the brightest in the constellation. It is marked on the star map, but its name is not given. It is the star that appears about half-way between Regulus and the three stars that form the small constellation Pyxis down near the southeastern horizon. Those three stars may be difficult to see if trees or lights block the southeastern horizon, but the brightest star in Hydra is easy to see. If you have good dark skies, it should be easy to see the five stars that form the head of the Hydra, as shown on the star map just below the stars of the constellation Cancer.

Canis Minor After finding Leo and Cancer and the head of the Hydra, it is easy to locate Canis Minor (Latin words for the Smaller Dog). Between the bright star Regulus in Leo, which is in the east, and the stars in the belt of Orion, which is in the south, there is only one very bright star. It is Procyon, the brightest star in Canis Minor. As the star map shows, there is only one other bright star in this small constellation. Like Sirius, Procyon also happens to be one of the stars that is near to our Solar System.

Monoceros Between Canis Minor and Canis Major is the constellation Monoceros (Latin word for Unicorn). There are no bright stars in this constellation and you may miss it entirely, if you are observing from a location that has city lights nearby. Challenge yourself; try to see all the stars shown on the star map. You will probably not see the shape of a unicorn in the pattern of stars; almost no one does!

Lepus and *Columba* Below Orion are two constellations representing wild creatures. The first one is the area of the sky known as Lepus (the Rabbit). You may under good conditions see all the stars marked on the map. However, if your skies are not very good, you will probably see only about four of them. Also, depending on your southern horizon, you may see all, some, or none of the stars in the constellation Columba (the Dove).

> **In the winter evenings a giant ring or circle of bright and dazzling stars is seen around the star Betelgeuse. They are Capella, Aldebaran, Rigel, Sirius, Procyon, Castor, and Pollux.**

The Great Circle Around Betelgeuse Many people have noticed that in the winter evening skies there are many bright stars, and some of the very brightest seem to form a giant ring around Betelgeuse, the star in the shoulder of Orion. This great ring or circle of stars is made up of Capella, Aldebaran, Rigel, Sirius, Procyon, Castor, and Pollux. Such a huge circle of brilliant stars is very easy to find because it has some of the brightest stars in the sky.

PRACTISE YOUR SKILLS

(a) Finding the Bright Stars

The following 12 stars are labelled on Map 1. They are easy to find in a clear sky. Check them off on this list as you find them.

- Sirius (the Dog Star in Canis Major, brightest star in the sky)

- Betelgeuse (the shoulder star in Orion)

- Rigel (the knee star in Orion)

- Aldebaran ("the eye of the bull" in Taurus)

- Castor and Pollux (The Heavenly Twins, the brightest stars in Gemini)

- Procyon (The Little Dog Star in Canis Minor)

- Regulus (brightest star in Leo)

- Capella ("the Goat Star" in Auriga)

- Polaris (the North Pole Star in Ursa Minor)

- Mira (the Wonderful Star in Cetus, a star that varies widely in brightness) (This is the one star on the list that may be too faint to see, if it happens to be at the faint part of its cycle.)

- Algol (a star in Perseus; it varies regularly in a period of about 2.9 days)

(b) 10 Interesting Objects for Binoculars

The following is a list of 10 objects that are very interesting to observe, and easy to find in binoculars. They are large and distinctive, and once you see them you will want to return to them many times. They are objects that a beginner should see and recognize before trying for other objects.

- Mizar and Alcor (The second star, counting from the end of the handle of the Big Dipper, along with the nearby fainter star that is shown on the star map, are the famous pair that give a test of good eyesight when viewed with the unaided eye. If you view them with binoculars, you will see that there also is a third star nearby. When viewed with large binoculars or a small telescope, Mizar, itself appears as a double star.)

- M45 (The Pleiades, the famous cluster in Taurus that often appears as six or seven stars to the unaided eye, shows a dozen or more stars in binoculars. The nebulosity around one or more of the stars may be seen in a telescope under good conditions.)

- M44 (The Beehive Cluster in Cancer is a "swarm of stars" in a good pair of binoculars. Enjoy the view.)

- M42 (Using binoculars or a small telescope, observe this nebula below the belt of Orion on a clear, dark winter evening. Notice the swirling mass of gas. Describe or draw the shape that you see. Does it look like a bird, or a small kite, or some such object?)

- M35 (This cluster of stars near the "feet of Gemini" is much smaller than M44. You may notice another fainter cluster of stars nearby.)

- Hyades Star Cluster (This huge cluster of bright stars near Aldebaran forms "the head of Taurus, the Bull." You can see some of these stars with the unaided eye. In binoculars, you will see dozens of stars, and in a small telescope, you may have to move the intrument a little in order to see all of them; otherwise they will not all fit into the field of view.)

- NGC869 and 884 (This Double Cluster in the Milky Way between Perseus and Cassiopeia will give you a very interesting sight in binoculars. Under good observing conditions, it can easily be seen naked-eye.)

- M41 (Not far below Sirius you will find this cluster of stars. Do you notice, in your binoculars, that there is one bright star near the centre of the group? What colour is it?)

- M31 (This famous Andromeda Galaxy is very distinctive in binoculars, and very easy to find since it can be seen with the unaided eye.)

- M33 (The first time you try, you may find it difficult to see this large galaxy in Triangulum, because it may be larger than you expect it to be.)

(c) Deep Sky Objects for the Small Telescope

The following list of 22 objects is a handy summary of all the deep sky objects marked on Map 1 (each indicated with a tiny circle of five dots). They are objects far beyond our Solar System, that is, galaxies, star clusters, or nebulae that may be seen with a small telescope or good-quality binoculars. A few of them can be seen easily with the unaided eye. The ones that can be seen in this way are mentioned below. Some of them will be easy for the beginner to find; others will be more difficult.

> This list of objects should be attempted *only after* completing the previous lists and becoming familiar with the use of a star atlas and a small telescope.

Charles Messier's list of deep sky objects, composed in the late 1700s, is still the most common list of such objects used by amateur astronomers today.

The names of many "deep sky objects" begin with the letter "M." This means that the object is from what is called the Messier Catalogue of 110 deep-sky objects. The French astronomer, Charles Messier, compiled the original version of this catalogue or list in the late 1700s; he was, in fact, drawing up a list of objects that could possibly be confused with comets because his main interest at the time was in searching for comets. Even though others added more objects to the list and there have been minor changes to it, the "M-objects" or "Messier objects" are still the most common of the deep sky objects observed by amateur astronomers. In fact, some amateurs have observed all of Messier's objects with binoculars.

The letters "NGC" indicate that the object is listed in The New General Catalogue of Non-stellar Astronomical Objects, originally published in 1888. Of course, that list of over 7800 deep sky objects (galaxies, star clusters, and nebulae) is over 100 years old, and is certainly no longer a new list, but the name and number are still used to identify those hundreds of objects. Some are bright enough to see naked-eye, as noted below; others are much fainter.

Check off each object when you have observed it.

– M41 (a cluster of stars in Canis Major, just south of the star Sirius)

– M47 (a cluster of stars just east of Canis Major)

– M93 (a cluster of stars found on map just below the "M" in the words Canis Major)

– M1 (a supernova remnant called the Crab Nebula, an expanding gas cloud in Taurus)

– M35 (a cluster of stars in Gemini)

– M37, M36, M38 (the three clusters of stars in Auriga)

– M45 (the famous Pleiades star cluster, easily seen naked-eye)

- M44 (the famous Beehive Cluster in Cancer; a naked-eye object)

- M67 (a small fainter star cluster in Cancer)

- M66 (a spiral galaxy marked below the triangle in Leo; nearby is another spiral galaxy, M65)

- M51 (the famous Whirlpool Galaxy in the constellation Canes Venatici; it is marked on the star map just below the end star in the handle of the Big Dipper.)

- M106 (a galaxy in Canes Venatici; it is marked on the map half-way between the cup of the Big Dipper and the stars of Canes Venatici)

- M63 (a galaxy in Canes Venatici; marked above the "C" in Canes Venatici)

- M101 (a large "face-on" galaxy in Ursa Major; marked above the end star in the handle of the Big Dipper)

- M81 (a spiral galaxy in Ursa Major; it is marked between the cup of the Big Dipper and the constellation Camelopardalis; near it may be seen the irregular galaxy M82, a fine sight in a small telescope)

- M31 (the famous Andromeda Galaxy; shown below the first "A" in the word Andromeda; it may be seen naked-eye under good conditions)

- M33 (a large "face-on" galaxy in Triangulum; it has been called the Pinwheel Galaxy; like M31, one of the nearest galaxies to our Milky Way)

- M39 (an open star cluster near the star Deneb, which is very low near the northwestern horizon. It will be better seen later in the year)

- M42 (the famous Orion Nebula; it is seen naked-eye below the "belt of Orion;" very fine object in a small telescope)

- NGC869 (part of the Double Cluster, along with NGC884); formerly called "h and X Persei; may be seen naked-eye; marked on the map half-way

> ## The Double Cluster in Perseus is bright enough to see naked-eye; yet it was not listed in Messier's catalogue. It is NGC 869 and 884.

between the constellations Perseus and Cassiopeia; dazzling in a small telescope)

The March-April Night Sky (Map 2)

Constellations and Naked-Eye Objects

For viewing objects in the sky during the times given on Map 2, you may use the following as your guide.

Some of the constellations previously seen in the western sky and marked on Map 1 have now disapppeared below the western horizon. Certain other constellations, that you did not previously see, have now appeared above the eastern horizon.

The constellations that are now no longer seen in the western sky are Cetus, Pisces, Pegasus, Andromeda, Triangulum, Aries, Eridanus, Lepus, and Columba.

The constellations that have appeared in the east are Bootes, Virgo, Corvus, Crater, and Corona Borealis. Parts of Hercules and Lyra are also visible in the northeast, as well as part of Serpens in the east, and Antlia in the Southeast.

With some adjustment, you can use the description of the constellations for Map 1, if you remember that all of them have moved westward. Use the following section for constellations and naked-eye objects that have risen in the east.

The Constellations of the Eastern Sky

Having found the Big Dipper in Ursa Major, as you have done previously, you can now proceed to all of the constellations of the eastern sky. You will have noticed that the Big Dipper is now high in the northeastern sky.

Bootes Follow the curve of the stars in the handle of the Big Dipper downward

> ### In modern times, most observers see in Bootes, not a herdsman or a shepherd, but the shape of a large kite flying in the wind.

and to the right. This will bring you to a bright reddish-yellow star called Arcturus, the brightest star in the northern half of the sky. Northward from this star is a pattern of stars that the ancient peoples associated with a herdsman or shepherd called Bootes. Many people nowadays see, not a person, but the shape of a large kite. If you have good observing conditions, you may notice five or six fairly bright stars enclosing the area of "the kite." Near Arcturus, as the star map shows, you will probably see five other stars that seem to make a stand for this kite which has been tipped over on its side. On the star map, they are the stars that surround the "A" in the word "Arcturus."

Virgo Retrace the curving line from the Big Dipper's handle to Arcturus and continue it on to the brightest star in the southeastern sky. This is Spica, the brightest star in the constellation Virgo. This large constellation was seen by the ancients as a goddess. As the star map shows, you may recognize a pattern of stars that seem to form a large box with two curving lines extending out from it toward the constellation Leo, which is higher in the sky, and which was described previously. Virgo is an area of the sky that contains many distant galaxies.

> **Following the curving line of stars, which is the Big Dipper's handle, leads to the very bright star Arcturus, and this curve then continues on to Spica, the brightest star in Virgo.**

Corvus and *Crater* Low in the southeastern sky and to the right from the star Spica is a distinctive pattern of four bright stars that seem to form a box tilted on its side. The two upper stars are almost in line with Spica. This pattern is called Corvus, a constellation that long ago was seen as a crow. This bird was drinking from a large cup situated nearby. Slightly up and to

> **Corona Borealis (The Northern Crown) is a pattern of stars that almost forms a circle, and does somewhat resemble a crown.**

the right from Corvus is Crater, the drinking cup. It seems to be tilted to the left toward the crow, which is drinking from it. Crater does not have any stars as bright as the four main stars of Corvus, and it may be difficult to recognize the pattern, if sky conditions are not good. You will notice, too, that these two star patterns, Corvus and Crater, seem to be riding on the back of Hydra, the sea monster whose body is shown by the long row of stars across the sky just above the southeastern horizon.

Corona Borealis If you move back to the eastern sky and look below the top end of "the kite" of Bootes you may see a pattern of stars that almost forms a circle. It is just rising in the east-northeast, and as the star map shows, is between Bootes and Hercules which has partly risen. Corona Borealis (Latin words for the Northern Crown) does somewhat resemble a crown. Some of the stars are like gems on a crown, and the brightest gem of all is called Alphecca. This star is marked on the star map, but it is not labelled. Some astronomers remember Corona Borealis as an area that has several famous variable stars.

PRACTISE YOUR SKILLS

(a) Finding the Bright Stars

The following 14 stars are labelled on Map 2. They are very easy to find in a clear sky since they are among the brightest of the stars. Check each one as you identify it.

- Sirius (the famous Dog Star in Canis Major, brightest star in the sky)
- Betelgeuse (the red giant, shoulder star in Orion)
- Rigel (the bright white knee star in Orion)
- Aldebaran (the "eye of the bull" in Taurus)
- Algol (famous variable star in Perseus with a regular period of 2.9 days)
- Castor and Pollux (the Heavenly Twins, brightest stars in Gemini)
- Procyon (the Little Dog Star in the constellation Canis Minor)
- Regulus (brightest star in Leo)
- Polaris (the North Pole Star in the constellation Ursa Minor)
- Capella ("the Goat Star" in Auriga)
- Arcturus (very bright, red giant star in Bootes)
- Spica (brightest star in Virgo)
- Vega (brightest star in Lyra)

(b) 8 Interesting Objects for Binoculars

Use the same checklist as for Map 1 (pages 35-36) with the following exception. Delete the last two objects, M31 and M33, because the area of the sky where they are found has now set.

(c) Deep Sky Objects for the Small Telescope

There are 27 Deep Sky Objects shown on Map 2.

> Before attempting to observe them, be sure to read the information above the list on pages 37-38.

Each object is indicated by a tiny circle of dots. They are the same as those shown for *Map 1* with the following exceptions:

(a) M31, M33, and M39 are *not* shown since they have set in the west.

(b) Since the areas of Coma Berenices, Virgo, and Hercules are up in the eastern sky, these *eight* objects are shown:

– M89, M84, and M58 (three galaxies in the constellation Virgo) (A small telescope can show many other galaxies, besides these three, in the area of

A telescope can show a dozen or more galaxies in the constellations Virgo and Coma.

Coma and Virgo where these three are marked. In fact, there is a large cluster of galaxies in this region of the sky.)

– M104 (a distinctive galaxy called "the Sombrero" because of its unusual appearance. Marked on the map between Virgo and Corvus)

– M13 (a large globular cluster in Hercules, marked on the map above the letter "s" in the word "Hercules")

– M92 (a globular cluster in Hercules, maked on the map above the first "e" in the word "Hercules")

– M3 (a globular cluster in Canes Venatici, marked on the map between the words "Bootes" and "Canes Venatici")

– M5 (a globular cluster in Serpens Caput, marked on the map just above and slightly to the right of the "E" indicating the eastern horizon)

The May-June Night Sky (Map 3)

Constellations and Naked-Eye Objects

For viewing the sky during the times given on Map 3, you may use the following as your guide.

You will notice that some of the constellations previously seen in the western sky and marked on Map 2 have now set below the western horizon. Certain other constellations, that you did not previously see, have now risen above the eastern horizon.

The constellations that are now no longer seen in the western sky are the "winter constellations": Orion, Canis Major, Canis Minor, Monoceros, Taurus, and part of Auriga.

The constellations that have appeared in the east are Hercules, Lyra, Cygnus, Aquila, Ophiuchus, Serpens, Libra, Scorpius, Sagitta, Delphinus, and Scutum.

For *most of the constellations shown on Map 3*, you can use the descriptions given for Maps 1 and 2, with one important adjustment. You must remember that all of them have moved westward a certain amount.

Use the following section for constellations and naked-eye objects that have risen in the east.

The Constellations of the Eastern Sky

Following the handle of the Big Dipper away from its cup, as you did previously, you come again to the very bright star Arcturus, which is now high in the sky. In fact, it is almost directly overhead. You will be able to use Arcturus as a guide to the constellations and stars of the eastern sky.

Hercules Facing east and directing your view downward and to the left from Arcturus, you will see first the semi-circle of stars called Corona Borealis,

> **Ancient peoples recognized the four stars of "the Keystone" as part of the body of the great hero, Hercules, who performed twelve enormous feats of strength.**

and then the large constellation named Hercules. The most distinctive pattern in this constellation is a group of four stars called "the Keystone," found on the star map above the last four letters of the word "Hercules." The ancient peoples recognized in this area the body of the great hero named "Heracles" or "Hercules," who was known for his strength and his success in performing twelve enormous tasks that no ordinary person would attempt.

In this area on the star map you will see marked two deep-sky objects, both of them globular clusters. They are called M13 and M92. Notice that this constellation extends down toward Ophiuchus. The line drawn in that direction stops at the star called Alpha Herculis or Ras Algethi. It is a famous double star that can be resolved into its two parts in a small telescope.

Lyra Continuing further downward toward the eastern horizon and slightly to the left you come to a very bright star named Vega. It is the brightest of the several naked-eye stars that form a distinctive parallelogram pattern known as the constellation Lyra. Actually, you will see that the parallelogram is below Vega, and Vega is part of a small triangle of stars. The star just to the left of Vega is the one astronomers call Epsilon Lyrae, or the "Double Double," since, in a small telescope, you can see that it is not just a double star, but that each star is itself a double. Many beginning observers also remember Lyra as a constellation that has a variable star which can be easily observed with the unaided eye. It is the star named "Beta Lyrae," and is the one shown on the star map closest to the letter "L" in the word "Lyra." (See page 140.)

Cygnus Low in the eastern sky, half-way between Vega and the horizon, is the large cross-like pattern of stars named Cygnus, the Swan or the Northern

> ## In Cygnus, the Swan, also called "the Northern Cross," the brightest star is named Deneb, and this whole constellation is within the Milky Way.

Cross. You can easily see that this cross seems to be tilted on its side. The brightest star named Deneb is at the top of the cross, and the whole constellation is in the Milky Way.

Among the many interesting objects in this constellation is a bright and very beautiful double star named Albireo. It is the star at the "bottom of the cross" or the "head of the swan" — the star that is marked just above the last letter of the word "Cygnus" on the star map. The two stars of this famous double are blue and gold in colour, and they are far enough apart to be clearly distinguished in binoculars.

Aquila Just barely rising above the eastern horizon is the star Altair, the brightest one in the constellation Aquila, the Eagle. This star is among the fifty stars closest to our Sun. The constellation pattern will be better recognized later in the year or later in the night when it is higher in the sky.

The Great Summer Triangle The three bright stars that you have just observed, Vega, Deneb, and Altair, are known as the Summer Triangle. During late

---

The three-star asterism — Vega, Deneb, and Altair — is known as the Summer Triangle.

---

spring, throughout the summer, and even into the autumn, these stars dominate the southern part of the sky and are easily recognized.

Ophiuchus and *Serpens* If, instead of moving down from the area of Hercules to Lyra and Cygnus, you move in a more southeasterly direction from Hercules, you will come to the large five-sided pattern of stars in the constellation Ophiuchus. This constellation was known to the ancient peoples as The Serpent Bearer, but nowadays no one sees a person holding a snake. Instead some people call it "The Coffin," because to them it looks like a large box. The brightest star in the constellation, Alpha Ophiuchi or Ras Alhague, is the one shown at the point formed by the star pattern at the left side of the constellation. This constellation contains a number of star clusters, none of which is marked on our star maps.

Extending out on both sides of Ophiuchus are parts of the constellation called Serpens, the Serpent or Snake. This is the only constellation that is broken into two parts. The head of the snake, Serpens Caput, has a row of stars extending upward from Ophiuchus toward Corona Borealis. The snake's tail, Serpens Cauda, extends downward from the southern part of Ophiuchus toward Aquila. The upper part of Serpens contains a well-known globular cluster of stars called M5, which can be seen in binoculars.

Libra About half-way between Arcturus and the southeastern horizon is the constellation Libra, the Scales, marked by four naked-eye stars. They form a box or square pattern with the two stars on the upper right being the brightest. The one shown closest to the letter "L" in the word "Libra" on the star map appears as a double star in binoculars. It has the interesting Arabic name "Zubenelgenubi." The star at the top of the square, with the equally interesting name "Zubeneschamali" is sometimes reported to appear greenish in colour

> # The two brightest stars of the constellation Libra have the interesting Arabic names: Zubenelgenubi and Zubeneschamali.

both when viewed naked-eye and with optical aid. Look at it carefully yourself, and record what colour you see.

Scorpius To the left of Libra and just rising above the southeastern horizon is Scorpius, the Scorpion. It is known for its bright red star Antares, a star that is as red as the planet Mars. The name of the star itself means that it is the rival of Mars. Some people claim that the pattern of the constellation actually resembles a scorpion with the bright stars between Antares and Libra forming the claws of the animal and the long row of stars to the lower left of Antares forming the tail. Marked on the star map just to the right of Antares is the cluster of stars called M4, a grouping that can easily be seen in binoculars.

PRACTISE YOUR SKILLS

(a) Finding the Bright Stars

The following 11 bright stars are labelled on Map 3. Check them off as you find them in a clear sky.

- Castor and Pollux (the Heavenly Twins, brightest stars in Gemini)
- Regulus (brightest star in Leo)
- Polaris (the North Pole Star in Ursa Minor)
- Capella ("the Goat Star" in Auriga)
- Arcturus (very bright, red giant star in Bootes)
- Spica (brightest star in Virgo)
- Vega (brightest star in Lyra)
- Deneb (brightest star in Cygnus or the Northern Cross)
- Altair (brightest star in Aquila)
- Antares (brightest star in Scorpius)

(b) 4 Interesting Objects for Binoculars

The following four are among the best of the deep sky objects. You should try to observe them before going on to others.

- M44 (the Beehive Cluster in Cancer with its dozens of bright stars)

- M4 (the globular star cluster in Scorpius just to the west of the star Antares)

- M11 (the open cluster of stars in Scutum; sometimes called the "Wild Duck Cluster")

- M13 (the large, bright globular cluster of stars in the "Keystone of Hercules")

(c) Deep Sky Objects for the Small Telescope

The following 22 Deep Sky Objects are labelled on Map 3.

> Before attempting to observe them, read the information above the list on pages 37-38.

- M81 (a spiral galaxy in Ursa Major; it is marked on the star map between the cup of the Big Dipper and the constellation Camelopardalis; near it may be seen the irregular galaxy M82; a fine sight in a small telescope)

- M106 (a galaxy in Canes Venatici; it is marked on the map half-way between the cup of the Big Dipper and the stars of Canes Venatici)

- M66 (a spiral galaxy marked below the triangle in Leo; near it is another spiral galaxy, M65)

- M63 (a spiral galaxy in Canes Venatici; marked on the map above the "n" in the first word of "Canes Venatici")

- M101 (a large "face-on" spiral galaxy in Ursa Major; marked above the end star in the handle of the Big Dipper)

- M51 (the famous Pinwheel Galaxy in the constellation Canes Venatici; it is marked on the star map just below the end star in the handle of the Big Dipper)

- M44 (the famous Beehive Cluster of stars in Cancer; near the middle of the constellation Cancer)

- M67 (another cluster of stars in Cancer; shown south of M44)

- M4 (a globular star cluster in Scorpius; just to the right of Antares)

- M5 (a globular star cluster in Serpens Caput; marked on the map half-way between the words "Ophiuchus" and "Virgo")

- M11 (an open star cluster in Scutum; marked on the map just above the eastern horizon and between the words "Aquila" and "Scutum")

- M27 (a planetary nebula called the Dumbbell Nebula; in the constellation Vulpecula; marked on the star map just above the "g" in the word "Sagitta")

- M89, M84, M58 (galaxies in the constellation Virgo; a whole cluster of galaxies may be found where these three are marked)

- M13 (a large, bright globular star cluster in Hercules)

> ## The globular cluster M13, in the constellation Hercules, is a great favorite of amateur astronomers. It is large, bright, and easy to find along one side of the four-sided "Keystone of Hercules."

- M92 (a globular star cluster in Hercules)

- M3 (a globular star cluster in Canes Venatici; marked on the map just below the letter "e" in the word "Bootes")

- M39 (an open cluster of stars near Deneb in Cygnus)

- M104 (the Sombrero Galaxy in the constellation Virgo; marked on the map just above the "r" in the word "Corvus")

- NGC869 (part of the Double Cluster, along with NGC884; formerly called "h and X Persei"; may be seen naked-eye; marked on the star map half-way between the constellations Perseus and Cassiopeia and very low near the northern horizon)

- NGC6960 (part of the Veil Nebula, along with NGC6979; found on the map near the "arm star" of the Northern Cross of Cygnus and low near the east-northeastern horizon; will be seen better later in the year when it is higher in the sky)

The July-August Night Sky (Map 4)

Constellations and Naked-Eye Objects

For viewing the summer sky during the times given on Map 4, you may use the following as your guide.

You will notice that some of the constellations previously seen in the western sky and marked on Map 3 have now set below the western horizon. Certain other constellations, that you did not previously see, have now risen above the eastern horizon.

The constellations that are now no longer seen in the western sky are some of the "spring constellations": Gemini, Cancer, and parts of Leo.

The constellations that have appeared in the east are Delphinus, Equuleus, Pegasus, Andromeda, and parts of Aquarius, and in the south Sagittarius and Capricornus.

For many of the constellations, you may use the descriptions given for Maps 2 and 3, if you remember that all of them have moved westward a certain amount.

The Constellations of the Northern Sky

Having read Chapter 3, you should be able to find the Big Dipper in the constellation Ursa Major. You will notice that it is in the northwest rather than due north, and that it is standing on its cup with the handle pointing upward. The "Pointer Stars" direct you to Polaris, the brightest star in Ursa Minor. You will notice that the Little Dipper is almost standing on its handle with its cup upward and toward the west. The stars of Draco wind between the two dippers and curl high in the sky with the head of the Dragon almost directly overhead. Tracing a line from the middle of the handle of the Big Dipper to Polaris and extending it on an equal distance brings you to the "W" of Cassiopeia, which is well up in the northeastern sky. If observing conditions are good, you will notice that it is in the Milky Way, the great band of millions of stars running across the sky. Below Cassiopeia and just at the northeastern horizon is the constellation Perseus. Above Cassiopeia and partly within the band of the Milky Way are some of the stars of the constellation Cepheus. As the star map shows, Cepheus with its five bright stars looks somewhat like a house that has been tilted to one side with the peak of its roof pointing almost to Polaris. The whole area of sky below Polaris is filled by two constellations that have no bright stars in them; because of this, they can be easily overlooked even though they occupy a fairly large area of sky. They are Camelopardalis, the Giraffe, and Lynx, the Lynx.

The Region of the Summer Triangle Taking the place of the bright star Arcturus that was previously high in the sky is a triangle of bright stars not far from the zenith. (You will see that Arcturus is now well down in the western sky and Spica has almost set at the western horizon.) As Star Map 4 indicates, *Vega* in Lyra, *Deneb* in Cygnus, and *Altair* in Aquila are the trio of brilliant stars close to the zenith. If the sky is dark enough, after twilight has ended, and a bright Moon is not interfering, and you are well away from the light pollution of a city, then you will notice something else about this area of the sky. The Milky Way is spread across the sky, running roughly from north to south. In fact, the Milky Way surrounds two of these three stars, completely enclosing the constellations Cygnus, the Northern Cross, and Aquila, the Eagle. The consellation Lyra is just outside the bounds of the Milky Way. We now know that the Milky Way is not a river of milk or a hazy cloud in the sky, but millions of stars; in fact, after the invention of the telescope about four hundred years ago, astronomers first saw what it really was, just as

> **The invention of the telescope about 400 years ago gave modern astronomers a chance to see that the Milky Way is, not a river of milk or a hazy cloud, but millions of stars.**

binoculars or a small telescope show us the innumerable stars in this galaxy of ours that we call the Milky Way. As you become more familiar with the sky, you will return to the area of Cygnus many times to explore the fascinating objects that are found there.

Between Cygnus and Aquila you may see four stars that form the small constellation named Sagitta, the Arrow. Near it are three other very small constellations. To the east, as you will see on your star map, are Dephinus, the Dolphin, and Equuleus, the Colt. The first of these contains six stars in

> **Near the small constellation named Sagitta, the Arrow, are three other very small constellations: Delphinus, the Dolphin; Equuleus, the Colt; and Vulpecula, the Fox.**

a pattern that actually does look like a small dolphin leaping out of the water. The second with four very faint stars does not look at all like a horse; in fact, many observers feel fortunate if sky conditions allow them to see any of the four stars. To the north and in the position between Sagitta and the last letter of the word "Cygnus," as shown on the star map, is the very tiny constellation referred to as Vulpecula, the Fox. It has only one star bright enough to be indicated on our star map. However, it does have one object well known to most astronomers, the deep sky object, M27 or the Dumbbell Nebula, which is an example of a planetary nebula.

The Star Clouds to the South As you move from Altair toward the southern horizon, you will notice, again if conditions are good, that the Milky Way becomes more dense and defined in certain spots. Here there are millions of stars in the central region of our galaxy. The densest regions can be seen in the constellation Scutum, the Shield, and in Sagittarius, the Archer, though the Milky Way extends to the right to include part of the constellation Scorpius, the Scorpion, which may be partly below your horizon, as shown on the star map. The constellation Sagittarius appears to most people not as a person but as a "teapot," with its spout to the right and handle to the left. As the star map indicates with the letters "GC" (for Galactic Centre) to the right of the spout, the centre of the Milky Way Galaxy is located in this direction. Many examples of nebulae and star clusters are found in this part of the sky.

Ophiuchus and Serpens The two constellations, Ophiuchus, the Serpent Bearer, and Serpens, the Serpent, were previously seen low in the southeast. Now they are high in the south and appear to dominate a large region of the sky. Ophiuchus contains a number of interesting star clusters that you can search for with binoculars. Serpens is a divided constellation, as the star map shows, with the head and part of the large snake's body to the right of Ophiuchus

> **Serpens is a divided constellation, with the head of the large snake on one side of Ophiuchus and the long tail on the other side.**

and its long straight tail to the left. On the star map, the two parts are labelled Serpens Caput (the Head) and Serpens Cauda (the Tail).

The Six Stars Maps

The Remaining Spring Constellations in the West The spring constellations that dominated the southern sky a few months ago are now sinking in the west. Most of Leo, the Lion, is below the horizon. Virgo, with the bright star Spica, is lying along the southwestern horizon, followed by the four stars that form the square of Libra.

The First of the Autumn Constellations Rising in the East Moving down from Cygnus to the eastern horizon, your eyes meet the Great Square of Pegasus. It actually looks like a huge diamond standing on one point just north of the eastern point on the horizon. The bright stars of Andromeda are stretched along the northeastern horizon. Two galaxies, M31 and M33, are close to the horizon, and on either side of the "middle star" of Andromeda. Two other constellations that will dominate the southern sky in the autumn are now just on the horizon. They are Pisces, whose one "fish" is just peaking above the horizon, and Aquarius, which is also only partly visible between the bright star Altair and the horizon. Also between Altair and the southeastern horizon are the stars of Capricornus, the Horned Goat, a large constellation that stretches between Sagittarius and Aquarius.

PRACTISE YOUR SKILLS

(a) Finding the Bright Stars

The following 7 very bright stars are labelled on Map 4. They are very easy to find in a clear sky. Check them off when you have found them. (You may notice that now there are fewer very bright stars to see than at any other time of the year. The winter sky certainly contains more than the summer sky. Compare the number on this checklist with that for Map 2 and Map 6.)

- Polaris (the North Pole Star, brightest star in Ursa Minor)
- Arcturus (very bright, red giant star in Bootes)
- Vega (brightest star in Lyra)
- Spica (brightest star in Virgo)
- Antares (brightest star in Scorpius; very reddish-orange in colour)
- Altair (brightest star in Aquila; only about 16 light-years away)
- Deneb (brightest star in Cygnus; 100 times as far away as Altair)

(b) 6 Interesting Objects for Binoculars

These are among the best of the deep sky objects currently visible. You should try to observe them before going on to others.

– M6 and M7 (These two open clusters in Scorpius are low in the south, but are excellent objects. They are rich in bright stars.)

– M22 (This globular cluster near the "top of the teapot" in Sagittarius is a beautiful bright object in steadily held binoculars.)

– M8 (The famous Lagoon Nebula is just above the "spout of the teapot" in Sagittarius. It shows both nebulosity and a star cluster.)

– M4 (This bright globular cluster is easy to find beside the star Antares.)

– M11 (This is a bright open cluster of stars in Scutum. Notice its unusual shape.)

(c) Deep Sky Objects for the Small Telescope

The following is a checklist of the 27 Deep Sky Objects shown on Map 4. Each one is indicated by a tiny circle of dots.

> Before trying to observe the objects on this list, be sure to read the information above the list on pages 37-38.

– M6 (bright star cluster in Scorpius)

– M7 (star cluster in Scorpius, near M6, and bright enough to see naked eye) (Both of these clusters are quite low in the southern sky.)

– M22 (globular star cluster in Sagittarius)

– M8 (Lagoon Nebula in Sagittarius)

– M17 (Omega Nebula in Sagittarius)

– M11 (open star cluster in Scutum)

– M4 (globular star cluster in Scorpius, just to the right of Antares)

– M89, M84, M58 (three galaxies in the constellation Virgo)
(The great cluster of galaxies found between the stars of Leo and Virgo is now low in the west and may be difficult to observe.)

– M5 (a globular star cluster in Serpens Caput)

– M13 (a bright globular cluster in Hercules, the one marked on the western side of this constellation)

- M92 (a globular cluster in Hercules, the one marked on the northern side of this constellation)
  (Hercules is now very high in the sky. This is a good time to view these two clusters.)

- M3 (a globular cluster in Canes Venatici)

- M27 (a planetary nebula in the constellation Vulpecula; found on the map above the "g" in the word "Sagitta")

- M51 (the famous Whirlpool Galaxy in Canes Venatici; it is marked on the map just below the end star in the handle of the Big Dipper)

- M101 (a large "face-on" spiral galaxy in Ursa Major; marked above the end star in the handle of the Big Dipper)

- M106 (a galaxy in Canes Venatici; marked on the map half-way between the cup of the Big Dipper and the stars of Canes Venatici)

- M63 (a spiral galaxy in Canes Venatici; marked on the map above the first letter in the words "Canes Venatici")

- M81 (a spiral galaxy in Ursa Major; marked on the star map between the cup of the Big Dipper and the constellation Camelopardalis)

- M2 (a globular cluster in Aquarius; marked on the star map half-way between the words "Equuleus" and "Aquarius")

- M15 (a globular cluster in Pegasus; marked on the star map just above the word "Equuleus")

- M31 (the famous Andromeda Galaxy; marked on the star map just below the third letter in the word "Andromeda")

- M33 (the famous Pinwheel Galaxy in Triangulum; marked on the star map just below M31 and near the horizon)
  (Both of these galaxies are now very close to the northeastern horizon; it is wise to wait until later in the night to have a better view of them.)

- M39 (an open star cluster near Deneb in Cygnus)

- NGC869 (part of the Double Cluster, along with NGC884; also called "h and X Persei"; may be seen naked eye and found between the stars of Perseus and Cassiopeia)

- NGC6960 (part of the Veil Nebula, along with NGC6979; it is now high in the sky and just below the "left arm" of the Northern Cross in Cygnus)

The September-October Night Sky (Map 5)

Constellations and Naked-Eye Objects

For viewing the sky during the times given on Map 5, you may use the following as your guide.

You will notice that some of the constellations previously seen in the western sky and marked on Map 4 have now set below the western horizon. Certain other constellations, that you did not previously see, have now risen above the eastern horizon.

The constellations that are now no longer seen in the western sky are some of the late spring and summer constellations: Virgo, Libra, Scorpius, most of Sagittarius, and part of Bootes.

The constellations that have appeared in the east are Auriga, Aries, Taurus, and Cetus, and Piscis Austrinus, which is in the south.

With some adjustment, you can use the description of the constellations for Map 4, if you remember that all of them have moved westward a certain amount.

The Constellations of the Northern Sky

Using the information you learned in Chapter 3, you will easily find the Big Dipper in the northern sky. The first thing that you will notice about it is that it is now low in the sky with the cup of the dipper very near the northern point of the horizon. After using the "Pointer Stars" to find Polaris, the North Pole Star, you will see that the Little Dipper in *Ursa Minor* stretches out toward the west and lies almost parallel to the northern horizon. The stars of *Draco*, the Dragon, extend to the westward between the two dippers, curl around the cup of the Little Dipper, and then extend again to the west where the head points to *Hercules*, which is now low in the western sky. Tracing an imaginary line from

> **Up and to the left from Cassiopeia is Cepheus with its pattern of stars resembling a "little house," but now this "little house" of Cepheus appears upside-down.**

the handle of the Big Dipper to Polaris and then extending it on an equal distance again brings us to the "*W*" of the constellation *Cassiopeia*, the Queen. This time we find that Cassiopeia is much higher in the sky, and it may now be easier to notice that it is inside the Milky Way, the great band of hazy brightness that extends across the dome of the sky. Slightly up and to the left from this star pattern is the "little house" of *Cepheus*, the King, with the "roof" of this five-star pattern pointing back down to Polaris as if the "house of Cepheus" is upside-down. Only part of Cepheus is within the Milky Way. The large area of sky extending down from Polaris to the northeastern horizon is occupied by the two "animal constellations," *Camelopardalis*, the Giraffe, and *Lynx*, the Lynx. None of their stars is very bright; you will be fortunate to see as many as are marked on the star map. In the northeast, Capella and the other bright stars of *Auriga* have risen enough to be easily seen, but further to the east, Aldebaran and a few of the stars of *Taurus* are so close to the horizon that they may not be noticed at all if there are trees or hills blocking the view. If it is possible to see bright, reddish Aldebaran and its companion stars in the Hyades cluster, you are catching a first glimpse of what the ancient peoples called the "rainy Hyades." When they saw them rising in the fall, they knew they should expect the rainy season of the year.

The Milky Way Crossing the Zenith As already observed, *Cassiopeia* and part of *Cepheus* are within the Milky Way and high in the sky. Following along this great wide pathway from Cassiopeia to Cepheus and continuing southwestward, you come to *Cygnus* or the Northern Cross, with its brightest

> **If observing conditions are good at this time of year, it will be easy to see that the Milky Way extends completely across the heavens from northeast to southwest.**

star, Deneb, very close to the zenith. If observing conditions are good, it will be easy to see that the Milky Way extends completely across the heavens from northeast to southwest. Follow its wide path to the southwest from Cygnus. Notice the short arrow called *Sagitta*, below Albireo, the star at the foot of the Northern Cross. Below it you will see *Aquila*, the Eagle, with the bright and relatively close star, Altair, the southernmost member of the Summer Triangle. Still further below it, you will see *Scutum*, the Shield, and the star clouds in and below this constellation.

The Summer Stars in the Western and Southwestern Sky The Summer Triangle of stars, Deneb, Vega, and Altair, are now well to the west of the zenith. Libra, Scorpius, and most of Sagittarius — the constellations that dominated the southern sky during the nights of summer — have now sunk below the western horizon. Only the handle of the "teapot of *Sagittarius*" remains visible in the southwest. Only parts of *Ophiuchus* and *Serpens* are above the west-southwestern horizon. *Hercules* is low in west, and below him, *Corona Borealis*, the Northern Crown, which will be difficult to see if there are trees or other obstructions near the western horizon.

Autumn's "Watery" Constellations in the South and Southeast As mentioned above, the ancient peoples knew the autumn as the rainy season. It is little wonder that the star patterns of this time of year are sometimes called the "watery constellations." In the southern and southeastern sky six creatures

> **At this time of year in the southern and southeastern sky, there are five constellations named after creatures from the depths of the ocean: Delphinus, Capricornus, Piscis Austrinis, Pisces, Cetus, and one constellation Aquarius, also associated with the watery realm.**

bear this association. Eastward from Altair is the small constellation named *Delphinus*, the Dolphin, which many observers claim actually looks like a dolphin leaping out of the sea. Southward from Altair is the constellation *Capricornus*, the Sea Goat or the Horned Goat. To the east of it is the large sprawling constellation *Aquarius*, the Water-bearer. Below Aquarius and low in the south is *Piscis Austrinus*, the Southern Fish, a small constellation of relatively faint stars except for one bright one named Fomalhaut. From our northern latitudes, this star is above the southern horizon for only a short while each year, but it is bright enough to be easily detected.

If you look from the zenith down toward the eastern horizon, you will notice first the Great Square of Pegasus and extending off to the left from it the three bright stars and other fainter ones in the constellation Andromeda. Below them are the final two "watery constellations," *Pisces*, the Fish, and *Cetus*, the Sea Monster or Whale. Pisces has no stars as bright as the Summer

Triangle. Careful observation will reveal a string of stars forming a large letter "V" pointing down to the horizon. The top ends of the "V" show two circles of stars, one below the Square of Pegasus and one below Andromeda. Cetus appears as a strange configuration of stars, some of them brighter than any in Pisces. Stretched along the eastern horizon, as the map indicates, Cetus has two patterns of four or five stars joined by a string of fainter stars. One of the stars in that string is the famous variable called Mira, the "Wonderful Star," one of the first stars noted to be variable. In fact, its variation in brightness is so great that at times it is as bright as the stars in the Square of Pegasus and at other times it is barely seen in ordinary binoculars. It is certainly one of the most interesting objects in the constellation Cetus. (See page 141.)

PRACTISE YOUR SKILLS

(a) Finding the Bright Stars

Check off the following 9 named stars when you observe them.

- Polaris (the North Pole Star, brightest star in Ursa Minor)
- Aldebaran (the "eye of the bull" in Taurus)
- Algol (famous variable star with a regular period of about 2.9 days)
- Mira (famous variable star in Cetus; varies widely in brightness)
- Fomalhaut (brightest star in Piscis Austrinus; always seen in the far southern sky from our northern latitudes)
- Altair (brightest star in Aquila)
- Deneb (brightest star in Cygnus)
- Capella ("the Goat Star," brightest in Auriga)
- Vega (brightest star in Lyra)

(b) 4 Interesting Objects for Binoculars

The following are among the most interesting objects to be seen at this time of year. Check them on this list, after observing them in binoculars.

- M15 (This bright globular cluster in Pegasus is easily seen in binoculars.)
- M11 (This open cluster in Scutum is a beautiful sight in binoculars. Note the pattern of the 4 stars beside it.)
- M31 (Steadily held binoculars will reveal some of the structure in this great galaxy in Andromeda.)

– M33 (This galaxy is not as bright as M31, but its large size always surprises beginning observers. It is in Triangulum.)

(c) Deep Sky Objects for the Small Telescope

There are 19 Deep Sky Objects shown on Map 5. The first 15 of them were more fully described on the checklist for Map 4 (pages 58-60).

> Before observing the objects on this list, be sure to read the information above the checklist on pages 37-38.

– M2 (globular star cluster in constellation Aquarius)

– M15 (globular star cluster in constellation Pegasus)

– M11 (open star cluster in constellation Scutum)

– M27 (planetary nebula in constellation Vulpecula)

– M13 (globular star cluster in constellation Hercules)

– M92 (globular star cluster in constellation Hercules)

– M101 (spiral galaxy in constellation Ursa Major)

– M51 (spiral galaxy in constellation Canes Venatici)

– M106 (galaxy in constellation Canes Venatici)

– M81 (spiral galaxy in constellation Ursa Major)

– M31 (famous naked-eye spiral galaxy in constellation Andromeda)

– M33 (spiral galaxy in constellation Triangulum)

– M39 (open star cluster in constellation Cygnus)

– NGC869 (part of double star cluster in constellation Perseus)

– NGC6960 (part of the Veil Nebula in constellation Cygnus)

– M36 (open cluster in constellation Auriga)

– M37 (open cluster in constellation Auriga)

– M38 (open cluster in constellation Auriga)
(As the star map shows, these three clusters are very low near the northeastern horizon. Wait until later for a better view of them.)

– M45 (This is the Pleiades Star Cluster. It has just risen above the eastern horizon and will be easy to observe over the coming months.)

The November-December Night Sky (Map 6)

Constellations and Naked-Eye Objects

For viewing the sky during the times given on Map 6, you may use the following as your guide.

You will notice that some of the constellations previously seen in the western sky and marked on Map 5 have now set below the western horizon. Certain other constellations, that you did not previously see, have now risen above the eastern horizon.

The constellations that are now no longer seen in the western sky are the "late summer constellations": Ophiuchus and Serpens, Corona Borealis, Hercules, Scutum, Capricornus, and most of Aquila.

The constellations that have appeared in the east are the "early winter constellations": Gemini, Orion, Monoceros, Canis Minor, Lepus, and Eridanus.

With some adjustment, you can use the description of the constellations for Maps 4 and 5, if you remember that all of them have moved westward.

The Constellations of the Northern Sky

From the information learned in Chapter 3, you will find that the Big Dipper in *Ursa Major* is very low near the northern horizon. In fact, the end of the handle is almost touching the horizon. After using the "Pointer Stars" in the cup of the dipper to point to Polaris, the North Pole Star, you will notice that the Little Dipper seems to be hanging on a hook in the sky. The cup of this dipper is almost directly below Polaris. *Draco* curls down toward the northwestern horizon, apparently searching for Hercules who has now disappeared from the sky. Tracing an imaginary line up from the Big Dipper's handle to Polaris and on toward the zenith brings you to the constellation *Cassiopeia*, the Queen, whose bright stars now look more like the letter "*M*" than a "*W*" to those who have been facing north. King *Cepheus* is now found below Cassiopeia and above Draco. To the eastward from Polaris, the zoo animals, *Camelopardalis*, the Giraffe, and *Lynx*, the Lynx, sprawl across a large area of sky with few bright stars until you notice the bright "twin stars," Castor and Pollux, that have now risen in the east.

The Summer Triangle Low in the West After dominating the sky for over six months, the Summer Triangle of stars, Altair in Aquila, Deneb in Cygnus, and Vega in Lyra, are now ready to set in the west. Notice that now the

W

Northern Cross, with Deneb at the top of it, is standing upright above the west-northwestern horizon. Altair and Vega are very low and may not be seen if trees or other obstacles interfere.

The Milky Way Stretching from East to West If observing conditions are good, you will notice that the Milky Way forms a great pathway across the sky from east to west. The rich star clouds of the Summer Milky Way have disappeared in the west. The less distinct Winter Milky Way is just rising in the east. Try to observe it carefully to notice where it widens and narrows as it crosses the sky.

The "Watery" Constellations Filling the Southern Sky Most of the star patterns in the southern half of the sky are the "watery" constellations seen on Map 5, with the addition of another member of the same group. To view all seven of them we can start with the Great Square of Pegasus, which is now west of the zenith. Between it and the western horizon is *Delphinus*, the Dolphin, which now seems to be rising out of a body of water on the western horizon. Equuleus, the Colt, is now scarcely noticeable since its few faint stars are so close to the horizon. Moving from the Great Square to the southwest brings you to *Aquarius*, the Water-bearer, and *Piscis Austrinus*, the Southern Fish, whose bright star, Fomalhaut, is barely above the horizon. Only a few stars of *Capricornus*, the Sea Goat or the Horned Goat, are still above the horizon; Star Map 6 shows only two of them. The southern point of the Great Square directs the way to Pisces, just as the "V" of *Pisces* directs the way to *Cetus*, the Sea Monster or Whale and the great river of stars called *Eridanus*. This large region of the sky contains many stars that are visible on a clear night but scarcely any that are very bright as viewed from our northern latitudes. (However, one star of Eridanus, seen only in southern latitudes, is among the brightest stars in the sky; it is known as Achernar and is found at the far southern end of the great river.) The upper end of the river seems to flow toward Rigel, the brightest star in Orion. The appearance of Orion is the signal that the stars of winter are about to make their appearance.

The Bright Stars of Winter Rising in the East From overhead where Cassiopeia and Perseus lie within the stars of the Milky Way, you should direct your attention eastward where many bright stars of winter are rising. Moving straight east from the curving row of stars in Perseus you come to the five bright stars of Auriga, the Charioteer, known for its collection of star clusters. Below it the constellation Gemini, the Twins, has risen, with Castor and Pollux shining brightly on the northern side of the constellation. Below them Cancer, the Crab, is peeking above the horizon, and Procyon, the brightest star in Canis Minor, the Small Dog, is also visible in a due easterly direction. South of Auriga, the head of Taurus, the Bull, is easily seen because of the bright reddish star, Aldebaran. Above it riding on the back of the bull are the

Pleiades, or Seven Sisters, a famous star cluster that is one of the brightest in the sky. Below Taurus, Orion, the Hunter, is making his appearance. He now

> # In the east, winter's bright stars, including the Twins, Aldebaran, the Pleiades, and the stars of Orion, are now rising.

seems to be lying on his back, but he will later stand upright and march across the sky. One of the most distinctive constellations of all, Orion has many bright stars, only two of which, Rigel and Betelgeuse, are labelled on the star map. To the south of the Hunter is Lepus, the rabbit, just above the horizon and appearing to accompany him across the sky. Keen sky watchers are always excited by the rising of Orion and his accompanying constellations; they bring a promise of many interesting objects to be seen in the winter skies. (See Photos 7, 8, and 9.)

PRACTISE YOUR SKILLS

(a) Finding the Bright Stars

The following 14 bright stars are labelled on Map 6. They are very easy to find in a clear sky. Check off each one when you identify it. (Compare the number of bright stars at this time of year with the number you saw during the summer when using Map 4.)

- Polaris (the North Pole Star, brightest star in Ursa Minor)
- Aldebaran (the "eye of the bull" in Taurus)
- Algol (variable star with a regular period of about 2.9 days)
- Mira (variable star in Cetus; known for its remarkable variation)
- Fomalhaut (brightest star in Piscis Austrinus; always seen in the far southern sky from our northern latitudes)
- Altair (brightest star in Aquila)
- Deneb (brightest star in Cygnus)
- Capella ("the Goat Star," brightest in Auriga)
- Vega (brightest star in Lyra)
- Castor and Pollux (the Twin Stars in Gemini)
- Procyon (the Little Dog Star in Canis Minor)

– Betelgeuse (the slightly variable red giant star in Orion)

– Rigel (the very bright "knee of Orion")

(b) 7 Interesting Objects for Binoculars

The following 7 are among the best of the deep sky objects to try to observe this time of year. Be sure to observe them before going to other objects.

– M31 (The Andromeda Galaxy is now high in the sky. With steady binoculars, its shape as a spiral galaxy is clearly seen.)

– M33 (If conditions are very good, you should try to find the famous Pinwheel Galaxy not far from M31 and also a member of the Local Group of Galaxies.
It is very large and "face-on," but not as bright as M31. Binoculars are better than a telescope for finding it.)

– M36, M37, AND M38 (Since the constellation Auriga is now high in the eastern sky, it is the ideal time to find these three open clusters, almost in a row, and in the central part of the constellation. Try to notice slight differences in the three of them.)

– M45 (The famous Pleiades Cluster is a delight in good binoculars. If conditions are good, challenge yourself to see some of the nebulosity near several of the brightest stars.)

– NGC869 (The Double Cluster between the stars of Cassiopeia and Perseus is now near the zenith. It is a dazzling sight in binoculars.)

(c) Deep Sky Objects for the Small Telescope

There are 19 Deep Sky Objects shown on Map 6. The first 15 of them were described on the checklists for Map 4 and Map 5.

Before trying to observe the objects on this list, be sure to read the information above the list on pages 37-38.

– M2 (globular star cluster in constellation Aquarius)

– M15 (globular star cluster in constellation Pegasus)

– M27 (planetary nebula in constellation Vulpecula)

– M101 (spiral galaxy in constellation Ursa Major)

– M51 (spiral galaxy in constellation Canes Venatici)

– M36 (open star cluster in constellation Auriga)

– M37 (open star cluster in constellation Auriga)

– M38 (open star cluster in constellation Auriga)

– M45 (famous Pleiades star cluster in constellation Taurus)

– M31 (naked-eye spiral galaxy in constellation Andromeda)

– M33 (large spiral galaxy in constellation Triangulum)

– M39 (open star cluster in constellation Cygnus)

– M81 (spiral galaxy in constellation Ursa Major)

– NGC869 (part of the double star cluster in Perseus)

– NGC6960 (part of the Veil Nebula in Cygnus)

– M1 (the Crab Nebula, a supernova remnant; marked on the map near the star that forms the "end of the horn" of Taurus)

– M35 (an open cluster in Gemini; marked on the map near the stars that form the "foot of Castor")

– M42 (the large, beautiful Orion Nebula, an emission nebula; marked on the map as part of the "sword of Orion")

– M44 (the Beehive Cluster, an open cluster in Cancer; marked on the map just below the second "c" in the word "Cancer")

7

Information about the Brightest Stars

Many observers of the night sky ask questions about the bright stars that they see night after night. They may be able to see that some of these stars, which are red or white, are different in colour from our Sun, which is a yellowish-orange colour, but they often want to know whether these stars are also different from our Sun in size, real brightness, and temperature. And how far away from our Solar System are they?

The following chart provides some basic information about the 19 bright stars named on our star maps. Note that these are NOT the 19 brightest or 19 nearest stars in the sky. A chart at the end of the book lists in order the 30 brightest stars, and among the 19 brightest there are several stars that are seen only in the southern skies, by observers in Australia, for example, stars that are not on our star maps. A list of the 30 nearest stars would include many stars that are not bright enough to see with the unaided eye; it would have only about 6 or 7 that are bright enough to see with the unaided eye even under good conditions.

These 19 stars are listed *in order of their brightness* in the *first column*. The *second column* gives their approximate *distance* in light years. (See the Glossary, page 184, for information about this unit of distance.) For some of these stars there is disagreement among the experts about the actual distance, but recent information from satellites that have measured the stars' brightness and position very precisely has helped establish the distance and other information with better accuracy than was known years ago.

The *third* column gives the approximate *surface temperature*. (The unit, degrees Kelvin, is similar to degrees Celsius, but it starts at -273 degrees Celsius.) Compare this temperature to our Sun's surface temperature, which is approximately 6000 degrees. Of course, within our Sun and within these stars also, where nuclear reactions are taking place, the temperature is many millions of degrees. Stars which have a higher surface temperature may be blue or white in colour. Stars which have a lower surface temperature may be red in colour.

The *fourth* column gives *additional information* about the star.

Besides noting how these stars compare with our Sun, it is interesting to note that *over half* of them have a "companion star," or are considered a "binary system," which means two stars gravitationally connected and in mutual orbit around each other. 10 of the 19 stars (Sirius, Capella, Rigel, Procyon, Aldebaran, Spica, Antares, Regulus, Polaris, and Algol) are in this category, and Castor is a "collection of stars." In this column, these abbreviations are used: lum. = luminosity (real brightness); mag. = magnitude (apparent brightness); rev. = period of revolution.

In the third and fourth columns, the numbers in brackets, that is (1) and (2), indicate that information is given about both stars in a two-star system.

The chart on the next two pages can help us draw several conclusions about the bright stars that we observe night after night. We have already noted that more than half of them are part of a "star system." Perhaps we may also have noted that there is very little relationship between the stars' brightnesses and their distances. Glancing at the chart tells us that the fifth star, Rigel, is slightly brighter than Procyon. Both stars are very prominent in the winter sky and are shown on Star Maps 6, 1, and 2. Even though Rigel may be brighter, we can see from the second column that it is over 70 times further away from us than Procyon. Rigel must be an extremely luminous object! Two other stars, also prominent in the southern sky during the winter season (and also found on Star Maps 6, 1, and 2) are Betelgeuse and Aldebaran. Betelgeuse in Orion is brighter than Aldebaran in Taurus, but Aldebaran is over 10 times closer to us than Betelgeuse. What conclusions might you draw?

Information about the Brightest Stars

Star	Approx. Distance From Sun (light years)	Approx. Surface Temperature (degrees K)		Notes
Sirius	8.6		10000	– brightest star in the sky – nearest star visible to naked eye from Canada – 2.35 X mass of Sun – 23 X lum. of Sun – 1.8 X diameter of Sun – has binary companion star of mag. 8, in 50 year period
Arcturus	37		4200	– yellow-orange – 25 X diameter of Sun – 115 X lum. of Sun – 4 X mass of Sun
Vega	25.3		9200	– bluish-white – 58 X lum. of Sun – 3 X mass of Sun
Capella	42	(1) (2)	6000 7500	binary, too close to observe Star A: 13 X diameter of Sun 90 X lum. of Sun Star B: 7 X diameter of Sun 70 X lum. of Sun
Rigel	815		12000	– bluish-white – 57000 X lum. of Sun – 50 X mass of Sun – 50 X diameter of Sun – Rigel has a companion star.
Procyon	11.4	(1) (2)	7000 white dwarf	– 2 X diameter of Sun – 6 X lum. of Sun – 1.7 X mass of Sun – very small; extremely dense – only 2 X diameter of Earth. – Rev.: 40.6 years.
Betelgeuse	652		3100	– red supergiant – pulsating, slightly variable – 8000 to 14000 X lum. of Sun – 160 million X vol. of Sun – 20 X mass of Sun – 1/10 millionth density of Sun

... continued

Star	Approx. Distance From Sun (light years)	Approx. Surface Temperature (degrees K)		Notes
Altair	16.8		8000	– 9 X lum. of Sun – rapid rotation: 6.5 hours
Aldebaran	65		3400	– red giant star – 40 X diameter of Sun – 120 X lum. of Sun – very slightly variable – has a companion star
Spica	275	(1) (2)	25000 20000	– eclipsing spec. binary – is very slightly variable
Antares	425		3100	– is slightly variable – a huge supergiant – has companion that appears close to it
Pollux	34		4500	– 35 X lum. of Sun – 4 to 5 X diameter of Sun
Fomalhaut	25.1		9000	– 14 X lum. of Sun
Deneb	1600		9000	– a supergiant – 60000 X lum. of Sun
Regulus	78		13000	– 160 X lum. of Sun – 5 X diameter of Sun – has a companion star, which is itself a double star
Castor	52	Double, each of which is a binary. Period of revolution: about 400 years. There is a third star, also a binary. Total: 6 stars		
Polaris	782		7000	– a Cepheid variable star – has a companion, mag. 9
Algol	105	(1) (2)	15000 5100	– the famous variable, which is an eclipsing binary with a period 2.8673075 days – varies from mag. 2.06 to 3.28
Mira	130		3300	– Long Period Variable, with a period of 332 days – varies from mag. 2.0 to 10.1

PRACTISE YOUR SKILLS

In the late spring sky, observe Deneb in the east and Regulus in the west. (See Map 3)

(1) Can you conclude from observation which is brighter? If so, which one?

(2) From the chart above, which one is brighter?

(3) What conclusion can you reach from knowing which is brighter and comparing their distances, as given on the chart above?

(4) In the summer sky, observe Arcturus in the west and Altair in the southeast. (See Map 4.) Answer the three previous questions in regard to these two stars.

(5) In the late autumn sky, observe Deneb in the west and Castor in the east. (See Map 6.) Answer the three questions above in regard to these two stars.

(6) In the winter sky, observe and compare the colour of Betelgeuse and Rigel.

(7) In the summer sky, observe and compare the colour of Antares and Vega.

8

Tips on Becoming a Better Observer

If you want to become a better-than-average observer, you should listen to the advice of many very experienced observers who are recognized as being good amateur astronomers. They will usually share with you important information about how to improve your skills and take advantage of the time you spend under the night sky.

Here are some of the tips that many skilled observers follow whenever they observe the night sky.

1. Before each observing session there are some important questions to be asked:

   What time of night will I be observing?

   Will the Moon be in the sky during that time of night?

   If so, will the Moon rise or set during that time?

   If the Moon will be up, will it be bright enough to interfere

   with what I want to observe?

   Depending on whether the Moon rises or sets, and when it rises or sets, you may be able to plan when you can observe certain objects, either before it rises or after it sets, if the objects are too faint to be easily seen while the Moon is in the sky. See the chapter about the Moon to find out *approximately* when the Moon will be rising or setting on a particular night.

2. Be sure to study a map of the constellations that will be up in the sky while you will be observing. Begin with the appropriate map from this guide. From this constellation map, and perhaps some other star maps, if you have them, you can plan what you want to observe.

3. Make a list of the lunar features (if you are going to observe the Moon), the planets, stars, and other objects that you want to observe. Leave a space after each one so that you can check them off when you observe them, and so that you can add a few comments about the appearance of each one or anything unusual about the appearance of each one. Take this list on a clipboard or in a notepad along with you to your observing site. Do not forget also to take a pen that has black ink or ink of a dark colour, certainly not red, since writing in red ink disappears under the light of a red flashlight, which you will probably be using.

4. When you get ready to go out to observe, remember the following:

   (1) Avoid looking at bright lights for about a half-hour before going out.

   (2) "Dark adapt" before going outdoors. This means that you should give your eyes a chance to become accustomed to the darkness. If possible turn off most or all of the lights in the room while you are preparing, so that you will not have to spend as long later becoming able to see faint objects. It takes the human eye about 15 minutes to become well enough accustomed to the dark to see objects as faint as most amateur astronomers want to see.

   (3) Dress warmly, especially if the weather is cold. It is extremely important to cover the head well, even if you feel there is no danger

of frozen ears. Do not take chances with the cold. Many experienced observers use winter clothes even in the summer. If you become warm, they can always be removed, as they should be, so that you avoid sweating. Dress "in layers." On a spring or summer evening, it is better to have two or three warm sweaters available than one heavy coat. The sweaters can be put on as the need arises.

(4) Take with you a dim, *red-light* flashlight to read your star maps — not a white-light flashlight. White light destroys the dark adaption that your eyes have acquired, and if you look at a white-light flashlight, it will be about 15 minutes more before you will again be able to see faint objects effectively. You do not need to buy an expensive red-light flashlight, if you do not have one. Simply convert the one you have. Either remove the bulb, paint it with a dark red paint or nail polish, and reinsert it, or cover the front of your regular flashlight with heavy red or brown paper.

When you are at your observing site, remember the following:

(1) Move slowly and cautiously when you are near tripod-mounted binoculars or a telescope. Sudden movements in the dark can cause you to hit an instrument and even damage it.

(2) When using hand-held binoculars always use the neck strap, for safety, to avoid dropping them. Move them slowly from one position to another. If the binoculars are mounted on a tripod, move the binoculars slowly and carefully and lock them securely in the required position before studying the object you want to observe. Sometimes when beginners are hand-holding their binoculars, they hold them too close to the eye-piece end of the instrument. Try to find the balance point of the binoculars and hold them at that point. You will see that it is closer to the "big end" than the "small end." This may seem like a small matter, but after a while you will find that it is much less tiring to do it this way, and you will be able to observe much longer and without having sore arms.

(3) Do not rush quickly from one object to another. Take your time to enjoy the view, and to appreciate and study each object.

(4) Check off each item on the list you prepared before the observing session. Add notes and make drawings showing what you are observing. Challenge yourself: in your drawings, try to show as much detail as you possibly can, even if it is a fairly faint object.

(5) If you are observing with tripod-mounted binoculars or a telescope, take a deep breath in order to relax and concentrate before looking at a faint or difficult object. While you are observing, try not to breathe

on the binoculars or the eyepiece if you are observing with a telescope. Your breath could cause condensation, which is often called "dewing" or "fogging" on the lens or eyepiece, or even "frosting" if the weather is cold. If "dewing" or "frosting" does happen, you should *not* take the instrument indoors immediately. That would only make the condition worse; instead, you should use a hair dryer carefully to circulate warm air over the surface where the condensation or frost is on the instrument.

(6) Find a location where there are no street lights or other outdoor lights glaring into your eyes. If you are observing from your backyard, find the spot that is the darkest.

(7) If the weather is very cold, go indoors every half hour to get warm. To avoid having to spend a while "dark adapting" all over again, have the indoor lights dimmed or turned out, if possible, when you go inside to get warm.

5. After the observing session is over, record your observations in your log or observing notebook as soon as possible. Use the checklist you prepared earlier and the notes and drawings you made while observing. Refer to the next chapter, Recording Observations, for one easy way of doing it.

9

Recording Observations

Why Record Observations?

Have you ever seen a bright meteor? Or a beautiful sunset? Or a display of the Northern Lights? You have? Really? When?

If you did not record somewhere these marvelous events, then, in a way, you have lost part of them. You might be able to describe the sudden flash and the long train of the meteor, or the lovely stratus clouds that accompanied the sunset, but what happens later on when you see another meteor or sunset and you try to compare the new sighting with the old one? Or what happens, if a friend tells you about a fabulous meteor or sunset that he or she saw two weeks ago and you do no know if the one you saw was on the same date as your friend's. You cannot find out because you did not record it.

There is another reason for recording your observations. Since you may often share your work with other people, you need to get the details straight so that they will understand clearly the beauty of what you saw, and they can compare it with what they have seen or did not see.

Besides, recording your observations is fun — to write, and to read later, perhaps many years later. A diary of your observing memories can last a lifetime, perhaps several lifetimes. Modern amateur astronomers find it very interesting to read the observing log kept by Charles Messier over two hundred years ago. He was a comet hunter who wrote such careful and exact notes that we can easily imagine what his observing sessions were like.

A Simple Method of Recording Observations

Exactly what type of records you keep is entirely up to you. Some observers like to use a simple notebook in which they write all notes and do all drawings one after the other. Other people, like me, like to use a science or laboratory type of notebook in which the left-hand page is blank and the right-hand page is lined, so that they can do their drawings and sketches on the left side, and write their notes on the right side. Whichever you choose is up to you, but you should have a notebook of some sort, get a new one when it is filled, and keep all your old ones in order in a safe place.

When I write my notes on the right-hand pages in my observing notebook, I use a simple code that I devised many years ago. Inventing a code for yourself, or borrowing one that someone else uses, can be very helpful. In that way you do not have to use many words over and over, because certain words *are* used very frequently.

The first thing you may want to write is a number of the observing session. Some observers have numbers that are up in the thousands, because they started keeping an observing notebook or log when they were quite young and first started observing things in the sky.

Next, many observers write a letter for the time of day or night of the observing session. The letters that can be used are: *e*, *n*, *m*, and *d*, standing for evening, night, morning, and daytime (since some astronomers do observe things in the sky in the daytime).

Most good observing logs contain five pieces of information about the observing session, often in code so that they appear on one line at the beginning of the entry: (1) date, (2) time, (3) location, (4) sky conditions, and (5) instrument used.

Concerning the *date*, if it is a night-time observing session, you should use a "double-date" because the date, as you know, changes at midnight. This is followed by the *start and end times* of the observing session. The *location* should be named unless all observing in the whole log is done from the same place.

Regarding *sky conditions*, some observers use a ten-point descriptive code. Such a scale may be used under both city and rural conditions. The range goes from very poor to very good. The number *0* means almost totally overcast or almost no sky visible. *1, 2,* and *3* refer respectively to a very cloudy, mainly cloudy, and partly cloudy sky. The digits 4 through 7 may apply to backyard observing from a city-bound site: very hazy or murky (*4*), hazy or murky (*5*), slightly hazy or murky (*6*), and acceptably clear (*7*). Under dark rural or country conditions, a person may use the numbers 8 through *10*: for a quite clear sky (*8*), a very clear sky (*9*), or an absolutely fantastic sky (*10*).

Then, you should indicate *how* you are observing, that is, whether it is with the unaided eye ("ne" for "naked eye"), or with binoculars ("b"), or with a telescope ("t"), in which case you should name the type of telescope or size and eyepiece used. All of this information can be given in one line *in coded form* and can be recorded in a few seconds after you become used to doing it.

Then, you should record the names of others who observed with you (if there was anyone with you). Finally and most important of all, you need to list the *objects* you observed or type of observation you did.

Here is an example of the recording of an observing session:

140n 1998, Jan.20-21 22:30-23:50EST backyard 7 ne & 10x50b Fred & Jane

ne:	– winter constellations
	– very bright meteor at 22:46, a bit brighter than Sirius going from the belt of Orion south past Lepus to Columba
10x50b:	– the Pleiades – beautiful (!)
	– Orion nebula – very nice
	– two clusters of stars in Auriga (M37 and M38)

In this entry from a "make-believe" observing log, the person was describing observing session number 140, which was on the night of January 20, 1998. The "double date" was used to avoid confusion caused by the change of date at midnight. The session began at 10:30 p.m. and ended at 11:50 p.m., just ten minutes before midnight. The writer used the 24-hour clock system. The letters "EST" indicates that it was Eastern Standard Time. There could be some confusion if the time system were not mentioned, especially during the summer months when Daylight Saving Time is used. The person was observing from his/her backyard. The only instrument was a pair of 10x50 binoculars and he/she was observing with friends, Fred and Jane. The wonderful meteor that they saw was recorded, and now it will not be forgotten because the observer took two minutes to write it down.

A More Advanced Method of Recording Observations

As you observe more and more objects, you will have an even greater need to record them, and so you will develop a more complete code for information that you want to write down. It may be helpful for you to write down in the back of your notebook the explanation for your code as it grows.

Here are some samples of a code that you may develop for places where you do your observations:

by	– my own *backyard*
Fob	– my friend, *Fred's observatory*
yc	– the *yard* at our summer *cottage*
lc	– the shore along the *lake* at our summer *cottage*
dn	– the *deck* on the *north* side of our cottage.

As you include other items in the code for sky conditions, you may expand that one to include such things as the following:

10.5	– more than superb conditions (!), the best I have ever seen in my life (This may have been from a place high in the mountains or very far from any city.)
cml	– *crescent Moonlight*
gml	– *gibbous Moonlight*
Fml	– *Full Moonlight.* (Moonlight conditions prevent an observer from seeing many stars and other objects that might otherwise be seen.)

Advanced observers should record the type of instruments they use, and may wish to use the following code:

11x80b	– *binoculars* of *11* power with lenses of *80* mm diameter
20cmrt	– a *reflecting* type of *telescope* with a mirror of *20cm* diameter
10cmra	– a *refractor* (lens) type of telescope with a lens of *10cm* diameter
20cmsct	– a *Schmidt-Cassegrain* type of *telescope* with a *20cm* aperture

The eyepiece or ocular used in the telescope should be listed also. For example:

> 28m-o – with a *28mm* eyepiece or *o*cular
>
> 19m-o – with a *19mm* eyepiece or *o*cular

Here is a sample section from the observing log of another observer:

982n 1998, May 24-25 23:20-02:20EST yc 9.5 ne & 10x50b & 20cmrt, 32m-o ____

> ne: – 20 constellations
>
> – meteor at 23:56EST as bright as Spica → SW from Lyr to Boo
>
> 10X35b: – M6 OC in Sco, M7 OC in Sco.
>
> 20cmrt: – Beta Cyg DS, M22 GC in Sag (!), M65 SG in Leo.

You can see that this person was observing alone for three hours in the yard at the summer cottage under superb conditions and using a 20cm relecting telescope with a 32mm ocular. Besides seeing many constellations, this person observed a bright meteor with the unaided eye and two objects with his binoculars, as well as three objects with the telescope. The meteor was as bright as the brightest star in the constellation Virgo and it *was moving* (→) *southwestward (SW)* from the constellation Lyra to the constellation Bootes. The objects observed with the binoculars were two large *open clusters (OC)* of stars (M6 and M7) in the constellation Scorpius. The objects observed with the telescope were the famous *double star (DS)* – Beta in the constellation Cygnus, M22 – a *globular cluster (GC)* in the constellation Sagittarius, and finally M65 – a *spiral galaxy (SG)* in the constellation Leo.

The exclamation mark after M22 indicates that the observer thought that it was a fabulous view of this object, perhaps the best view that this person had ever seen of this star cluster. If the observer wanted to, he or she could also have written other personal notes about this object or others.

As observers become more skilled year after year, they usually continue to invent even more advanced codes to describe more completely the sky conditions (naming both the transparency and the "seeing," or lack of turbulence in the atmosphere) and to state more the details about the appearance of the objects observed, whether they are planets, galaxies, star clusters, or comets.

By using simple codes such as these, a great deal of information can be recorded in your observing log in a very short while, and it can be very useful to you later.

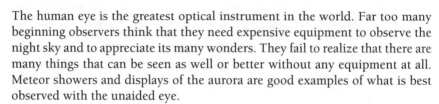

10

The Importance of Binoculars

The human eye is the greatest optical instrument in the world. Far too many beginning observers think that they need expensive equipment to observe the night sky and to appreciate its many wonders. They fail to realize that there are many things that can be seen as well or better without any equipment at all. Meteor showers and displays of the aurora are good examples of what is best observed with the unaided eye.

Many beginning observers also think that they need an expensive telescope to observe many distant objects in the sky, and they fail to realize that hundreds of objects can be observed just as well *or better* with binoculars than with a telescope.

There are many advantages to owning a pair of binoculars. Binoculars are versatile instruments. Many models may be used at sporting events or when one is vacationing or sight-seeing. In fact, some people may find that they already have a pair that was once used at spectator sporting events, and is quite suitable for enjoying views of the night sky.

Binoculars are sometimes the best possible instrument for viewing certain objects such as large star clusters like the Pleiades or the Hyades, for locating many objects especially if the area of the sky is not well-known, for finding the planets Uranus and Neptune, which cannot be seen with the unaided eye, for locating the brighter planets in twilight, and for studying bright comets or the Moon during a lunar eclipse.

Binoculars allow the observer to use both eyes — a definite advantage over telescopes. When using both eyes you can relax in a way that is not possible when using only one eye. The two eyes can assist and complement each other. Faint objects will appear brighter than they will in a telescope, and the viewer can have a better sense of the realism of the object being viewed.

When choosing a pair of binoculars, one should keep a few things in mind. Most binoculars are designated by two numbers with an "X" between them. The first number indicates the magnification or the "power" that they give you. Objects in "7 power" binoculars appear seven times closer or larger than they do to the unaided eye. The second number tells you the diameter in millimetres of the main or larger lens. The larger the diameter of the lenses, the greater ability they have to gather light. This "light gathering ability" is very important for all binoculars and telescopes. The more light they can gather, the brighter the objects will appear. The first number, the magnification, is important, also, but perhaps not as important as most people think. You must remember that the *higher* the magnification, the *smaller* the "field of view" or area of the sky that you will see. There is not much point in having high magnification, if you can not find most of the things that you want to view, or have to spend most of your time searching for objects and then, after you find them, discover that that you can see only a small part of the object because it is too big to fit into the field of your binoculars. Binoculars with high power are also extremely difficult to hand-hold. The objects that you want to see appear to "jump all over."

What binoculars are best for observing objects in the night sky? 7X50 or 10X50 binoculars give a wide field and generally give bright images. 8X40s are also good. These three are well suited to astronomy, as well as being suitable for other purposes. "Zoom" binoculars, that is, those with variable magnification, such as 7-15X35, are *not* recommended; they are often poor quality instruments.

Should binoculars be mounted on a tripod? It is recommended that a tripod be used with binoculars over 7X, if you are using them for longer than just a few minutes. A tripod steadies the images and makes studying them much easier. Some binoculars have tripod adapters already on them; others do not. If your binoculars do not have a tripod adapter, you may buy one at a camera

> ## A tripod is strongly recommended for binoculars of over 7x; it is an absolute necessity for binoculars of over 10x.

store. A good sturdy tripod is well worth the investment. It makes your binocular observing sessions much more enjoyable. A tripod is an absolute necessity if you have large astronomical binoculars, such as 11X80 instruments.

When thinking about buying good quality binoculars, you should expect to pay from $60 or $80 to several hundred dollars depending on the size of the instrument. It is often said that price is a good indicator of quality when comparing instruments of the same size. Paying a slightly higher price will often mean obtaining instruments that have good quality optics and sturdy construction.

Owning and using a pair of good quality binoculars is suggested as a major step toward a lifetime of enjoying the views of the night sky.

When to Buy a Telescope

Most beginning astronomers do not need a telescope as soon as they think they do, and too many beginners buy a telescope before they are prepared to use one properly. Sometimes, because they are not yet really prepared to use one, they become frustrated when it does not magically perform for them. Then they put it aside, and eventually lose interest. They lose out on a chance to view hundreds of wonderful objects in the sky.

The major reasons that beginners are unprepared to use a telescope are that they are not yet totally familiar with the sky, they do not yet know what objects in the sky are best viewed in a specific type of telescope, and they do not realize that most telescopes allow them to view only a very small piece of the sky at once. Some beginners also expect that, with a small telescope, they will see objects in exactly the same way as those objects have been photographed by the largest telescopes in the world and pictured in textbooks or magazines.

Before buying any telescope, a person should become familiar with the sky, should learn about what can be seen in certain areas of the sky and during certain seasons of the year, and should find as many objects as possible with a pair of binoculars. This means that you should study star maps, learn all the constellations that can be seen at a certain time, and try to identify as many of the very bright stars as possible. It also means that you should be able to identify the bright planets that can be seen at certain times.

Then you will be able to use *binoculars* to view more challenging things. You will be able to use them to search for the star clusters marked on the star maps in this book, such as the three that are found in the constellation Auriga. You will use them to view M31, the spiral galaxy in the constellation Andromeda. You will be able to find the globular cluster M13 in the constellation Hercules. You will be able to find the huge nebula of hydrogen gas called M42 in the sword of Orion, the great winter constellation in the southern sky.

Only then, *after* you have been able to identify these things and find them *both* with the unaided eye *and* with binoculars, should you consider buying a telescope. Even then, buying a telescope should not be a hasty decision. Perhaps it would be best to join an astronomy club, such as a Centre of the RASC (See Chapter 21.) In the club you will meet people who own and use many kinds of telescopes. They can give you advice on the best type of telescope for your needs.

There are several things that always need to be considered when a person thinks he or she is ready to purchase a telescope. They can be listed as follows:

(a) *PORTABILITY*   There is no need to buy a huge telescope if you live in an apartment and need to travel for an hour every time you set it up and use it. It is better to own a small, very portable telescope that could be used every clear night, rather than a huge one that would be used only once a month.

(b) *EASE OF USE*   A simple telescope for beginners is better than one with advanced features that would require a long time to learn about. There is a place for complicated and sophisticated technology, but a beginner needs to concentrate on finding objects in the sky, not to be spending precious time, particularly on cold winter nights, leaning how to operate certain unnecessary options on an untested telescope.

(c) *PRICE*   The cost, or initial investment, is an important consideration for most people. That is why this chapter began with the warning that too many people buy telescopes too soon in the course of their venture into astronomy. A good quality telescope is an *important* investment; a good quality telescope, properly used and maintained, should last a lifetime, yes, for forty or fifty years. Many telescopes that are much older than that are still being used, and their owners would never want to get rid of them.

There is a real danger that a beginner will spend money on a very poor quality "department store" telescope, one that will prove quite unsatisfactory. Then the money spent will be wasted, if the telescope is set aside and never used again. Most telescopes sold in department stores for $400 or less are not worth bringing home. On the other hand, some second-hand telescopes, available from members of astronomy clubs, because the original owner simply wanted to move on to a different type of telescope, are real bargains and may be exactly what a beginner should buy *if* he or she is ready to own a telescope. Such a telescope may be available for the same amount, or even less than a person would spent in a department store for a telescope that would prove almost worthless.

(d) *SUITABILITY FOR YOUR KIND OF OBSERVING*   Certain types of telescopes are more suitable for some kinds of observing than others. A 100mm refractor may be very suitable for observing lunar craters and bright planets, but would not be a good telescope for observing faint galaxies. A fairly large reflector might be very good for observing faint galaxies but might not be a good telescope for observing detail on the surface of the planets. There are other considerations about the suitability of telescopes that you can learn from consulting with experienced telescope users.

Indeed, there are many considerations to take into account. The best advice is to consult with experienced observers, and consider your purchase and your needs very carefully.

In summary, you should probably purchase a telescope *only after* you have passed certain steps on the the road to becoming familiar with the sky, and with binocular observing. To find out whether you are ready for such a step, you can ask yourself the following eight questions:

1. Can I name four circumpolar constellations? (These are constellations in the northern sky that never set from locations in the Earth's northern hemisphere. They appear on all the star maps in this book.)

2. Can I name three constellations that are seen in the southern sky in each of the four seasons of the year?

3. Can I name or explain the location of each of the following:
   (a) 4 double stars,
   (b) 4 variable stars,
   (c) 5 star clusters,
   (d) 5 nebulae or galaxies?

4. Have I seen all of the above objects (in # 3), either with the unaided eye or with binoculars?

5. Can I find all of the above objects by myself (using binoculars, if necessary)?

6. Have I found all the bright stars on the maps in this book *and* the binocular objects listed for each star map? (This means you will have spent at least a year studying the sky with the unaided eye and with binoculars.)

7. Am I familiar with the use of at least one star atlas in addition to the maps in this observing guide?

8. Am I sure that I want to spend time learning how to operate a telescope in order that I may observe hundreds of fainter and more challenging objects?

If you can answer "Yes!" to *all eight* of these questions, then you may indeed be ready to own a telescope.

Additional Considerations When Buying a Telescope

Many experienced amateur astronomers are aware of what happened when they first considered purchasing a new telescope. If they did not know a few other amateur astronomers at the time, they were often tempted to buy a department store telescope as their first instrument. If they knew other astronomers at the time, such friends usually discouraged them from doing such a thing. If they did not have such friends and went ahead and did it, they almost always regretted it for a long time. Their advice, after such an event, is invariably this: "Don't even think of buying a department store 'scope with its flashy box under the big sign advertising '600 power'!" They may sometimes continue by saying: "I found that the mount was flimsy, the optics poor, the eyepieces small and inferior, and the field of view too small to include what I wanted to see or even to find what I wanted to see. Do you want me to continue with my list of objections to such a purchase?"

Usually, their advice is to discuss your specific observing interests with an experienced observer, and then decide which type of telescope you really want. Then make the purchase from a reputable telescope dealer. Consider whether you really want a refractor, or reflector. Consider whether you want an equatorially mounted telescope with a clock drive to follow the stars as you observe, or photograph, them, or do you want an alt-azimuth telescope that can be easily moved from one object to another in as simple a way as you choose? Consider whether you want a Newtonian with its possibility of large aperture for increased "light-gathering ability," or a catadioptric (popularly called a Schmidt-Cassegrain or a Maksutov, depending on some technicalities of design — See the Appendix.), which allows for a shorter and more portable instrument than a Newtonian of the same size.

Remember always that the primary purpose of a telescope is to gather and to magnify starlight so that we may study an object — firstly, *to gather it*, and that is so important! The more you can gather the better! Secondly, you must have the ability to magnify it to the amount that is ideal for gaining the most information. Therefore, generally speaking, the primary rule is the greater the aperture the more desirable the instrument. [Aperture is the diameter of the primary mirror or objective (primary lens) of a telescope.] However, the focal length is also an important consideration in a telescope. A telescope with a longer focal length will generally give better views when used at higher magnification. On the other hand, some observers may choose a telescope with a shorter focal length because they want to view extended objects that require a slightly larger field of view. As is readily seen, there are always "tradeoffs"; there is always the ever-present process of "give and take."

Summary of Some Advantages and Disadvantages of the Telescope Types

Refractors:

Advantages:
    – have a simple design and are usually easy to maintain,
    – have no obstruction at all in the light path to interfere with the incoming light,

              – give sharp, clear images, if the lenses are well made,

              – are often preferred by discriminating planetary viewers.

Disadvantages: – quite expensive, when "per unit of aperture" is considered,

              – do not have the large apertures that many astronomers want for faint objects.

Newtonian Reflectors:

Advantages: – least expensive, when "per unit of aperture" is considered,

              – have, generally, a smaller obstruction in the light path than other reflectors,

              – have a design that allows for small, medium, and large apertures.

Disadvantages: – are larger, less portable than some other designs with the same aperture,

              – may require frequent collimation and other maintenance,

              – usually require a time for "cooldown" that is longer than for other designs.

Catadioptric (Schmidt-Cassegrain and Maksutov types):

Advantages: – with their folded light paths, have a tube length that is shorter, more compact, and more portable than other designs,

              – with their shorter tubes, can be used with a steady "fork mount,"

              – can be easily used with cameras and other accessories.

Disadvantages: – have a smaller field of view than some other telescope types,

              – have a longer "cooldown" time than some other telescope types,

              – have a larger obstruction in the light path than other reflectors,

              – may be subject to dewing problems, if humid conditions are prevalent.

> **The list of pros and cons of each telescope type means that the beginner should think seriously before buying.**

Useful Telescope Magnification:

Having learned that the clear aperture (usually the diameter) of the objective or of the main mirror of the instrument is what determines the light gathering ability of the instrument, beginning observers should then learn that it is the combination of (a) the focal length of the telescope and (b) the focal length of the eyepiece, which determines the magnification of the instrument. If the same units, such as millimetres, are used, and if (a) is divided by (b) for each eyepiece being used, then the observer has a list of the magnifications obtained when he or she used each eyepiece. For example, with a telescope of focal length 2000 mm, a person using a 40-mm and a 25-mm eyepiece would have 50 power and 80 power for the respective eyepieces. (2000/40 = 50, and 2000/25 = 80.)

There is a limit to the useful power that any telescope can deliver. If the power is extremely low in most telescopes, the beam of light from the eyepiece will be too wide to enter the pupil of the observer's eye, even when the observer is dark adapted, although on some "rich field telescopes" it is possible to go lower than the suggested limit. If the power is extremely high, the telescope simply magnifies everything in the field, including things that we do not want magnified, such as turbulence in the atmosphere. On only rare occasions is the atmosphere above most sites steady enough to allow an observer effectively to

> **Be wary of very high power. Only rarely is the atmosphere steady enough to allow 400x or more.**

use more than 400 power. (Little good using 500 power, if the object looks as if it is being seen through a river of boiling water!) A formula for Useful Magnification Range (UMR) may be stated approximately in this way:

$$UMR = 0.2D \text{ to } 2D,$$
where D is the diameter of the objective, or of the main
mirror, of the telescope, expressed in millimetres.

In other words, for a typical telescope whose objective, or main mirror, is 200 mm in diameter, the useful range of magnification is from 40 power to 400 power (0.2 X 200 = 40, and 2 X 200 = 400.).

Do not be too hasty in making a purchase. Talk to several owners of different types of telescopes. Decide what is best for you and your circumstances. Be prepared to take the time to learn how to operate it properly. Your long-term rewards over future years of observing will probably be determined by whether you take the time to make the right decisions *before* purchasing your telescope.

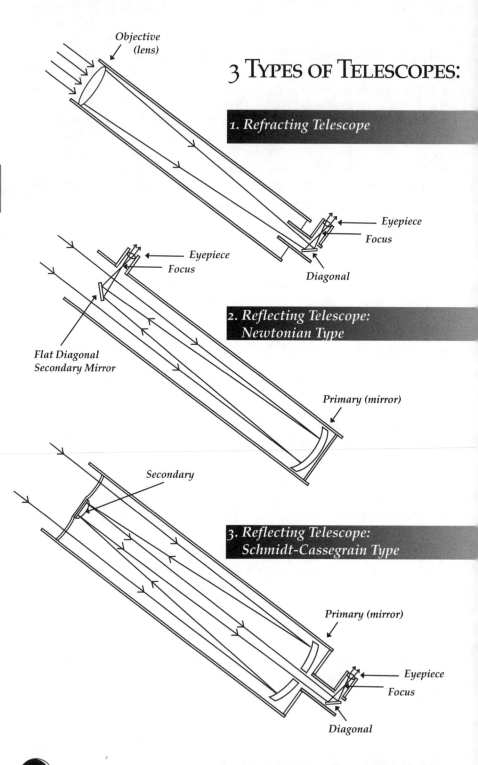

3 TYPES OF TELESCOPES:

1. Refracting Telescope

Objective
(lens)

Eyepiece
Focus
Diagonal

2. Reflecting Telescope: Newtonian Type

Eyepiece
Focus

Flat Diagonal
Secondary Mirror

Primary (mirror)

3. Reflecting Telescope: Schmidt-Cassegrain Type

Secondary

Primary (mirror)

Eyepiece
Focus
Diagonal

A High Quality Refractor:
Aperture: 127 mm (5")

- *for a serious observer who wants superb views of the planets*

- *fairly expensive*

Newtonian Reflector:
Popular Dobsonian Mount
Aperture: 254 mm (10")

- *easy to operate*

- *maximum aperture for the price*

- *a good investment*

Schmidt-Cassegrain Reflector
Aperture: 300 mm (12")
(also similiar models of aperture 200 mm, 250 mm, 350 mm, and 400 mm)

- *"computer-technology controlled" to drive accurately, even for photography*

- *compact tube and fork mount*

- *requires very sturdy tripod (shown)*

- *requires electrical power source*

- *expensive, not reccomended as a "first scope"*

12
An Introduction to Astrophotography

Many of those who are just starting to pursue an interest in astronomy think that it will be a long time before their knowledge of techniques and their mastery of complicated equipment will allow them to produce good photographs of astronomical objects, in other words, to do astro-photography. A few other beginning astronomers may have expectations that, within a very short time, they should easily be able to match the astrophotography done by experienced veterans of the craft and even have their results displayed in the well-known astronomy magazines. Neither one of these ideas is likely to be correct, and neither one is the proper approach for a beginner who wishes to record images of some of the great celestial objects or events that she, or he, has seen.

Only a small amount of equipment is actually needed to be introduced to astrophotography, and the beginner may actually be surprised at how easily that equipment may be obtained. In regard to the required expertise, a reasonable understanding of only a few simple techniques is all that is necessary to begin enjoying elementary astrophotography. Of course, the beginner may well wish to continue to more advanced levels of the craft, that is, to learn about other ways, and even more advanced modes, of recording images of the sky. The beginner, also, may quickly discover that this aspect of the hobby becomes quite addictive.

The person who is just starting out must, indeed, have reasonable expectations, since, with the limited equipment and resources usually available to the beginner, he, or she, in most cases, will not quickly be able to match the results of the very experienced astrophotographer. This fact makes it all the more important for the beginner to keep good records of what he or she does, and thereby learn from his or her mistakes, in addition to consulting experienced astrophotographers for their suggestions in overcoming unexpected problems that may arise. For the beginner, then, a balanced approach is here suggested, one that requires only:

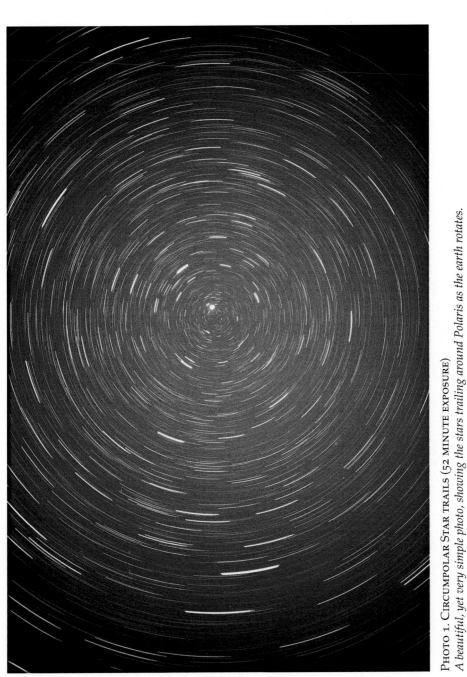

PHOTO 1. CIRCUMPOLAR STAR TRAILS (52 MINUTE EXPOSURE)
A beautiful, yet very simple photo, showing the stars trailing around Polaris as the earth rotates.

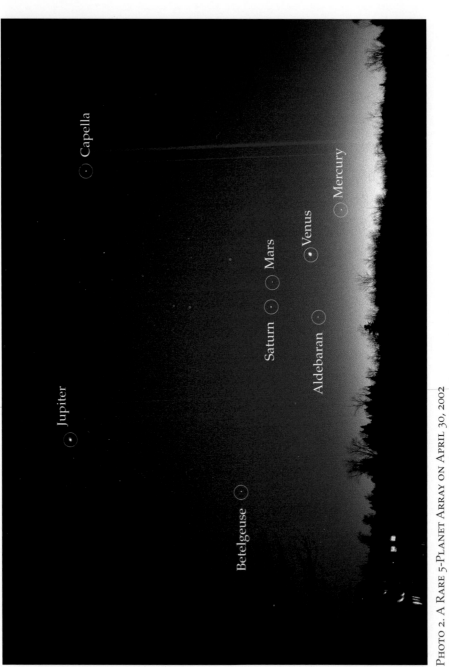

PHOTO 2. A RARE 5-PLANET ARRAY ON APRIL 30, 2002
A 28 mm lens photo of all 5 "naked-eye" planets in the western evening sky.

PHOTO 3. A 5-PLANET ARRAY ON MAY 3, 2003
In three days the planets have moved.

PHOTO 4. A BRIGHT METEOR IN SAGITTARIUS
As this 15-second exposure of the Teapot was being taken on August 12, 2001, a bright Perseid lit up the sky.

PHOTO 5. AURORA
An Aurora can be impressive, as was this one on September 3, 2002. So easy to photograph!

PHOTO 6. AN AURORA AT SOLAR MAX

An Aurora of March 9, 1991 from near the time of the 1990 solar maximum. Note Big and Little Dipper.

Photo 7. Orion
A very simple photo using a 50 mm lens with the camera on a tripod.

PHOTO 8. ORION RISING OVER THE TREES
The stars of Orion trail for 2 minutes (85 mm lens), in a very simple, but beautiful photograph.

– simple equipment that may be easily available,

– the basic 'know-how' to use it for maximum results,

– enough planning and attention to details to obtain reasonable results from the outset, and

– a knowledge of what is reasonable to photograph, and under what conditions to do it.

Various Types of Astrophotography

Amateur astronomers who use film to record images of objects and phenomena (events) of the sky make use some of the following types of photography:

1. "Simple unguided astrophotography," in which the camera is mounted on a tripod,

2. "Piggy-back astrophotography," in which the camera is mounted on an 'equatorial' telescope, (and with the telescope's clock drive operating, the camera is able to follow an object in the sky as the Earth rotates), to take exposures that are often longer than just a few seconds or even a few minutes,

3. "First-Focus astrophotography," in which the camera is attached directly to the telescope without any eyepiece being used in the telescope, a method that requires accurate guiding by a good-quality clock drive in order to produce acceptable photographs,

4. "Eyepiece-projection astrophotography," in which an eyepiece is used in a telescope and the light coming through it is projected onto the film in a camera which is attached to the eyepiece holder by means of a tube, and

5. "Afocal astrophotography," in which a camera with an appropriate lens is held in front of an eyepiece and a photograph is made of the object seen in the eyepiece, with the camera being held either by hand for extremely short exposures or by a metal holding device.

Besides these methods of recording objects and events in the sky, some astronomers use special techniques to keep the film very cold and employ a device called a "cold camera." Others use film that his been subjected to a process known as "hypersensitization" in order that the film may record images at a faster rate than otherwise.

Within the past decade some astronomers have used "electronic imaging" instead of film to record the sky and its splendours. "CCD cameras" (for imaging using what is called a "charged couple device") have enabled them to produce marvellous images of celestial objects.

The Equipment Needed for Simple Unguided Astrophotography:

– a camera: – 35 mm (or possibly "medium format") preferred

– NOT the newer "fully automatic" or "point-and-shoot" models, which do not allow the exposure times or apertures to be controlled

– a camera with a "B-setting," NOT one with a completely electronic shutter

– a camera with manual film-winding, since the automatic winding feature prevents multiple exposures on the same frame

– "mirror lock-up" — a preferred feature, but not absolutely necessary

– "10-second delay" timer — a preferred feature, but not absolutely essential

– a "fast lens," or several of them, for the camera, if possible, meaning that, for a 50-mm lens, it should be f/1.8, or f/1.4, or even f/1.2.

– a tripod: – an absolute necessity. (A model that is large, solid, and steady is definitely preferred. A very solid tripod is a wise investment.)

– proper film: another necessity. (A huge array of film is available. However, since most beginning astrophotographers want images of star fields and constellations to be captured in short exposures lasting only a few seconds, a "fast film," such as one with an ISO rating of 200 to 800, is generally preferred.)

– cable release: This inexpensive device is needed to operate the camera properly, that is, without having to hold a finger on the shutter release button during an exposure that may last several seconds or several minutes.

– a watch with a second hand or digital display for seconds. (Do not forget to wear it when you are photographing, since knowing the length of your exposures is important.)

– a notebook, other than your observing log, in which to record, in a "code format," the following information for each of your photographs: (1) date, (2) time, (3) lens used, (4) film used, (5) object, (6) exposure time, and

(7) camera setting, that is, focal ratio (and focal length, if the lens is a "zoom").

It is not necessary for many beginners to purchase a new camera. In fact, the idea of purchasing of a new camera may lead them to acquiring a type of camera that is quite unsuitable for doing what they really want to do. In many cases, a camera of the type they should be considering may be found stored away in their own homes and unused for many years, but still in good condition. Alternatively, they may find one, in good condition and at a very good price, at a used camera store. Experienced astrophotographers are often asked about what brands are recommended, and they often say that, among the used cameras that are 20 to 40 years old, they would recommend ones such as the Nikon F2, the Pentax K1000, the Olympus OM1, the Canon F1, and the Ricoh KR-5 Super II. When one buys a camera, it is wise to inquire if additional lenses are available. As we will learn, a choice of interchangeable lenses allows the astrophotographer to do a variety of kinds of photography, and sometimes a used camera shop has a number of lenses, which accompany a given camera.

From among the selection of films available, many astrophotographers recommend some of the following brands: (for slides) Kodachrome 200, Fujichrome 400 Sensia and 400 Provia, Ektachrome 400, Elitechrome 400, and (for prints) Fujicolor 200 and 400 and G800. In the past, great photographs have also been taken using Agfa 1000 (though it is somewhat grainy), 3M 1000, Konica 3200, Ektachrome P1600, Ektachrome P 800/1600, ScotchChrome 800 – 3200, though these films may be difficult or impossible to find in many places. They do illustrate the fact that a very wide variety of films exists. The beginner should choose one near the top of the list, and become familiar with its characteristics before experimenting with others further down the list.

"Camera Awareness"

When beginning to do astrophotography, many people do not have a good idea about "how big a piece of sky" they will have in any one photograph they might take. The answer to the question about the area of sky that can be photographed is that it depends entirely on two things:

1. the Focal Length of the camera lens or telescope used, and

2. the size of the film.

Interchangeable camera lenses are available in a wide variety of sizes or Focal Lengths. The so-called "35-mm camera" has a film size of 36 mm X 24 mm for each frame. The mathematical formula for the "angle of the sky photographed," in degrees, is $A = (57.3S)/F$, where S is film size (36 mm AND 24 mm), and F is Focal Length. Similar calculations may be done to determine the area or sky photographed with a "medium-format" camera and with cameras that use film of other sizes.

The Area of Sky Photographed With a 35-mm Camera Using Various Lenses:	
Lens:	**Area of Sky:**
24 mm lens	86 deg. X 57.3 deg.
28 mm lens	73.7 deg. X 49.1 deg.
50 mm lens	41.2 deg. X 27.5 deg.
85 mm lens	24 deg. X 16 deg.
105 mm lens	20 deg. X 13 deg.
135 mm lens	15 deg. X 10 deg.
200 mm lens	10 deg. X 7 deg.
400 mm lens	5 deg. X 3 deg.
2000 mm "lens" (the 20 cm SCT)	1 deg. X 0.7 deg.

How Big Will an Object Appear in a Photograph?

In determining how big the Moon, for example, will appear on a photograph, we should recall that the Full Moon is ½ degree in diameter. If we use a 50-mm lens to photograph an area of sky that includes the Moon, the Moon will occupy only a tiny fraction of the 41.2 degrees of sky shown in the "longer dimension" of the frame. How tiny will the Moon be? It will be (½ X 1/41 X 36) mm, or 36/82 mm. That is 0.44 mm, or less than ½ mm. The image of the Moon on the film will be *extremely* tiny. If, on the other hand, we use a 400-mm lens, we see that the "piece of sky" in the photograph will be 5 degrees wide, as measured across the "longer dimension" of the frame. At ½ degree in diameter, the Moon will occupy 1/10 of the 36 mm, or 3.6 mm. That is a more respectable size, though still not one that dominates the photograph. By using a 20-cm Schmidt-Cassegrain Telescope as a lens to photograph the Moon, we have a case in which the Moon will completely dominate the photograph because its 0.5 degree diameter disk will barely fit within the "shorter dimension" of the frame of the photograph which shows only 0.7 degrees of sky. This explains why the 20-cm SCT is a popular instrument for photographing the Full Moon at the time of a lunar eclipse.

On the other hand, we may want to show a large area of sky in order to capture an extensive display of the Aurora Borealis. We may wish to show an area extending from the northern horizon up to the star Polaris, and depending on our latitude, the altitude of Polaris may be 45 degrees or more. Glancing at the chart above, we can see that a 28-mm lens is ideal for such purposes, since it can show an expanse of sky 49 degrees across in its "shorter dimension" and over 70 degrees in its "longer dimension."

If we wish to consider whether a certain lens is the right one to use to photograph a certain constellation, we should be aware of the size of the constellation or of the distance, in degrees, between certain stars of that constellation. Consider the Big Dipper. We already know, from Chapter 4, the angular distance between the bright stars that form the Big Dipper. If we wish to include the "cup" of the Big Dipper in a photograph, we should remember that the distance between the two stars at the "top of the cup" is 10 degrees, and the whole Big Dipper is 25 degrees from end to end. Glancing at the chart above quickly tells us that the whole Big Dipper can be easily included in a photograph, if we use a 24-mm, a 28-mm, or a 50-mm lens. With an 85-mm lens, it may fit, if we angle the Big Dipper to show it in a "corner-to-corner" orientation; otherwise, it will probably not fit in the frame, which allows for only 24 degrees X 16 degrees. The "cup of the Dipper" will fit in photographs taken with an 85-mm, a 105-mm, or a 135-mm lens. However, the 200-mm lens would probably not be suitable for the "cup of the Dipper," since the frame of the photograph can accommodate only 10 degrees in the "longer dimension." Those "top stars" may be shown if the camera were "oriented" or "tilted" to show them, but even then they would still be quite close to the edge of the frame. Obviously, the 400-mm lens, as well as the 20-cm SCT with its 2000-mm focal length, would both be unsuitable for photographing the "cup of the Big Dipper."

Astrophotographic Projects

Many beginning astrophotographers are eager to find projects that are suitable for their stage of development and skill in this craft. Surprisingly, there are many projects that are quite suitable for those who have just begun to use this method of capturing the beauty of the sky. A selection of the right project should be based on interest, weather conditions, season of the year, lunar phase, and equipment available.

Keep in mind that, to produce a good photograph, the camera must be very steady throughout the exposure. That is why a very solid tripod has already been stressed. Placing it in a good location is equally important.

In photographing "night sky objects," waiting until the very end of astronomical twilight is important, unless it is a photograph designed to show the "remaining twilight" above the western horizon. Besides the glow of twilight, the effects of light pollution, even if not in the immediate vicinity, can have a damaging effect on a photograph. As a result, trying to do your astrophotography in a very dark location is of great importance. From many locations, the sky will become "washed out" at some point in the exposure, and increasing the length of the exposure time only increases the damage to the image from the "sky glow." At what point that happens is very difficult to state, because it depends on a large number of factors, such as: (1) the amount of "ambient light" and "sky glow" in the area, (2) the possible presence of some "twilight," though a person may think that astronomical twilight has ended in the evening or not yet begun in the morning, (3) the presence of mist or water vapour in the air, (4) the generally poor sky transparency at the site, (5) the film used, (6) the lens used, and (7) the length of the exposure.

Experience will teach a beginning astrophotographer a great deal about these matters, and he, or she, must be willing to learn from those lessons. If so, the rewards will be considerable.

Suitable Projects for Simple Unguided Astrophotography:

Projects to show:

- circumpolar star trails, that is, the great circular trails of stars in the polar region of the sky, when long exposure photographs are made (See Photo 1.)
- planetary groupings and conjunctions of planets in a certain area of the sky (See Photos 2 and 3.)
- meteor showers (See Photo 4.)
- the Aurora Borealis, which can be very impressive! (See Photos 5 and 6.)
- constellations, especially short exposures showing only the brightest stars (See Photos 7, 9, 10, 11, 12, 13, and 15.)
- star trails for a single constellation (See Photo 8.)
- the Earth's shadow rising in space, in the east, after sunset, something that can be done as a series of photographs at one-minute intervals (See Photo 14.)
- the Zodiacal Light (See Photo 16.)
- large areas of the sky in a certain season of the year

- large multi-star asterisms, such as the Summer Triangle or the Winter Hexagon
- multiple exposures (on a single frame) of a lunar eclipse
- Moonrises and Moonsets

With so many choices available for someone who wishes to photograph the sky, there should be little hesitation in choosing one, or several of them, even if a person has never before used a camera after dark.

13

Observing the Moon

Most people have observed the Moon and been fascinated by it at one time or another. Not everyone, however, knows in advance what to expect from the Moon on a certain night when he or she might wish to go out and observe what is in the night sky.

Will the Moon be visible in the sky tonight? Will it be rising, or setting, or high in the sky when I want to observe? Will it be so bright or so close to an object I want to observe that it will interfere with my seeing that object? After reading this chapter carefully you should easily be able to answer all of those questions.

What should I expect from the Moon tonight? To answer that question, you always need to know what time it is *in the Moon's cycle* or where the Moon is in its monthly orbit around the Earth. Our word "month" comes from the word "Moon." Long ago our ancestors learned to measure the Moon's cycle very accurately, and they found out that it was about 29 1/2 days between times when the Moon was at the same phase. For example, it was 29 1/2 days between two New Moons or two Full Moons. We all know from looking at calendars that there are four major phases listed: New Moon, First Quarter, Full Moon, and Last Quarter, and then the cycle repeats itself. The time of New Moon is really the beginning of the "lunar month." That is why we say that a Moon that is only 2 days old is a "very young Moon," and one that is 28 days old is a "very old Moon." A Moon's life cycle is only 29 1/2 days! Then a new life cycle begins. We can also see why the time between each one of the four major phases is about one week. Since the four major phases occur when the Moon is at the beginning and is about 1/4, 1/2, and 3/4 through its life cycle, the time between each major phase is about 1/4 of 29 1/2 days or a little more than seven days.

In order to know what we should expect from the Moon at any one time, we should ask what phase of the Moon occurs today? Or, between which phases are we now?

Depending on the answer, we should follow these guidelines in order to know approximately what to expect from the Moon.

Between the Time of New Moon and First Quarter

On the day of New Moon, the Moon will appear too close to the Sun to be seen at all.

During the week following New Moon, the Moon will become visible in the evening in the western or southwestern sky. This will happen a half hour to an hour or more after sunset as the sky gets darker. One, two, or three days after

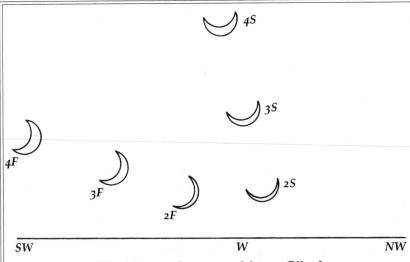

The Young Crescent Moon Climbs Into the Western Evening Sky

The young crescent Moon appears in quite different locations in the sky depending on the season of the year. From the latitudes of southern Canada and northern United States, the Moon climbs a steep path from night to night *in the springtime* and a very gradual path *in the fall*. The Moon's approximate locations above the western horizon about an hour after sunset are shown for 2-, 3-, and 4-day-old Moons in early spring (2S, 3S and 4S) and in early fall (2F, 3F, and 4F). Note that as the Moon climbs in the sky, its crescent is becoming larger or "waxing." During winter and summer, the crescent Moon climbs along a pathway that is between those shown for spring and fall.

New Moon, it will be a small crescent, gradually growing in size as the days go by. It is called a "waxing crescent Moon." ("Waxing" means "growing.") The "horns of the crescent" will point away from the Sun and upward or toward the south or southeast — toward the observer's left. As the crescent grows in size from night to night, it will appear brighter and become easier to spot in the sky. You may start to see it before sunset. As the days go by, instead of seeing it for only an hour or so, you will see it for 3 or 4 hours.

On about the date of First Quarter, the Moon will be about 1/4 of the distance around the sky (as measured from the Sun) in its orbit around the Earth. Half of the Moon's disk now appears lighted — the half that is westward or to our right as we look at the sky. At sunset the Moon will now appear up in the sky in the South (since the Moon rose at about mid-day). You can expect that the Moon will set at about midnight.

Between the Time of First Quarter and Full Moon

During the week from First Quarter until Full Moon you will see the lighted part of the Moon growing and becoming much brighter. Now it is called a "gibbous Moon" or a "waxing gibbous Moon." Gibbous is the term used when the lighted part of the Moon is more than half the disk. It is now much easier to see in the daytime. At sunset a bright Moon is seen first in the southern sky. Later as the week goes by, it is seen in the southeastern sky, and then in the eastern sky just before the time of Full Moon. As this week goes by, expect to see the Moon setting later and later, between midnight and the time of sunrise. In other words, it will set just a short while after midnight on the first day or two after First Quarter, and almost at the time of sunrise on the day or two before Full Moon.

On the day of Full Moon, expect the great round Moon at its very brightest to rise approximately in the east at about the time of sunset. It will be in the sky all night, and will be highest at about midnight, and will set in the west at about the time of sunrise.

Between the Time of Full Moon and Last Quarter

During the week between the times of Full Moon and Last Quarter, the lighted part of the Moon gets smaller. It is now called a "waning Moon" - meaning one that is growing smaller. It is called a "gibbous Moon" at this time also, but it looks different from a "waxing gibbous Moon." Now the "bright side" of the Moon is on the left as we see it, or to the East, if we refer to the directions in the sky. Putting the two ideas together, we call it a "waning gibbous Moon." As the week goes by, the Moon interferes less with our observing if we want to observe faint objects in the evening or early night, since the Moon rises later and later every night. On the first night or two after Full Moon, it will usually rise within an hour or two after the time of sunset, and it will be highest in the sky an hour or two after midnight, and set in the west an hour or two after sunrise.

As the week goes by, the Moon rises later and later until near the time of Last Quarter, when it rises at about midnight. During this week also, you should expect to see the Moon in the daytime before noon in the southwestern or western sky.

On the day of Last Quarter, you can expect that the Moon will rise at about midnight or a little after, will be highest in the sky at about the time of sunrise or a little after, and will set at about noon. Be sure to look for the Moon in the southwestern or western sky a couple of hours before noon. It may be a challenge sometimes, but you may also be able to see it easily at other times.

Between the Time of Last Quarter and New Moon

During the period of time between Last Quarter and New Moon, the Moon is waning fast; it is becoming a small crescent again.

It does not interfere with the observing plans of most observers because it is not seen in the evening sky at all and is seen only after midnight, or in the "wee hours" of the morning, or in the early dawn when it sometimes presents a very beautiful sight.

In the first few days after Last Quarter the Moon rises in the east within a few hours after midnight and is highest in the sky a few hours after sunrise and sets in the early afternoon. As the week goes by, the Moon continues to rise later and later. Two or three days before New Moon, the Moon rises just a couple of hours before sunrise. Within the last few days before New Moon, it is a crescent that is growing smaller and smaller in the eastern part of the sky and it disappears from view when the Sun rises. (The "brighter part" of the Moon appears so small that the Moon's overall brightness is much less than it was a week or so earlier.) Now the "horns of the crescent" are pointing upward away from the Sun or to the south or southwest — toward the observer's right. In the last two or three days before New Moon, the Moon's crescent is so small that many people will not see it at all. Even experienced observers may see it only for a short time, unless they are using binoculars to spot it and follow it as it moves up in the sky before the Sun rises. On the last day before New Moon, when it appears very close to the Sun, probably no one will see it rise just a short while before the Sun.

Of course, on the day of New Moon, we do not observe the Moon at all, except on the rare occasions when we see a solar eclipse. Now that the Moon is back to New Moon, we are ready to begin the lunar cycle all over again.

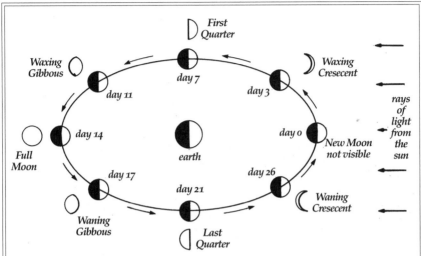

Phases of the Moon

This diagram shows the Moon at eight points in its orbit around the Earth, as viewed from a point high above the orbit. Imagine yourself an observer on Earth at the centre of the diagram and looking toward the Moon at intervals of a few days. The outer figures show the appearances of the phases of the Moon as viewed by an observer on Earth, at the corresponding times during the lunar month. Note that at New Moon the lighted side of the Moon is not seen from Earth. At the time of First and Last Quarter (Day 7 and Day 21), only half of the lighted half of the Moon is seen. At the time of Full Moon (Day 14), all of the Moon's lighted half is seen. The time between phases is approximate; the exact time from one New Moon until the next is slightly more than 29 1/2 days.

The chart on the following page gives the date and Universal Time for each New Moon and Full Moon from 2003 through 2010. Converting to Standard Time for any North American time zone simply means subtracting a certain number of hours. When Daylight Saving Time applies, 1 hour is then added.

Dates of New Moon and Full Moon from 2003 to 2010

To help in using the above guidelines for observing the Moon, here are the dates and times for New Moon and Full Moon from 2003 to 2010, given in Universal Time (UT). To convert to Standard Time for the North American time zones, *subtract* the following number of hours: NLST − 3 ½; AST − 4; EST − 5; CST − 6; MST − 7; PST − 8. (For example, in the Eastern Time Zone, the February 6, 2004, Full Moon is at 3:47 Eastern Standard Time, and the December 5, 2006, Full Moon is on December 4, 2006 at 19:25 (or 7:25 p.m.) Eastern Standard Time.) The dates for First Quarter and Last Quarter are 7 or 8 days *after* the dates for New Moon and Full Moon respectively, and may be filled in, as you wish, on this chart.

For 2003:

NEW MOON		F.Q.	FULL MOON		L.Q.
Jan. 2	20:23	___	Jan. 18	10:48	___
Feb. 1	10:48	___	Feb. 16	23:51	___
Mar. 3	2:35	___	Mar. 18	10:34	___
Apr. 1	19:19	___	Apr. 16	19:36	___
May 1	12:15	___	May 16	3:36	___
May 31	4:20	___	Jun. 14	11:16	___
Jun. 29	18:39	___	Jul. 13	19:21	___
Jul. 29	6:53	___	Aug. 12	4:48	___
Aug. 27	17:26	___	Sep. 10	16:36	___
Sep. 26	3:09	___	Oct. 10	7:27	___
Oct. 25	12:50	___	Nov. 9	1:13	___
Nov. 23	22:59	___	Dec. 8	20:37	___
Dec. 23	9:43	___			___

For 2004:

NEW MOON		F.Q.	FULL MOON		L.Q.
		___	Jan. 7	15:40	___
Jan. 21	21:05	___	Feb. 6	8:47	___
Feb. 20	9:18	___	Mar. 6	23:14	___
Mar. 20	22:41	___	Apr. 5	11:03	___
Apr. 19	13:21	___	May 4	20:33	___
May 19	4:52	___	Jun. 3	4:20	___
Jun. 17	20:27	___	Jul. 2	11:09	___
Jul. 17	11:24	___	Jul. 31	18:05	___
Aug. 16	1:24	___	Aug. 30	2:22	___
Sep. 14	14:29	___	Sep. 28	13:09	___
Oct. 14	2:48	___	Oct. 28	3:07	___
Nov. 12	14:27	___	Nov. 26	20:07	___
Dec. 12	1:29	___	Dec. 26	15:06	___

For 2005:

NEW MOON		F.Q.	FULL MOON		L.Q.
Jan. 10	12:03	___	Jan. 25	10:32	___
Feb. 8	22:28	___	Feb. 24	4:54	___
Mar. 10	9:10	___	Mar. 25	20:58	___
Apr. 8	20:32	___	Apr. 24	10:06	___
May 8	8:45	___	May 23	20:18	___
Jun. 6	21:55	___	Jun. 22	4:14	___
Jul. 6	12:02	___	Jul. 21	11:00	___
Aug. 5	3:05	___	Aug. 19	17:53	___
Sep. 3	18:45	___	Sep. 18	2:01	___
Oct. 3	10:28	___	Oct. 17	12:14	___
Nov. 2	1:24	___	Nov. 16	0:57	___
Dec. 1	15:01	___	Dec. 15	14:15	___
Dec. 31	3:12	___			

For 2006:

NEW MOON		F.Q.	FULL MOON		L.Q.
		___	Jan. 14	9:48	___
Jan. 29	14:15	___	Feb. 13	4:44	___
Feb. 28	0:31	___	Mar. 14	23:35	___
Mar. 29	10:15	___	Apr. 13	6:51	___
Apr. 27	19:44	___	May 13	6:51	___
May 27	5:26	___	Jun. 11	18:03	___
Jun. 25	16:05	___	Jul. 11	3:02	___
Jul. 25	4:31	___	Aug. 9	10:54	___
Aug. 23	19:10	___	Sep. 7	18:42	___
Sep. 22	11:45	___	Oct. 7	3:13	___
Oct. 22	5:14	___	Nov. 5	12:58	___
Nov. 20	22:18	___	Dec. 5	0:25	___
Dec. 20	14:01	___			

For 2007:

NEW MOON		F.Q.	FULL MOON		L.Q.
		___	Jan. 3	13:57	___
Jan. 19	4:01	___	Feb. 2	5:45	___
Feb. 17	16:14	___	Mar. 3	23:17	___
Mar. 19	2:43	___	Apr. 2	17:15	___
Apr. 17	11:36	___	May 2	10:09	___
May 16	19:27	___	Jun. 1	1:04	___
Jun. 15	3:13	___	Jun. 30	13:49	___
Jul. 14	12:04	___	Jul. 30	0:48	___
Aug. 12	23:02	___	Aug. 28	10:35	___
Sep. 11	12:44	___	Sep. 26	19:45	___
Oct. 11	5:01	___	Oct. 26	4:52	___
Nov. 9	23:03	___	Nov. 24	14:30	___
Dec. 9	17:40	___	Dec. 24	1:16	___

For 2008:

NEW MOON		F.Q.	FULL MOON		L.Q.
Jan. 8	11:37	___	Jan. 22	13:35	___
Feb. 7	3:44	___	Feb. 21	3:30	___
Mar. 7	17:14	___	Mar. 21	18:40	___
Apr. 6	3:55	___	Apr. 20	10:25	___
May 5	12:18	___	May 20	2:11	___
Jun. 3	19:23	___	Jun. 18	17:30	___
Jul. 3	2:19	___	Jul. 18	7:59	___
Aug. 1	10:13	___	Aug. 16	21:16	___
Aug. 30	19:58	___	Sep. 15	9:13	___
Sep. 29	8:12	___	Oct. 14	20:02	___
Oct. 28	23:14	___	Nov. 13	6:17	___
Nov. 27	16:55	___	Dec. 12	16:37	___
Dec. 27	12:22	___			

For 2009:					For 2010:				
NEW MOON	F.Q.	FULL MOON	L.Q.		NEW MOON	F.Q.	FULL MOON	L.Q.	
		Jan. 11	3:27	___					___
Jan. 26	7:55	___	Feb. 9	14:49	___	Jan. 15	7:11	___	Jan. 30	6:18	___
Feb. 25	1:35	___	Mar. 11	2:38	___	Feb. 14	2:51	___	Feb. 28	16:38	___
Mar. 26	16:06	___	Apr. 9	14:56	___	Mar. 16	21:01	___	Mar. 30	2:25	___
Apr. 25	3:23	___	May 9	4:01	___	Apr. 14	12:29	___	Apr. 28	12:18	___
May 24	12:11	___	Jun. 7	18:12	___	May 14	1:04	___	May 27	23:07	___
Jun. 22	19:35	___	Jul. 7	9:21	___	Jun. 12	11:15	___	Jun. 26	11:30	___
Jul. 22	2:35	___	Aug. 6	0:55	___	Jul. 11	19:40	___	Jul. 26	1:36	___
Aug. 20	10:02	___	Sep. 4	16:03	___	Aug. 10	3:08	___	Aug. 24	17:05	___
Sep. 18	18:44	___	Oct. 4	6:10	___	Sep. 8	10:30	___	Sep. 23	9:17	___
Oct. 18	5:33	___	Nov. 2	19:14	___	Oct. 7	18:44	___	Oct. 23	1:36	___
Nov. 16	19:14	___	Dec. 2	7:30	___	Nov. 6	4:52	___	Nov. 21	17:27	___
Dec. 16	12:02	___	Dec. 31	19:13		Dec. 5	17:36	___	Dec. 21	8:13	___

Guide to the Map of the Moon

To assist in your observations of the Moon, especially if you are using binoculars or a small telescope, the accompanying map is provided. With it are listed some of the many named features on the Moon. They include craters, mountains, and maria. Craters are roughly circular features, many of which have been

Many lunar craters have been formed by impacts of meteors and asteroids striking the lunar surface over millions of years.

made by the impact of meteors and asteroids striking the surface of the Moon over many millions of years. The maria (a Latin word meaning "seas") are not

The Moon's maria (Latin: seas) are not seas or water of any kind since there is no water on the surface of the Moon, but they are large plains formed by lava flows several billion years ago.

seas or oceans at all, because there is no water on the Moon, but they are the large dark areas probably formed by the flow of lava billions of years ago.

The numbers before the names of the features indicate their position by number on the map of the Moon. No 0's are used in the numbers to avoid confusion with the round craters marked on the map. The numbers after the

> **The numbers after the names of the features indicate the number of days after New Moon when that feature will be near, or on, the terminator and best seen in binoculars or a small telescope.**

features refer approximately to *the number of days after the new Moon* when that feature is best seen in binoculars or a small telescope. Most observers prefer to observe craters and mountains when they are near the terminator (the line dividing the dark side from the light side). At the time of First Quarter, as seen from the Earth, this line is nearly straight and is seen running from the Moon's north pole to its south pole.

For several reasons, these numbers are only approximate. They are given in the form "7-8" meaning that you should try to find this feature "*about 7 or 8 days after the date of New Moon*," which is approximately when the terminator or "sunrise line" will be crossing that feature.

For some features, two sets of numbers are given. This means that there are two times when this feature may be seen near the terminator. For example, after the crater Hercules, are the numbers "3-4" and "15-17." This means that this crater is near the terminator or "Sunrise line" about 3 or 4 days after New Moon, and it is near the "Sunset terminator" about 15 to 17 days after New Moon or several days after Full Moon. You will soon notice that, if you wish, you may study many features between the time of New Moon and Full Moon when the "Sunrise terminator" is crossing them *or* later in the Moon's month when the "Sunset terminator" is crossing the same place. Of course, if you study the features later in the Moon's month, you will have to observe later in the night when the waning Moon is in the sky.

Features Marked on this Map of the Moon

Craters

21 Albategnius (7-8)	44 Eratosthenes (8-9)	66 Maurolycus (6-7)
22 Alphonsus (8-9)	45 Eudoxus (5-6)	67 Mersenius (11-12)
23 Arago (5-6)	46 Fracastorius (4-5)	68 Newcomb (3-4)
24 Archimedes (8-9)	47 Furnerius (15-17)	69 Petavius (15-16)
25 Aristarchus (11-12)	48 Gassendi (11-12)	71 Piccolomini (4-5)
26 Aristillus (7-8)	49 Grimaldi (13-14)	72 Plato (8-9)
27 Aristoteles (5-6)	51 Halley (7-8)	73 Plinius (5-6)
28 Arzachel (8-9)	52 Hercules (3-4 & 15-17)	74 Posidonius (4-5)
29 Atlas (15-16)	53 Herschel (8-9)	75 Ptolemaeus (8-9)
31 Autolychus (7-8)	54 Hevelius (13-14)	76 Reinhold (9-10)
32 Bessel (6-7)	55 Hipparchus (7-8)	77 Ross (5-6)
33 Bullialdus (9-10)	56 Julius Caesar (5-6)	78 Schickard (11-12)
34 Cassini (7-8)	57 Kepler (11-12)	79 Schiller (11-12)
35 Catharina (5-6)	58 Langrenus (15-16)	81 Snellius (15-16)
36 Clavius (9-10)	59 Lansburg (9-10)	82 Stevinus (15-16)
37 Cleomedes (15-16)	61 Longomontanus (9-10)	83 Taruntius (3-4)
38 Cook (15-16)	62 Macrobius (3-4)	84 Theophilus (5-6)
39 Copernicus (8-9)	63 Maginus (8-9)	85 Timocharus (8-9)
41 Cyrillus (5-6)	64 Manillius (6-7)	86 Tycho (8-9)
42 Delambre (5-6)	65 Maskelyne (4-5)	87 Wilhelm (9-10)
43 Endymion (3-4 & 15-17)		

Mountains

A Alpine Valley (7-8)	K Haemus Mts. (5-6)	V Speitzbergen (8-9)
B Alps Mts. (7-8)	M Jura Mts. (10-11)	W Straight Range (9-10)
E Altai Mts. (5-6)	N Pyrenees Mts. (4-5)	X Straight Wall (8-9)
F Apennine Mts. (7-8)	R Rheita Valley (15-17)	Y Taurus Mts. (3-4 & 16-18)
G Carpathian Mts. (10-11)	S Riphaeus Mts. (9-10)	Z Teneriffe Mts. (8-9)
H Caucasus Mts. (6-7)		

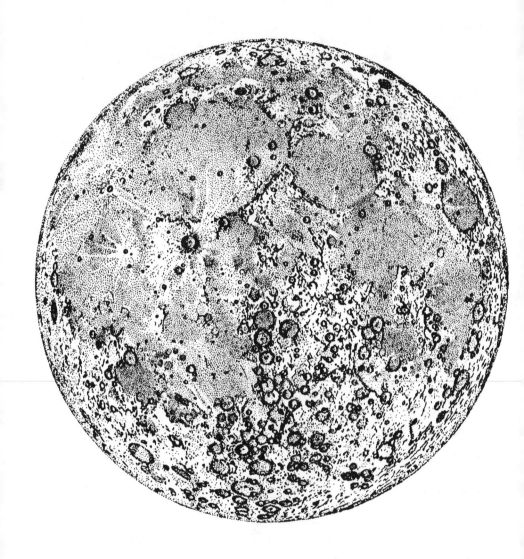

Moon as Seen from Earth

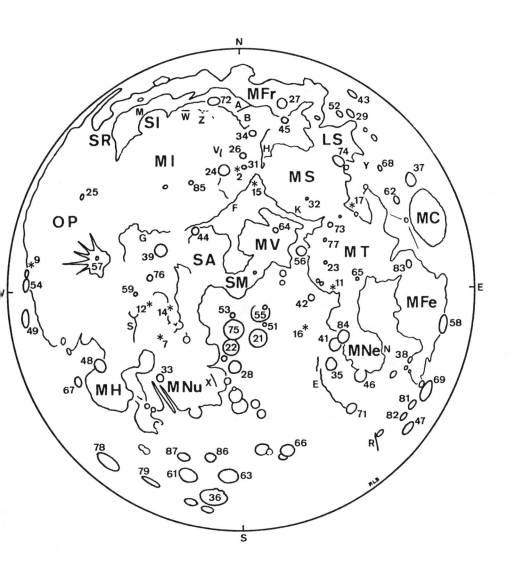

The Moon   See List of Named Features

"N" and "S" Indicate Approximate
Position of North and South Poles

Maria

LS	Lacus Somniorum (Lake of Dreams) (3-4 & 15-17)
MC	Mare Crisium (Sea of Crises) (3-4 & 15-17)
MFe	Mare Fecunditatis (Sea of Fertility) (3-4 & 15-17)
MFr	Mare Frigoris (Sea of Cold) (7-8)
MH	Mare Humorum (Sea of Moisture) (11-12)
MI	Mare Imbrium (Sea of Rains) (8-9)
MNe	Mare Nectaris (Sea of Nectar) (4-5)
NNu	Mare Nubium (Sea of Clouds) (8-9)
MS	Mare Serenitatis (Sea of Serenity) (4-5 & 16-18)
MT	Mare Tranquillitatis (Sea of Tranquility) (4-5 & 16-18)
MV	Mare Vaporum (Sea of Vapors) (7-8)
OP	Oceanus Procellarum (Ocean of Storms) (10-12)
SA	Sinus Aestuum (Seething Bay) (8-9)
SI	Sinus Iridum (Bay of Rainbows) (9-10)
SM	Sinus Medii (Central Bay) (8-9)
SR	Sinus Roris (Bay of Dew) (13-14)

Sites Associated with Various Lunar Missions

2 Luna 2, First to reach the Moon (Sep. 1959) (in MI)

7 Ranger 7, First close pictures (Jul. 1964) (between MNu and OP)

9 Luna 9, First soft landing (Feb. 1966) (in OP)

11 Apollo 11, First men on Moon (Jul. 1969) (in MT)

12 Apollo 12, (Nov. 1969) (between MNu and OP)

14 Apollo 14, (Feb. 1971) (between MNu and OP)

15 Apollo 15, (Jul. 1971) (near Apennine Mts.)

16 Apollo 16, (Apr. 1972) (near Crater Halley)

17 Apollo 17, (Dec. 1972) (between MS and MT)

14

Observing the Planets

Some of the easiest objects in the sky to observe are the members of our own Solar System. The Solar System is made up of the Sun at the centre, the nine major planets (counting Earth) and their Moons or satellites, thousands of minor planets or asteroids, hundreds of comets, and a great quantity of tiny dust particles.

Of the nine planets, five can be easily observed with the unaided eye because they are very bright objects. Two others are bright enough to be seen with binoculars. Only one planet, far-away Pluto, is too faint to be seen in binoculars and can be seen only with a large telescope.

Venus is immediately recognized because it is brilliantly white and much brighter than any star in the sky.

Jupiter, too, is whitish and brighter than any star, even Sirius.

Mars is usually an orangish-brown colour and can be about as bright as Sirius when it is near the Earth, but at other times, it may be much less brilliant, even fading to about the same brightness as Dubhe, the star at the end of the cup in the Big Dipper.

Saturn is often seen as slightly yellowish in colour and varying from about the brightness of Rigel, the brightest star in Orion, when it is most brilliant, to the brightness of Spica, the brightest star in Virgo.

Mercury sometimes appears with the brightness of the stars of the Big Dipper, and sometimes it is even brighter than Sirius, the brightest star of all, but usually its great brilliance is not noticed because it appears in the twilight where its dazzling brightness cannot be appreciated.

The planets are different from the stars and other objects in the night sky. Because they travel around the Sun, we cannot mark them on an ordinary star map and say that they will be seen in a certain place at a certain time of year. We need to describe their positions in a different way because their motion around the Sun means that they will be in a different place from year to year, and sometimes from month to month.

The Cycles of the Planets

Sometimes people assume that they should be able to observe a planet based on what they did a number of years before a certain date. Perhaps you have heard someone say: "I saw Mars for many nights in a row three years ago. It was during the summer time. I will have time to look for it again this summer when I am at the cottage." You may also hear someone say, "I saw Venus last winter in the western evening sky. It was very bright. I am going to look for it there again this winter." Both of these people are bound to be disappointed at not being able to observe the planet they hope to see at the time they expect to see it. Neither Mars nor Venus has a yearly cycle of the type that these two people expect it to have.

There are many opportunities throughout the year to see most of the planets, and in some years, to see all of the planets. On rare occasions, we are even able to see all of the bright planets at once, such as occurred on those memorable evenings in late April and early May, 2002. On those fabulous evenings, the cycles of the five bright planets brought them together in the western evening sky, and for several weeks we could observe, and photograph, five planets of our Solar System doing a kind of "dance" above the western horizon from night to night, as their orbits carried each of them around the Sun and as the view from planet Earth, also travelling around the Sun, changed from night to night. (See Photos 2 and 3.)

The cycle of each one of the planets is different from that of the other planets. The inferior planets will be considered first, that is, those inside the orbit of planet Earth, namely Mercury and Venus. Then the superior planets, those outside Earth's orbit, will be considered.

The Inferior Planets

The inferior planets, Mercury and Venus, are seen only at a limited distance from the Sun, never at a large distance from the Sun or at opposition to the Sun. They may appear east of (or to the left from) the Sun, OR they may appear to the west of (or to the right from) the Sun.

When either Mercury or Venus is to the east of the Sun (that is, to the left from the Sun as viewed from planet Earth), and far enough away from the Sun to be easily seen, it appears in the western sky after sunset, and for a while it appears to move higher and higher from evening to evening, and then it appears to move downward, or sunward, from evening to evening. The moment when it is farthest out from the Sun (and usually about the same time as it appears highest in the evening sky) is called its **Greatest Eastern Elongation**.

When either Mercury or Venus is to the west of the Sun (that is, to the right from the Sun as viewed from the Earth), and far enough away from the Sun to be easily seen, it appears in the eastern sky before sunrise, and it appears to move higher and higher from morning to morning, and then it appears to move downward, or sunward, from morning to morning. The moment when it is farthest out from the Sun (and usually about the same time as it appears highest in the morning sky) is called its **Greatest Western Elongation**.

Mercury:

Mercury is often seen in the western evening sky for a week or two or maybe three weeks, and then not seen for a month or so, and then it is seen in the eastern morning sky for a week or two or maybe three weeks, and then not seen for about 2 months or more, and then the cycle repeats.

Mercury as Observed for Several Years in the Past:	
Eastern Elongations from the Sun: (Periods of western evening sky observations)	Western Elongations from the Sun: (Periods of eastern morning sky observations)
Late Feb. 2000 Early Jun. 2000 Sep. and early Oct. 2000 Late Jan. 2001 May 2001 Sep. 2001	Late Mar. and Early Apr. 2000 Late Jul. 2000 Late Nov. 2000 Early Mar. 2001 Early Jul. 2001 Late Oct. And Early Nov. 2001
Early Jan. 2002 Late Apr. and Early May 2002 Early Sep. 2002 Late Dec. 2002	Late Feb. 2002 Late Jun. 2002 Late Oct. 2002
Apr. 2003 Aug. 2003 Early Dec. 2003	Early Feb. 2003 Late May and Early Jun. 2003 Late Sep. and Early Oct. 2003

As seen from the above information, there are three, sometimes four, periods of time each year when Mercury may be seen in the western evening sky after sunset, alternating with the three, sometimes four, periods of time each year when it may be seen in the eastern morning sky. Usually there is a period of about a month, or month and a half, between the "*western evening sky observation period*" and the "*eastern morning sky observation period.*" Also, there is usually a period of about two months between the "*eastern morning sky observation period*" and the "*western evening sky observation period.*" The length of time for a complete cycle (which includes both the evening sky observation period and the morning sky observation period) is about 116 days, which is slightly less than 4 months. Therefore, there are 3 such complete cycles in any year, with some time for a small part of an additional cycle.

Which of these periods of time are most favourable for observing the planet Mercury, (that is, which one presents the greatest chance of seeing it on a good number of occasions)? The most favourable elongations (that is, those with the greatest chance of being observed on a good number of occasions) are the evening sky observations *in the springtime*, AND the **morning sky observations** **in the autumn**. The reasons for this are the same as those given for the "*steep climb of the Crescent Moon in springtime*" (See page 105.) and for the "*sooner-than-expected rising of the Harvest Moon in autumn.*" (See page 174.).

Venus:

Venus as Observed for Several Years in the Past:

For the last 8 months of 1977, Venus was observable in the evening twilight. Then, except for January, it was a brilliant eastern, morning sky object for the first 9 months of 1998. From the last few days of 1998 to early August 1999, Venus dominated the western evening twilight, being particularly brilliant in the late winter and spring. Venus was then in the eastern morning sky before sunrise for 8 months from September 1999 through April 2000. It was not seen then by northern-hemisphere observers until August, when it became visible in the western evening sky, where it was visible until March 2001, appearing high and very brilliant in late winter evenings. In March 2001, Venus appeared lower from evening to evening until it disappeared, but almost immediately it appeared in the eastern morning sky and was seen there until the end of 2001, being particularly brilliant in May and June. After over two months' absence from our 'northern latitude skies', it reappeared in March 2002 in the western evening sky and remained there until the end of October, being very brilliant in the late summer. In early November Venus became visible in the eastern morning sky where it was a dominant object throughout the winter and remained visible until late July 2003. In September 2003, it appeared in the western twilight sky and it was a dominant object there through the autumn and winter and into the spring of 2004.

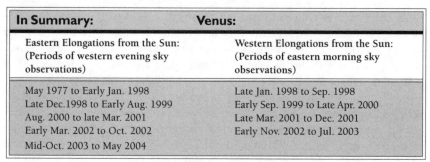

In Summary:	Venus:
Eastern Elongations from the Sun: (Periods of western evening sky observations)	Western Elongations from the Sun: (Periods of eastern morning sky observations)
May 1977 to Early Jan. 1998	Late Jan. 1998 to Sep. 1998
Late Dec.1998 to Early Aug. 1999	Early Sep. 1999 to Late Apr. 2000
Aug. 2000 to late Mar. 2001	Late Mar. 2001 to Dec. 2001
Early Mar. 2002 to Oct. 2002	Early Nov. 2002 to Jul. 2003
Mid-Oct. 2003 to May 2004	

As can be readily seen, Venus is observed in the western evening sky for a period of about 8 to 9 months, and then after a period of a few days to a couple of weeks, it emerges in the eastern morning sky. It is then seen there for a period of about 7 $\frac{1}{2}$ to 9 months, after which it is not usually seen at northern latitudes for a period of two to three months, after which its appearance in the western evening sky marks the beginning of the cycle once again. This complete cycle (which includes both the evening sky observation period and the morning sky observation period) lasts more than 19 months, actually, on average, 584 days.

On occasion, observers have been able to record seeing Venus beyond the times suggested in this brief summary. For example, in 2001, some observers were able to spot Venus very low in the morning sky on March 29 (and for a few people, on several mornings before and after that date), having observed it in the evening twilight only about 10 hours previously. The apparent passage of Venus, at that time, 8 degrees north of the Sun (at the time of its inferior conjunction with the Sun) allowed it to be seen for several days in both the evening and morning sky. This "twice a day sighting" can occur only at the time Venus's passing from being "*an evening sky object*" to being "*a morning sky object*." On the other hand, there is always an extended period of time, for northern hemisphere observers, often a couple of months, or more, when Venus is not seen at all during the interval between its being "*a morning sky object*" and being "*an evening sky object*."

The Superior Planets

The superior planets, those outside the orbit of planet Earth, (that is, Mars, Jupiter, Saturn, Uranus, Neptune, and Pluto) may be seen all around the sky, since they orbit the Sun and are outside the Earth's orbit. When they appear on the far side of the Sun as viewed from the Earth (though not necessarily eclipsed by the Sun), they are said to be **in conjunction** with the Sun. When their orbit puts them at an angle of 90 degrees from the Sun, they are said to be in "**quadrature**" (with the Sun). When they are in the opposite part of the sky (180 degrees) from the Sun, they are said to be "**at opposition**."

There is a great range in the orbital periods of the outer planets. The orbital period of Mars is less than 2 years, but that of Saturn is over 29 years, and that of Pluto is over 247 years. (See page 191 for each planet's Period of Revolution around the Sun.) A "nearer planet," like Mars, appears to move a much larger angular distance across the sky in a certain period of time, such as a month or two, than a more distant planet, like Uranus or Neptune. For example, if the Earth overtakes Mars in January of one year, it will not do it again for over two years because, as the Earth is orbiting the Sun, Mars also in its orbit is covering a large angular distance across the sky, but if the Earth passes by Jupiter in January of one year, as these two orbit the Sun, then in the next year it will be only a month or so later than January when the Earth again passes "on the inside" of that planet. The far outer planets, like Uranus, Neptune, and Pluto, that appear to move only a small angular distance in their orbits each year, will be only a small angular distance farther east in the sky in the following year, and the Earth will pass them only a few days later in the following year (from the date when it passed them the previous year). This "*passing of each outer planet*" takes place at the time of "opposition," when the Earth and the other planet are on the same side of the Sun, so that the outer planet is exactly opposite the Sun in the sky, as viewed from planet Earth. At the time of this "*passing of the outer planet,*" or as astronomers say "**at opposition,**" there is what is called "retrograde motion" of the planet in the sky for a certain period of time. This is similar to what happens at a turn on a race track, during a horse race, when a rider on an inside horse looks over his shoulder to the outside and sees a horse and rider in the outside lane *appear* to be moving backwards in relation to the crowd of spectators in the background. The outside horse may, in fact, be moving just as fast as the inside horse , but because it has to travel farther, it *appears*, on the turn, to be going backwards as viewed against the crowd of spectators who are outside the track. This temporary backward or "**retrograde motion**" happens for a certain period of time before and after the date of opposition of each individual outer planet. After moving eastward in the sky for a long period of time, the planet *appears* to stop moving eastward, *appears* stationary for a moment, *appears* to retrograde for a certain period of time, *appears* stationary again, and then again *appears* to move eastward in its regular motion around the sky.

The Retrograde Motion of Mars

   This diagram illustrates the orbits of Earth and Mars, as viewed from high above the Solar System. The inner circle represents Earth's orbit. The position of Earth, over a 6-month period at about the time of a Mars opposition, is shown by the numbers from 1 to 7 with each number representing the Earth's position — at 1-month intervals. The corresponding positions of Mars in its orbit are represented by the numbers on the outer circle which represents the orbit of Mars. As seen from Earth which is "overtaking Mars", Mars appears to be moving backward even though it is actually moving forward as usual. The numbers at the top of the diagram represent the position of Mars as seen among the background stars at the times corresponding to the times numbered on Earth's orbit. Mars is at opposition at the point marked "4," and as illustrated, for about a two-month period, (from the point marked "3" to the point marked "5") Mars appears to move from East to West among the background stars. At the point marked "5," Mars again resumes its usual apparent motion from West to East in the sky.

   Similar events occur near the times of opposition of the other superior planets.

   This diagram is not to scale. (See the Appendix for a proper scale model of the Solar System.)

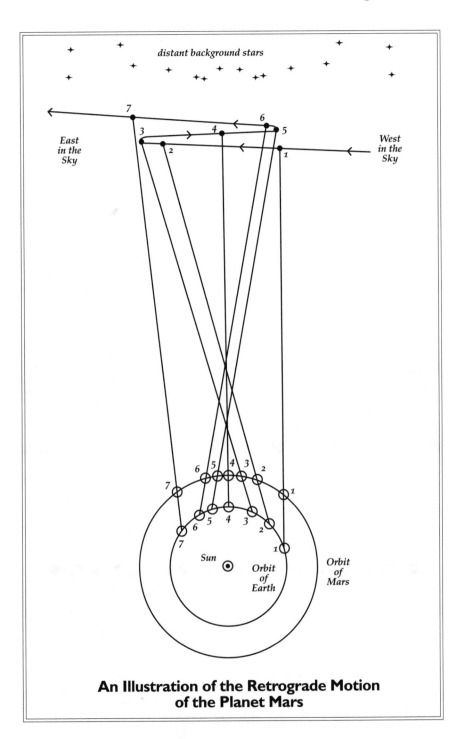

**An Illustration of the Retrograde Motion
of the Planet Mars**

The Periods of Retrograde Motion for the Superior Planets for Several Years in the Past:

	Stationary and Begins retrograde (Westward) motion	Date of Opposition (from Sun)	Stationary and Begins forward (Eastward) motion again
2000:			
Mars	_____	_____	_____
Jupiter	Sep. 21	Nov. 28	Jan. 25, 2001
Saturn	Sep. 12	Nov. 19	Jan. 25, 2001
Uranus	May 25	Aug. 11	Oct. 26
Neptune	May 8	Jul. 27	Oct. 15
Pluto	Mar. 16	Jun. 1	Aug. 22
2001:			
Mars	May 11	Jun. 13	Jul. 19
Jupiter	Nov. 2	(See below.)	(See below.)
Saturn	Sep. 27	Dec. 3	Feb. 27, 2002
Uranus	May 29	Aug. 15	Oct. 31
Neptune	May 11	Jul. 30	Oct. 17
Pluto	Mar. 18	Jun. 4	Aug. 25
2002:			
Mars	_____	_____	_____
Jupiter	_____	Jan. 1	Mar. 7
Saturn	Oct. 11	Dec. 17	Feb. 22, 2003
Uranus	Jun. 3	Aug. 20	Nov. 4
Neptune	May 13	Aug. 2	Oct. 20
Pluto	Mar. 21	Jun. 7	Aug. 27
2003:			
Mars	Jul. 30	Aug. 28	Sep. 29
Jupiter	Dec. 4, 2002	Feb. 2	Apr. 4
Saturn	Oct. 26	Dec. 31	Mar. 8, 2004
Uranus	Jun. 7	Aug. 24	Nov. 8
Neptune	May 16	Aug. 4	Oct. 23
Pluto	Mar. 23	Jun. 9	Aug. 30

	WHEN *OPPOSITION* OCCURS:	DURATION OF *RETROGRADE MOTION*:
Mars:	EVERY 26 MONTHS	– for about 2 to 2½ months
Jupiter:	about 5 weeks later than previous year	– for about 4 months
Saturn:	about 2 weeks later than previous year	– for about 4½ months
Uranus:	about 4 days later than previous year	– for about 5 months
Neptune:	about 2 or 3 days later than previous year	– for about 5¼ months
Pluto:	about 2 or 3 days later than previous year	– for about 5¼ months

PRACTISE YOUR SKILLS:

Having studied the information given about the cycles of the planets in past years, it should be possible to make approximate, but fairly accurate, predictions about what can be expected regarding *the visibility of the planets in future years.* Remember *to use* these predictions for the visibility of the planets, since the dates for *the elongations of the inferior planets* and the dates for the *opposition and retrograde motion of the superior planets* are actually, in a very practical way, the statements about *the very best times to observe each of the planets.*

(1) List the approximate periods of time when the planet **Mercury** will be (a) visible in the western evening sky, and (b) visible in the eastern morning sky in 2004.

(2) As can be seen from the information given above, the planet **Venus** may be observed in the western evening sky in the early part of 2004. (a) List the approximate period of time when **Venus** will be visible in the eastern morning sky in the year 2004. (b) List the approximate periods of time when **Venus** will be visible in the western evening sky and in the eastern morning sky during the years 2005 and 2006.

(3) As can be seen from the information given above, there will be no **Mars** opposition in 2004, 2006 or 2008. List the approximate dates for (a) the **Mars** oppositions of 2005, 2007, and early 2010, and (b) the beginning and the end of **Mars's** retrograde motion in the years 2005, 2007, and early 2010.

(4) The dates for **Jupiter's** opposition from 2000 through 2003 are given above. (a) Using the known interval between successive oppositions of this planet, list the dates of **Jupiter's** opposition from 2004 to 2010. (b) List also the dates when **Jupiter** may be observed in its retrograde motion during each of those years.

(5) **Saturn** does not come to opposition in the year 2004, though it may be observed in the early and late parts of that year. (a) List the dates for **Saturn's** opposition in the years 2005 through 2010. (b) List also the dates in those years when **Saturn's** retrograde motion may be observed.

(6) **Uranus, Neptune,** and **Pluto** are all at opposition during the summer and early autumn from the year 2000 through the year 2015. From the information given above, list the approximate date of opposition for each one of these planets for the years 2004 through 2010.

Locating the Inferior Planets

Having learned about the cycles of the inferior planets, and having tried to predict their future appearances from their past performances, we may now examine the predicted times for observing Mercury and Venus between the years 2003 and 2010.

Mercury:	
Eastern Elongations from the Sun: (Periods of western evening sky observations)	Western Elongations from the Sun: (Periods of eastern morning sky observations)

2003:
  Early and Mid-Apr.
  Mid-Aug.
  Early Dec.
	2003: Early Jan.
	  Early Jun.
	  Late Sep. and Early Oct.

2004:
  Late Mar and Early Apr.
  Late Jul.
  Late Nov.
	2004: Mid-Jan.
	  Mid-May
	  Early and Mid-Sep.
	  Late Dec.

2005: Early and Mid-Mar.
  Early Jul.
  Early Nov.
	2005: Late Apr.
	  Late Aug.
	  Mid-Dec.

2006: Late Feb. and Early Mar.
  Mid- and Late Jun.
  Mid-Oct.
	2006: Early Apr.
	  Early Aug.
	  Late Nov.

2007: Early and Mid-Feb.
  Late May and Early Jun.
  Mid- and Late Sep.
	2007: Mid- and Late Mar.
	  Mid- and Late Jul.
	  Early Nov.

2008: Late Jan.
  Early and Mid-May
  Early and Mid-Sep.
	2008: Early Mar.
	  Late Jun. and Early Jul.
	  Mid- and Late Oct.

2009: Early Jan.
  Mid- and Late Apr.
  Late Aug.
  Mid-Dec.
	2009: Mid-Feb.
	  Mid-Jul.
	  Late Sep. and Early Oct.

2010:
  Late Mar. and Early Apr.
  Early Aug.
  Late Nov. and Early Dec.
	2010: Late Jan.
	  Late May
	  Mid- and Late Sep.

Venus:	
Eastern Elongations from the Sun: (Periods of western evening sky observations)	Western Elongations from the Sun: (Periods of eastern morning sky observations)
2003: Mid-Oct. to May 2004 2005: May to Dec. 2007: Jan. to Jul. 2008: Aug. to Feb. 2009 2010: Mar. to Oct.	2003: Jan. to Jul. 2004: Jun. to Dec. 2006: Feb. to Sep. 2007: Sep. to Mar. 2008 2009: Apr. to Oct. 2010: Nov. to May 2011

Locating the Superior Planets

Having learned about the cycles of the superior planets and the times for best observing them, we may now locate the superior planets among the background stars at the times of their oppositions and when they are in their retrograde motion. Each planet has its own cycle in this way also.

Mars: Each successive time that Mars comes to opposition (as it does 26 months after its last opposition) it is *approximately 60 degrees further around the sky, as measured along the ecliptic* (which is marked on all the star maps with letters representing the months, in order to show the apparent position of the Sun during the year). This mean that Mars, at an opposition, is, roughly speaking, *two constellations eastward along the ecliptic* from where it was at the last opposition. Here is a list of the dates when the planet Mars is at opposition between 2003 and 2010, along with the dates when its retrograde motion can be observed (though Mars can also be observed for several months both before and after the times of its retrograde motion), and the constellations within which Mars is to be found at those times:

Mars:			
Year:	In Retrograde Motion:	At Opposition:	In the Constellation:
2003	From Jul. 30 to Sep. 29	on Aug. 28	Aquarius
2005	From Oct. 9 to Dec. 7	on Nov. 8	Aries
2007	From Nov. 25 to Jan. 23, 2008	on Dec. 23	Taurus-Gemini area
early 2010	From Dec. 9, 2009 to Feb. 8	on Jan. 28	Cancer-Leo area

Refer to Star Map 5, Star Map 6, and Star Map 1 for the regions of the sky where Mars will be found at the times of these four oppositions, including the times of the planet's retrograde motion before and after opposition.

Jupiter: Each successive time that **Jupiter** comes to opposition it is *approximately 30 degrees further around the sky, as measured along the ecliptic*. This means that **Jupiter**, at opposition, is, roughly speaking, *one constellation eastward along the ecliptic* from where it was at the last opposition. Here is a list of the dates when the planet Jupiter is at opposition between 2003 and 2010, along with the approximate dates when its retrograde motion can be observed (though Jupiter can also be observed for several months both before and after the times of its retrograde motion), and the constellations within which Jupiter is to be found at those times:

Jupiter:			
Year:	**In Retrograde Motion:**	**At Opposition:**	**In the Constellation:**
2003	Early Dec. 2002 to early Apr.	Feb. 2	Cancer
2004	Early Jan. to Early May	Mar. 4	Leo
2005	Early Feb. to Early Jun.	Apr. 4	Virgo
2006	Early Mar. to Early Jul.	May 5	Libra
2007	Early Apr. to Early Aug.	Jun. 6	Scorpius
2008	Early May to Early Sep.	Jul. 9	Sagittarius
2009	Early Jun. to Early Oct.	Aug. 15	Capricornus
2010	Early Jul. to Early Nov.	Sep. 21	Aquarius

Refer to Star Map 1, Star Map 2, Star Map 3, and Star Map 4 for the regions of the sky where Jupiter will be found at the times of these oppositions, including the times of the planet's retrograde motion before and after opposition.

Saturn: Each successive time that **Saturn** comes to opposition, it is *approximately 12 degrees further around the sky, as measured along the ecliptic*. This means that **Saturn**, at opposition, is, roughly speaking, *only about a "half-constellation" eastward along the ecliptic* from where it was at the time of the last opposition. Here is a list of the dates when the planet Saturn is at opposition between 2003 and 2010, along with the approximate dates when its retrograde motion can be observed (though Saturn can also be observed for several months both before and after the times of its retrograde motion), and the constellations within which Saturn is to be found at those times:

Saturn:			
Year:	In Retrograde Motion:	At Opposition:	In the Constellation:
2003	Late Oct. to mid-Mar. 2004	Dec. 31	Gemini
2005	Mid-Nov. 2004 to Late Mar.	Jan. 13	Gemini
2006	Late Nov. 2005 to Early Apr.	Jan. 27	Cancer
2007	Early Dec. 2006 to Mid-Apr.	Feb. 10	Leo
2008	Mid-Dec. 2007 to Late Apr.	Feb. 24	Leo
2009	Early Jan. to Mid-May	Mar. 8	Leo
2010	Mid-Jan. to Late May	Mar. 22	Virgo

Uranus, Neptune, and Pluto: Each successive time that these three planets come to opposition they are only a very short distance further around the sky, as measured along the ecliptic. Generally speaking, Uranus is only about 4 degrees, Neptune is only about 2 degrees, and Pluto is only about 1.5 degrees further eastward along the ecliptic from where each one of them was at the time of the last opposition. Sometimes these planets may appear within the boundaries of a single constellation for 5, or 10, or more years, and in the case of Pluto, it may remain within a single constellation for as long as 25 to 30 years.

Uranus and Neptune are generally considered to be too faint to see with the unaided eye, although a few people claim to have seen Uranus without any optical aid. Both planets may be seen in binoculars, though they usually look much like stars. A telescope of moderate size, however, shows them to be small disks rather than just tiny dots.

The parts of the sky where these two planets are found are best seen in the late evening during the summer months. For those who wish to search for Uranus and Neptune with binoculars or a small telescope, a map showing their exact location may be found in the *Observer's Handbook*, a publication of the Royal Astronomical Society of Canada.

Uranus: At the time of its *opposition of 2003*, Uranus will be in the constellation Aquarius, "above the tip of the left horn of the goat" of Capricornus, having just recently crossed the constellation-border from Capricornus. Uranus will remain *in Aquarius until 2009* when it will cross the constellation-border into Pisces. (See Star Maps 4 and 5.) Here is a summary of approximate dates when Uranus is at opposition each year between 2003 and 2010, along with the approximate dates when its retrograde motion can be observed, and the constellations within which this planet is found:

Uranus:			
Years:	In Retrograde Motion:	At Opposition:	In the Constellation:
2003 to 2009	Late Jun. to Late Nov.	Late Aug. to Early Sep.	Aquarius
Year 2010	Early Jul. to Early Dec.	Mid-Sep.	Pisces

Neptune: At its *opposition of 2003*, Neptune will be in the central part of the constellation Capricornus, near the mid-point between the two "horns of the goat" of Capricornus, and it will remain *in the constellation Capricornus until 2013*, when it also will cross the constellation-border into Aquarius. Between 2003 and 2010 Neptune will be slowly crossing "the left horn of Capricornus." (See Star Maps 4 and 5.) Here is a summary of approximate dates when Neptune is at opposition each year between 2003 and 2010, along with the approximate dates when its retrograde motion can be observed, and the constellation within which this planet is found:

Neptune:			
Years:	In Retrograde Motion:	At Opposition:	In the Constellation:
2003 to 2010	Late May to Late Oct.	Mid-Aug.	Capricornus

Pluto: At the time of *its opposition in 2003*, Pluto will be near the bright star at the southern-eastern corner of *the constellation Ophiuchus* (See Star Map 4.), near the point where the four constellations, Ophiuchus, Serpens Cauda, Sagittarius, and Scorpius, meet. From there it will move very slowly, *between 2003 and 2012*, toward a point near the top of the teapot of Sagittarius. (See Star Map 4.) For all of those years it will be a very faint object among the many stars of the Milky Way that are found in that area of the sky.

Pluto is far too faint to be seen with the naked eye or with a pair of binoculars. Even in the largest and best telescopes in the world, it appears as only a tiny dot of light. It is difficult to distinguish Pluto from the millions of faint stars that also appear as dots of light, unless a person observes it with a large telescope for several nights in a row and notices that one of the tiny dots has moved. Then the person knows which one is Pluto.

The best time for observing the "*Ophiuchus-Scorpius-Sagittarius*" part of the sky is after midnight on a Moonless night in May, June, or July. Maps showing the precise location of Pluto among the stars are published in astronomy magazines and in the *Observer's Handbook*, a publication of the Royal Astronomical Society of Canada.

Answers to **PRACTISE YOUR SKILLS** questions:

(1) In answering this question, a person should note that, for **Mercury**, the last observing period given was a western evening one in early December 2003. The *next one will be an eastern morning one in January 2004.*

(a) **Mercury** may, later, be visible in the western evening sky in March 2004, in late June 2004, and in early November 2004.

(b) Following its January eastern morning appearance, **Mercury** may also be visible in the eastern morning sky in late April 2004, in early August 2004, and in late December 2004.

(2) (a) **Venus** will be visible in the eastern morning sky from early June 2004 until the end of the year, and into January 2005.

(b) **Venus** will be visible in the western evening sky from March until November 2005, and in the eastern morning sky from December 2005 until August 2006.

(3)

(a) **Mars's opposition dates:**	(b) **Mars's retrograde motion periods:**
2005, Nov. 8,	2005, Oct. 9 to Dec. 7,
2007, Dec. 23,	2007, Nov. 25 to 2008, Jan. 23,
2010, Jan. 28.	2009, Dec. 29 to 2010, Feb. 28.

(4)

(a) **Jupiter's opposition dates:**	(b) **Jupiter's retrograde motion periods:**
2004, Mar. 7,	2004, Jan. 9 to May 8,
2005, Apr. 9,	2005, Feb. 11 to Jun. 7,
2006, May 12,	2006, Mar. 15 to Jul. 10,
2007, Jun. 15,	2007, Apr. 16 to Aug. 12,
2008, Jul. 18,	2008, May 20 to Sep. 16,
2009, Aug. 22,	2009, Jun. 25 to Oct. 20,
2010, Sep. 25.	2010, Jul. 28 to Nov. 22.

(5)

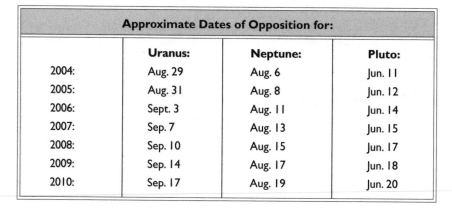

(a) **Saturn's opposition dates:**	(b) **Saturn's retrograde motion periods:**
2005, Jan. 13,	2004, Nov. 7, to 2005, Mar. 19,
2006, Jan. 27,	2005, Nov. 21 to 2006, Apr. 2,
2007, Feb. 10,	2006, Dec. 5 to 2007, Apr. 15,
2008, Feb. 24,	2007, Dec. 15, to 2007, Apr. 28,
2009, Mar. 8,	2009, Jan. 1 to May 12,
2010, Mar. 22.	2010, Jan. 15 to May 27.

(6)

	Approximate Dates of Opposition for:		
	Uranus:	**Neptune:**	**Pluto:**
2004:	Aug. 29	Aug. 6	Jun. 11
2005:	Aug. 31	Aug. 8	Jun. 12
2006:	Sept. 3	Aug. 11	Jun. 14
2007:	Sep. 7	Aug. 13	Jun. 15
2008:	Sep. 10	Aug. 15	Jun. 17
2009:	Sep. 14	Aug. 17	Jun. 18
2010:	Sep. 17	Aug. 19	Jun. 20

Transits: Venus in 2004 and Mercury in 2006

On most occasions when Mercury or Venus moves from being an object in the evening sky (that is, to the left of the Sun) to being an object in the morning sky (that is, to the right of the Sun), the planet passes above or below the Sun. When the planet Mercury or Venus is at this position in its orbit, that is, between the Sun and the Earth, it is said to be *at inferior conjunction*. Because the plane of the orbit of both Mercury and of Venus is inclined to the plane of the Earth's orbit, it is only *on rare occasions* that either Mercury or Venus actually *passes directly across the face of the Sun*, as viewed from the Earth. Such events are called *transits*. A transit may last from only an instant, if the inferior planet passes over the edge of the Sun's disk in what is known as a graze, to about 8 hours, if the planet passes close to, or over, the centre of the Sun's disk. In a transit, the planet travels from left to right, that is from east to west on the sky, as it crosses the face of the Sun.

Transits of Mercury happen generally 13 times per century. Transits of Venus are much rarer events, 10 times rarer, in fact, happening generally 13 times per millennium.

Mercury: The most recent transit of Mercury occurred on 2003, May 7. The next two transits of Mercury across the disk of the Sun will be on **2006, November 8** and **2016, May 9**. In the 2006 event, Mercury will cross the Sun's disk somewhat below the mid-point of the disk, in an event lasting **about 4 ½ hours**. In the 2016 event, Mercury will cross the Sun's disk only slightly below the mid-point of the disk, in an event lasting **about 8 hours**. Details about the precise times and the best locations from which to view these two events will be published in the popular astronomy magazines and journals in the months before these events.

Venus: No living person has seen a Venus transit. The last one occurred on

> # The previous transit of Venus across the Sun was in the 19th Century (1882); there was none in the 20th Century; there will be two in the 21st Century (2004 and 2012).

1882, December 6. The next two transits of Venus across the disk of the Sun will be on **2004, June 8** and **2012, June 6**. In the 2004 event, Venus will cross the lower part of the Sun's disk well south of the mid-point of the disk, in an event that will last **about 5 ½ hours**. In the 2012 event, Venus will cross the upper part of the Sun's disk about half-way between the mid-point of the disk and the northern limb, in an event lasting **about 6 hours**. Details about the precise times and the best locations from which to view these events will be published in the popular astronomy magazines and journals in the months before these events.

Safety, First and Foremost: Because observing a transit of Mercury or Venus involves observing the Sun, it is extremely important to observe all the rules about safe solar observations, as outlined in Chapter 20. Never look directly at the Sun. Never use binoculars or a telescope to observe the Sun unless the instrument is properly fitted with an approved solar filter. For those who do not use binoculars or a telescope, using arc welder's glass # 14 and wearing approved mylar "eclipse glasses" are two of the very few safe methods of solar observing. Because of the apparent size of Mercury, binoculars or a telescope, properly filtered, of course, are needed to observe a transit of Mercury. A transit of Venus can be detected even without binoculars or a telescope, but the proper filters must always be used, just as for viewing solar eclipses.

15

Observing Eclipses

During some years, skywatchers are lucky and we are able to observe an eclipse right from our own backyard. In other years there are no eclipses that are visible from our part of the world. Sometimes, too, there are parts of eclipses that are visible from parts of the country and they can easily be seen if the weather is good. In these cases, our luck depends completely on where we live and the type of weather we have.

Observers are encouraged to note carefully the dates of eclipses that can be seen from their locations *and* to mark them on a calendar so that they do not miss them.

There are two types of major eclipses — *Solar Eclipses* and *Lunar Eclipses*.

A *Solar Eclipse* occurs at least twice during a calendar year and at the time of a New Moon. It happens because the Moon passes between the Sun and the Earth and hides at least part of the Sun from our view. Some solar eclipses are seen by very few people because they are visible only from certain remote places on Earth.

There are several kinds of Solar Eclipses. (a) The best known are Total Eclipses, in which the Sun is totally hidden by the Moon as seen from certain places on Earth. The last Total Solar Eclipse visible from Canada occurred in 1979. (b) Partial Solar Eclipses are ones in which the view of the Sun is partly hidden for some locations on Earth. (c) Annular Eclipses occur when the Moon is a little farther from the Earth than usual so that it appears a little smaller than usual; in this case, during the eclipse, the Moon cannot completely cover the Sun. When this kind of eclipse happens, a "ring of the Sun" can be seen around the Moon, when viewed from some locations on Earth.

A *Lunar Eclipse* may occur only at the time of a Full Moon, and it happens when the Moon partly enters, or completely passes through, the shadow of the Earth. Lunar Eclipses are usually easy to see if the Moon is visible in the sky, but they cannot be seen if Full Moon occurs at about noon in our location, because the Full Moon is not visible in the sky during the daytime. Such eclipses would be visible from other locations on Earth.

The main types of Lunar Eclipses are: (a) Total Lunar Eclipses, in which the Moon completely enters the shadow or umbra of the Earth and the whole disk of the Moon becomes dark (See Photo 15.), (b) Partial Lunar Eclipses, in which the Moon partly enters the Earth's shadow or umbra and only part of the Moon's disk appears dark, and (c) Penumbral Lunar Eclipses, in which the Moon enters only the faint "outer shadow" or "partial shadow" that surrrounds the Earth's umbra.

Eclipses do not occur randomly during the year. In fact, in each year there are *usually* two periods during which eclipses happen. Each of these two periods is about a month in length, and these periods are about, but not exactly, six months apart. (In fact, they are about 10 days less than six months apart, and so these periods come a little earlier each year.)

These two periods are sometimes called *the eclipse seasons*. In 1999, for example, the first eclipse season was in late January and February, and the second one was in late July and August. In some years, such as the year 2000, when the first eclipse season came in January, a third season began before the end of December.

North American Eclipses from 2003 to 2010

This list does not include Penumbral Lunar Eclipses, which are often undetectable or barely detectable.

2003 – The two eclipses visible from North America are the May 15-16 Total Lunar Eclipse, the middle of which will be at 12:40 a.m. EDT, and the November 8 Total Lunar Eclipse, the middle of which will be at 8:19 p.m. EST.

2004 – The only eclipse visible from North America is the October 27 Total Lunar Eclipse, the middle of which will be at 11:04 p.m. EST.

2005 – The only eclipse visible from North America is the April 8 Partial Solar Eclipse, visible in the U.S. south of a line from Los Angeles to Pittsburg.

2006 – There will be no eclipses visible from North America, although a Total Solar Eclipse will be visible in northern Africa and Turkey on March 29.

2007 – The two eclipses visible from North America are the March 3 Total Lunar Eclipse, visible in the eastern part of the continent centred at 6:20 p.m. EST, and the August 28 Total Lunar Eclipse visible in western part of North America, and centred at 3:37 a.m. PDT.

2008 – The two eclipses visible from North America are the February 20 Total Lunar Eclipse, centred at 10:26 p.m. EST and the August 1 Total Solar Eclipse visible in the Canadian High Arctic.

2009 – There are no eclipses visible from North America, although a Total Solar Eclipse on July 22 is visible from China.

2010 – The only eclipse visible from North America is the December 21 Total Lunar Eclipse, the middle of which will be at 3:17 a.m. EST.

16

Observing Variable Stars

There are thousands of variable stars (that is, stars whose brightness changes) that deserve our attention, either from what can be learned through studying them, or from a desire to assist professional astronomers who need such data but do not have the time to devote to this field of astronomy. In other words, it is a field of astronomy in which the amateur, even the beginning amateur, may make a genuine contribution to the "science of astronomy." The beginner will soon find that there is a great array of variable stars; many "variables" indeed can be easily observed with the unaided eye (such as three of the four highlighted here, and those listed in this book's Appendix); thousands more can be followed through their cycle of brightness changes with ordinary binoculars; and still thousands more are best observed with a small, or medium-size, telescope, since their range in brightness takes them down to a level that can not be detected in binoculars.

The beginner should first become proficient at observing those in the "naked-eye" category. Then he or she will be able to move on to the "binocular variables," but still use many of the techniques employed for the former group, while learning a few new techniques necessary to monitor the fainter ones being observed with binoculars and eventually with a small telescope.

Where to Begin: After carefully reviewing the ideas concerning stellar brightness and magnitude in Chapter 4 (See pages 19 to 21.), the beginner should become acquainted with the information given for the four variable stars highlighted in this chapter and should begin a program of observing their brightness changes. Then, he or she should proceed to the list of 10 "naked-eye" variable stars, given in the Appendix. To accompany this practical beginning, there are probably no better introductory resources than the summary of variable star types and lists presented in the *Observer's Handbook* (a publication of the Royal Astronomical Society of Canada) and the excellent text, **Observing Variable Stars**, both of which are listed at the end of this chapter.

When to Begin: An observer who is new to variable star observing can begin at any time. One of the four "beginning variables" introduced here (Delta Cephei) is a star that is circumpolar from all parts of Canada, that is, it is always above the horizon. All four of the "recommended beginner's variable stars," that are introduced here, are prominently placed and easily visible in the autumn evening sky, and in addition, some of them are also visible at other times in the year, as can be seen from checking the various star maps for the constellations in which these stars are found. Whether it is autumn, or any other season, begin your program of *observing variables* as soon as possible, if you have not already done so, and make it a time of learning, exploration, and enjoyment! (See Photos 10, 11, 12, and 13.)

How to Begin:

1. Using *the accompanying charts* for the four "beginner's variable stars" and *the star maps of this book* to locate their constellations, **locate each of these four stars**. (This is to be the beginning of a program of monitoring these stars *on a number of consecutive nights* or "as-close-as-possible-to-consecutive" nights.) Be sure that you orient the accompanying charts correctly. On each chart there is an arrow pointing North, which in the sky means pointing toward the North Celestial Pole, or in practical terms, toward the star Polaris. Hold the chart in front of you so that the arrow points toward Polaris, regardless of the orientation of the book. At this time, you may notice that the variable star is slightly reddish or orange-red in colour, since many of the variable stars are that colour.

2. Having found the variable star, **locate the other stars** that are marked and numbered on the chart. The numbered stars are the "comparison stars." Their brightness is given to the tenth of a magnitude, with the decimal point removed to avoid confusing it with a star. (For example, "29" means "magnitude 2.9.") Take care to *notice the brightness of these stars*, and to notice that "the *brightness of these stars makes sense*," that is, that a star numbered "19" appears brighter than a star numbered "29."

3. Do a ***rough comparison*** between the variable star and the numbered *comparison stars*. (For example, in the case of the first of the variables listed below, Beta Persei, there are 5 comparison stars. A rough comparison may tell you that Beta Persei appears fainter than Gamma Andromedae (mag. 2.2) but brighter than Zeta Persei (mag. 2.9).

4. *Refine the brightness estimate* of the variable star by asking (a) *to which one* of these two stars *does it appear closer* in brightness, if to either, and (b) *where does its brightness fit* on a line between the brightness of these two stars? If you decide that the variable, Beta Persei, is closer in brightness to Zeta, and that it is about 3/4 of the distance along the "brightness range" between Gamma Andromedae and Zeta Persei, then you should write in your notes the time of the observation and the following: "Beta Persei: "2.2 – 3/4 – 2.9", which is a code for the estimate just made. You can then complete the calculation indoors later when you write your observation report. A simple calculation will show that Beta Persei was at mag. 2.7. As you become proficient at observing, you will become more adept at writing

the magnitude of the variable stars, perhaps without having to write out the code just mentioned. With this star, if a change from its usual maximum brightness is noticed, then you should perhaps observe it again later in that same observing session, to record any possible further changes in its brightness.

The Recommended Beginner's Variable Stars

The four variable stars presented below are chosen for several reasons. They have been known as variables for a very long time, and at least three of the four are important historically. They are relatively easy to locate, and at maximum, certainly, they may be seen even in relatively light-polluted skies. From moderately dark skies, three of them can be followed throughout their cycles of variation in brightness. Only one of them (the star Mira) requires binoculars to follow it throughout its entire cycle, but learning about it, as a prototype (an ideal example) of a Long Period Variable, is very important, even for the beginner.

Within a very few nights of starting to observe them, you should notice that three of these four stars are variable stars, and you should start to have some appreciation for their periods and ranges of brightness. For one of these four (the star Mira), it will take longer than a few nights to notice its variability, but you will still notice it, if you continue to follow it for a longer period of time.

After you have observed, and recorded on several occasions, these stars' changes in brightness, you should begin constructing a simple graph to show their brightness, or magnitude, plotted against the dates of your observations. Make these graphs a part of your own observing records, and try not to be influenced by the graphs representing the observations of these stars by many other observers over many years. (Such graphs are provided with this chapter as examples of the information that is known about these variable stars, that have been monitored for many years.)

The graphs just mentioned may be called "variability charts." In fact, because of the information that they present, they are often referred to as "the light curve for the star _____," and a variable star, such as Beta Persei, may be named, as an example. Note that on the horizontal axis of the graph the time is given in hours or in days. In fact, along this axis, each unit may represent 1 day, 4 days, or 20 days, depending on the cycle of the star. Along the vertical axis, the brightness of the star is represented, in terms of the magnitude estimates made by observers. Each dot along the curving line represents a careful observation made by an observer. Note that each unit along this axis represents three-tenths of a magnitude or two-tenths of a magnitude, or, in the case of the star Omicron Ceti, two magnitudes.

MAPS FOR FOUR VARIABLE STARS

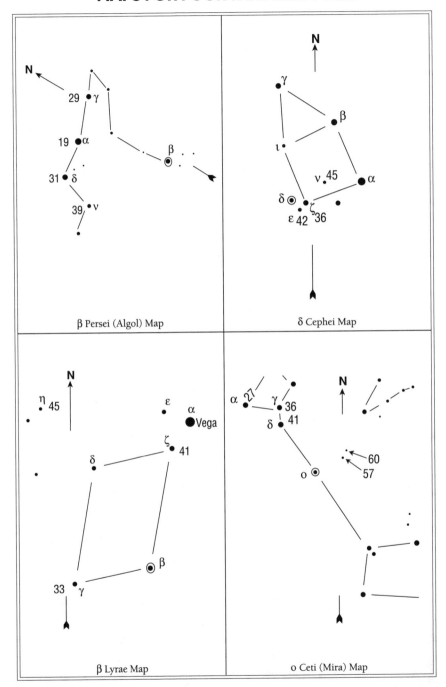

β Persei (Algol) Map

δ Cephei Map

β Lyrae Map

o Ceti (Mira) Map

THE "VARIABILITY CHARTS" OR "LIGHT CURVES" OF FOUR VARIABLE STARS

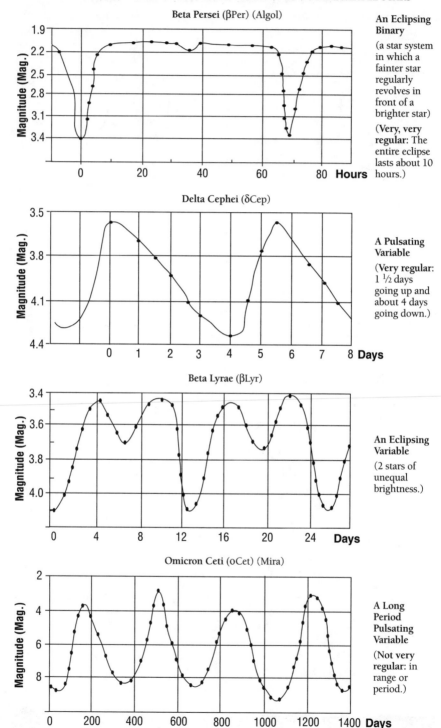

Beta Persei (βPer) (Algol)

An Eclipsing Binary

(a star system in which a fainter star regularly revolves in front of a brighter star)

(**Very, very regular:** The entire eclipse lasts about 10 hours.)

Delta Cephei (δCep)

A Pulsating Variable

(**Very regular:** 1 ½ days going up and about 4 days going down.)

Beta Lyrae (βLyr)

An Eclipsing Variable

(2 stars of unequal brightness.)

Omicron Ceti (oCet) (Mira)

A Long Period Pulsating Variable

(**Not very regular:** in range or period.)

(1) **Beta Persei**: This star is also called by its Arabic name, **Algol** – "the winking demon," and may have been known in mediaeval times, or even antiquity, as a variable star. It is easily seen in the constellation Perseus, and in the autumn evening sky is just to the right of the Alpha Persei group of stars, as if Perseus is holding up the flashing Gorgon's head, which so regularly changes in brightness!

Over the many, many years when it has been observed, Algol has been seen to be *extremely regular* in its variability (range of brightness) and in its period (the time over which it changes in brightness). In astronomy texts, its period is given as 2.867315 days (and with the great accuracy possible with this long number, it may be converted to 2 days, 20 hours, 48 minutes, 56.02 seconds!). Simply amazing in its regularity! How easy it is to see that, on the night when Bayer recorded this star in his atlas in 1603 (See page 23.), it was not at its minimum. When at its maximum, Algol is, very obviously, the second brightest star in the constellation Perseus, and therefore, of course, was designated Beta by Bayer. However, when seen on a night of its drop to minimum, it is just as obviously the fourth or fifth brightest star in the constellation. It is very easy to monitor. No wonder it has been seen "winking" for centuries! (See Photo 10.)

Summary: Period: 2.867315 days
Range of Variability: mag. 2.1 to 3.3
Comparison stars: Alpha Persei (mag. 1.9); Gamma
Andromedae (mag. 2.2); Zeta Persei (mag. 2.9);
Delta Persei (mag. 3.1); Nu Persei (mag. 3.9).

(2) **Delta Cephei**: This is one of the three 'naked-eye stars' that form one of the bottom corners of the five-sided "stick-figure" that outlines a house, (and to the modern skywatcher, it is certainly not the outline of a king on his throne, which our ancient ancestors, with their more active imaginations, were able to see!) This "stick-figure house" is in the northeastern, evening autumn sky above the constellation Cassiopeia. (See Map 5.) Of course, as the night advances, the orientation of the "stick-figure house" changes, and in the late autumn evenings it is almost upside down as it moves above the North Star, Polaris. However, being a circumpolar constellation, Cepheus goes through every possible orientation over the course of a year, as it constantly "circles the Pole Star." Among the little triangle of 'naked-eye stars' that mark the left edge of the "floor of the stick-figure house," Delta is the one that is farthest from the "floor of the house." Its discovery as a variable star was a significant event in the history of astronomy and cosmology, since in the case of this star and similar pulsating variables, the relationship between their period of variability and their actual luminosity or brightness (no matter in what part of the galaxy they are found) provides, through a simple calculation, the distance scale of the galaxy. This fact can be used to calculate even the distances to other nearby galaxies in which stars like Delta Cephei can be observed and monitored.

Historically, this star and its discovery as a variable were extremely important in the science of astronomy! Try to keep that in mind as you observe its very regular changes in brightness.

Careful monitoring of this star over many years has shown that it takes about four days to descend to minimum brightness and 1 ½ days to climb back up to maximum. With its great regularity, which has been known for many decades, its period is listed as 5.366341 days (or 5 days, 8 hours, 47 minutes, 32 seconds!). During that time, the range in brightness is from magnitude 3.5 to 4.4. Estimates are very easy to make because the "comparison stars" are so close to Delta Cephei. Two of them are the other members of the trio mentioned above (Epsilon and Zeta Cephei), and a third is nearby also, right near the "floor of the house," as mentioned above. Delta Cephei is a very important prototype (the ideal and primary member) of a class of variable stars; they are pulsating stars whose period is much shorter than that of the Long Period Variables (LPV's). Their periods are usually from about a half-dozen days to about two dozen days. (See Photo 11.)

Summary: Period: 5.366341 days
            Range of variability: mag. 3.5 to 4.4
            Comparison stars: Epsilon Cephei (mag. 4.2); Zeta Cephei
            (mag. 3.6); Nu Cephei (mag. 4.5)

(3) **Beta Lyrae**: The "corner star" of the parallelogram of stars that outline the Lyre is not far from Vega, the brightest star in the Great Summer Triangle. Beta Lyrae is on the side of the parallelogram farthest away from Vega, and of the two stars on that side, it is the one that is slightly closer to Vega.

Beta Lyrae also has a period that is very regular, and its range in brightness is also very regular! Its period is usually given as 12.939854 days (which can be converted to 12 days, 22 hours, 33 minutes, 24 seconds!). The range is from about magnitude 3.3 to 4.4. Two of the three other stars in the parallelogram mentioned above are used in making its brightness estimates. Not very difficult to do! These comparison stars are so easy to find! Beta Lyrae is a two-star system involving stars of unequal brightness. Careful monitoring of its brightness has shown that there are two "drops of brightness" in its cycle, a large one when the fainter star is almost completely blocking the other one, and a smaller one when the geometry of the two eclipsing stars is such that we have the brighter member partially blocking our view of the fainter one. (See Photo 12.)

Summary: Period: 12.939854 days
            Range of variability: mag. 3.3 to 4.4
            Comparison stars: Gamma Lyrae (mag. 3.3); Zeta Lyrae
            (mag. 4.1); Eta Lyrae (mag. 4.5)

(4) **Omicron Ceti** (also called Mira or Stella Mira – "The Wondrous Star") This star is located "in the neck of the great sea monster, Cetus," which, in the autumn evening skies, stretches along the southeastern horizon. The monster appears to lie prostrate above the trees, as if just slain by Perseus in the myth of his heroics. For part of its cycle, Mira is easily seen with the unaided eye, about half-way along the "neck of the monster," between the group of stars on the left that outline its head and the group on the right that outline its huge body.

Omicron Ceti, or Mira, is a very interesting contrast to the three variable stars just described, both in regard to its range of variability and its period. It ranges from about magnitude 3.4 (though even that changes from time to time, and occasionally it has been seen as bright as a magnitude 2 star!) to magnitude 9.3 which is much too faint to be seen with the unaided eye. Because of its wide range in brightness, it is easy to understand why binoculars are needed in order to follow this star as it fades toward its time of minimum brightness (since the unaided eye rarely sees beyond sixth magnitude stars, even under superb skies). Its period, or cycle, is also much greater than that of the stars described above. For Mira, the period is about 332 days, which is about 11 months. Because of its slow change, it is not necessary to monitor this star every night; doing so on a weekly basis is usually sufficient. This star is the prototype of long period variability (that is, of stars with periods usually over several hundred days) caused by a star's pulsation. (See Photo 13.)

Summary: Period: about 332 days
            Range of variability: (about mag. 3.4, rarely 2, to about 9.3,
                rarely 9.6)
            Comparison stars: Alpha Ceti (mag. 2.7); Gamma Ceti
                (mag. 3.6); Delta Ceti (mag. 4.1); and other stars (See star
                chart.).

Guidelines for "Variable Star Observing"

After several months in which you have monitored the four stars described above, you may wish to move on to the next step, which will be to observe and record the brightness changes for the remainder of the 10 "naked-eye" variables" listed in the Appendix of this book. (As explained on page 193, these stars are easily found, using the most elementary star atlas. Most of them, in fact, are actually marked on the star maps in this book, though they are not labelled.)

After another period of several months in which you become familiar with all 10 of those "naked-eye" variables, you will doubtless want to move on the observation of "binocular variables," and eventually to those that can be followed best using a small telescope. In exploring these challenges, you will be able to use the techniques you have mastered in making "naked-eye" variable estimates.

However, in all of your variable star observing, you should keep a few guidelines in mind:

1. Always estimate the variable star's magnitude *in an unbiased way*, that is, from honestly comparing its brightness to that of the comparison stars, not from a preconceived notion of what you think the star should be doing or what magnitude it should be displaying at a certain time. Three of the four stars presented above are very regular in their performance, but many that you will eventually observe will be very irregular in both their range and period. For such stars, any prior notions of what you will see may adversely affect your estimates of their brightness.

2. *Do not stare* at the variable star. Keep your eyes moving. Staring at a red

> ## Avoid staring at a variable star when attempting to estimate its brightness.

   star makes it appear brighter than it should (an effect known as "*the Purkinje effect*," from its discoverer) by comparison with other whiter stars, and most variables are reddish in colour.

3. When you graduate to using binoculars or a telescope, try to use *a field of view* that allows you to view, at one time, both the variable and one, or more, of the comparison stars.

4. If possible, position the variable star and the comparison star *near the centre of the field of view* of the binoculars or telescope, to avoid several

> ## In binoculars or telescope, try to have the variable and comparison star near the centre of the field.

   problems that may be associated with the edges of the field. If, in a single wide field of view, they are both very near the edge because of their distance apart, you may simply have to observe them separately, unless you can change to a telescope eyepiece that gives a larger field of view.

5. If possible, orient the instrument, or even your own position, so that an imaginary line joining the two stars being observed is *a horizontal line, not a vertical line*. Experienced observers have found that this practice makes for better estimates.

6. Some observers have found that, if they *"defocus" the image* in their mounted binoculars or telescope, they are better able to estimate a variable

> **"Defocusing" is a trick used by some observers to help them estimate a star's brightness.**

star's brightness in comparison with another star. If both stars cannot be accommodated in one field of view, "defocus" both the variable and its comparison star, in their separate fields of view, until both images are about the same size, and then estimate their relative brightness in the method suggested above. This may help considerably in making a correct estimate of brightness.

Many observers become fascinated by variable star observing, and over many years, they become committed to monitoring a number of variable stars. Some choose a small number, maybe a dozen or more, and follow their changes for a long time; others choose a large number, maybe a hundred or several hundred or even more, and are able to follow their activity for years. However you choose to arrange your variable star observing in the future, enjoy the venture!

Other Resources to Assist in Future Variable Star Observations

The following additional resources can be of great assistance to variable star observers at any level of experience:

1. The Variable Stars section of the current annual edition of the *Observer's Handbook*, a publication of the Royal Astronomical Society of Canada, is available by mail from the address given elsewhere in this book or from the Society's Web site: www.rasc.ca. This section contains a list of the types of variable stars, along with the characteristics of each type, and there are lists of variable stars that can be observed within several of those types.

2. An excellent and very highly recommended guide is the book *Observing Variable Stars* by David H. Levy, published by Cambridge University Press.

3. Information pages and variable star maps are available by mail from The American Association of Variable Star Observers (AAVSO), 25 Birch Street, Cambridge MA 02138-1205 USA, or from the Web site: www.aavso.org. Membership in this organization is also encouraged.

17

Observing Meteors and Meteor Showers

As our planet Earth travels around the Sun every year, it meets up with large amounts of dust, usually tiny particles that are no bigger than a grain of sand. These pieces of dust are called meteoroids. A strange event occurs when one of these particles and the Earth's atmosphere encounter each other. The fast movement of the particle through the atmosphere causes the surrounding air to glow brightly. As astronomers say, the air surrounding the fast moving dust particle is being "ionized." When we look up at this event from below, we see a meteor flashing across the sky. Many people used to call them "shooting stars" or "falling stars." Actually, it is more correct to avoid these names and use the proper term — "meteors." Stars are extremely distant and very massive objects like our Sun, usually many times more massive than our Earth. Meteors are glowing particles travelling through our Earth's atmosphere.

Observing meteors is easy and fun. It does not require binoculars, or a telescope, or any special equipment. However, you do concentrate on a certain area of the sky for up to an hour at a time, in order to get a good idea of the number of meteors flashing through the atmosphere. In this way meteor observing can be challenging. It will also help an observer to become more familiar with the sky and the constellations.

Meteors can appear on any night of the year, but, as we will see later, they are much more common at certain times of the year. They are more likely to be seen on nights when there is no Moon in the sky and when you are observing in a dark country location far away from the bright street lights of a city. Under such conditions, at times when there is no meteor shower at all, an observer can expect to see from 5 to 8 "sporadic" or stray meteors per hour. In fact, that number increases after midnight.

Sometimes we may see extremely bright meteors that are brilliant enough to cast a shadow on the ground. These are called fireballs or bolides, especially if they appear to break up into several pieces. Sometimes they even "explode" into a number of fragments. Occasionally, too, they appear to glow in different colours, such as green or red. Sometimes a trail, called a train, is left behind when the original flash from the meteor has disappeared. This train, which may appear slightly smokey, may last for five or ten seconds or even longer, if the meteor has been an extremely bright one. If we notice any of these events accompanying a meteor, we should carefully record it (or them), and we should

Photo 9. Orion with 135 mm lens
Note the smaller field with this longer lens. This photo was guided to avoid star trails.

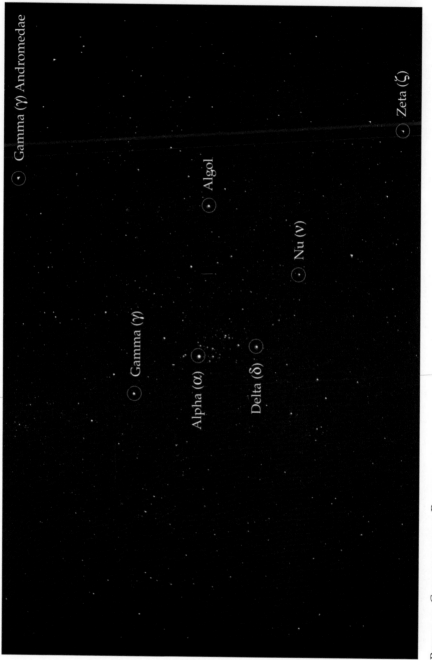

Photo 10. Constellation: Perseus

A very simple 50 mm photo showing Perseus and the famous variable star Algol.

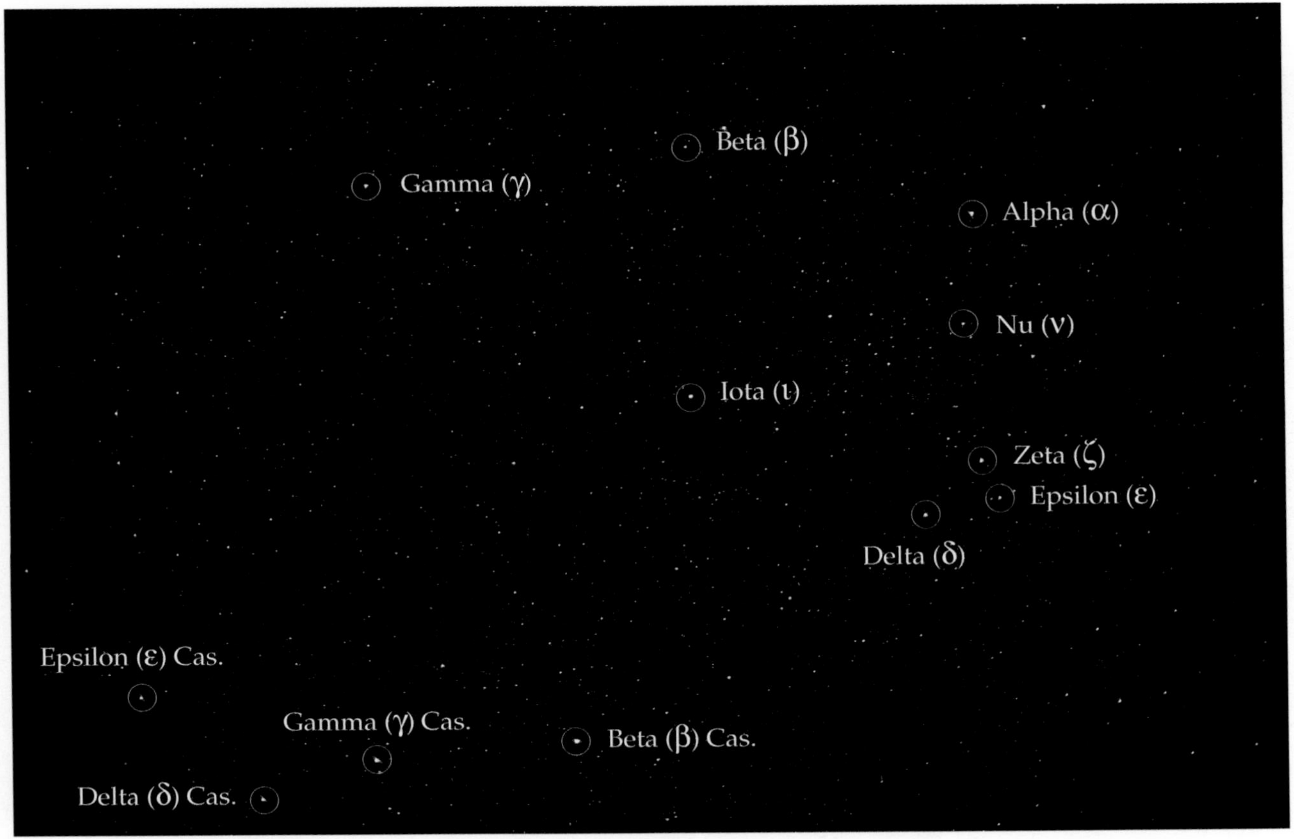

PHOTO 11. CONSTELLATION: CEPHEUS
King Cepheus circles the celestial pole ahead of his queen Cassiopeia. His most famous star is Delta.

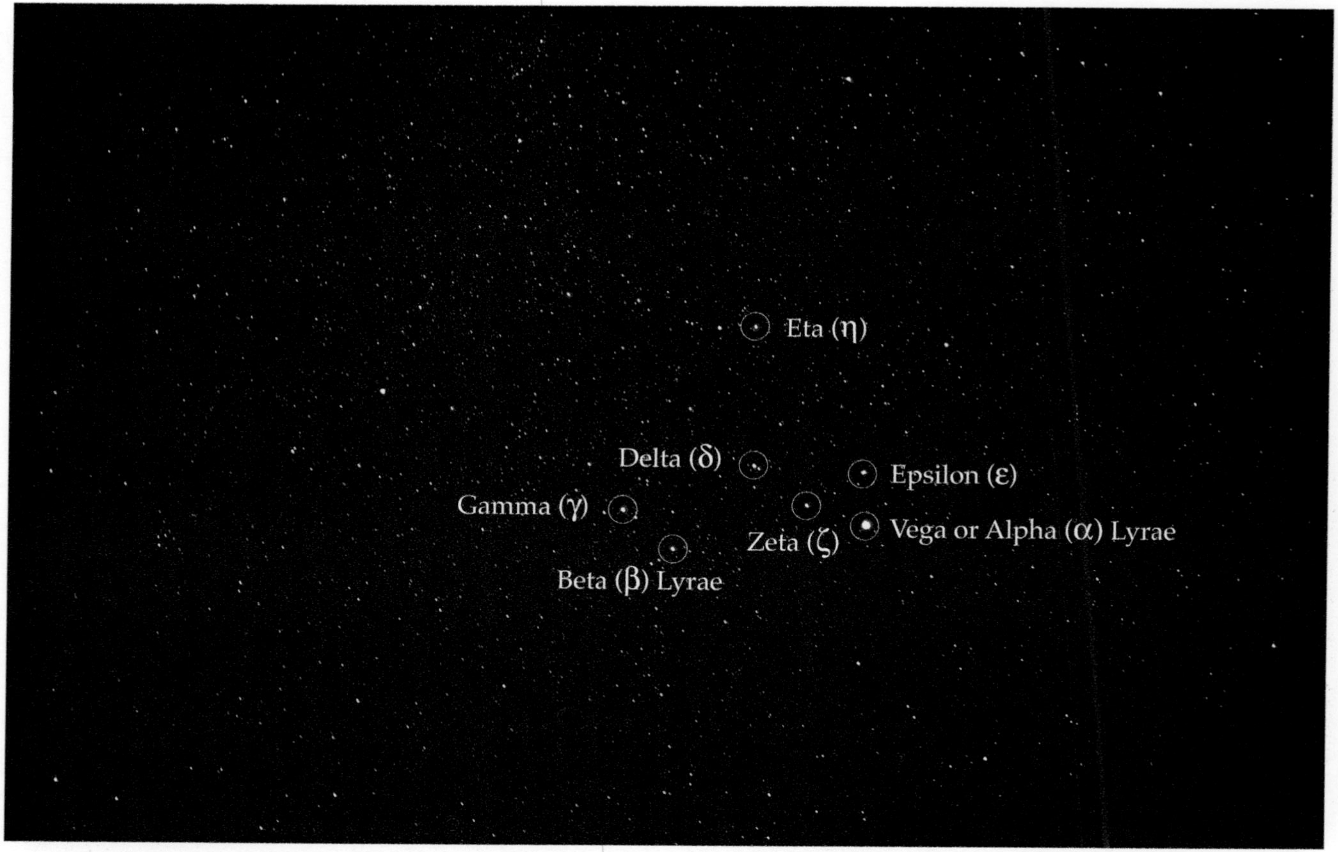

Photo 12. Constellation: Lyra
This simple photograph of the brilliant star Vega and the constellation Lyra, shows the variable, Beta Lyrae.

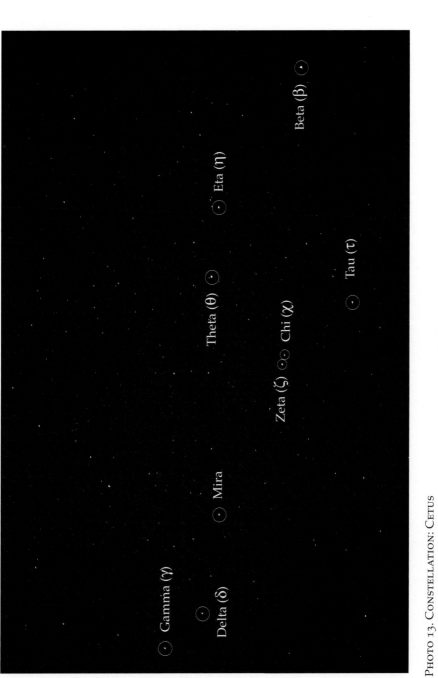

Photo 13. Constellation: Cetus
This huge constellation is difficult to show in a 50 mm lens photo. The famous variable star Omicron Ceti (Mira) can be easily seen here.

Photo 14. Earth Shadow Rising
On a very clear evening, the earth's shadow is seen rising in the east for 20 minutes after sunset.

Photo 15. Eclipsed Full Moon in Taurus!
Remembering that a Full Moon, during a total lunar eclipse, is no brighter than a bright star, we can do amazing, but very simple, photography. This 50 mm photo was guided, but for only 55 seconds, using ISO 400 film.

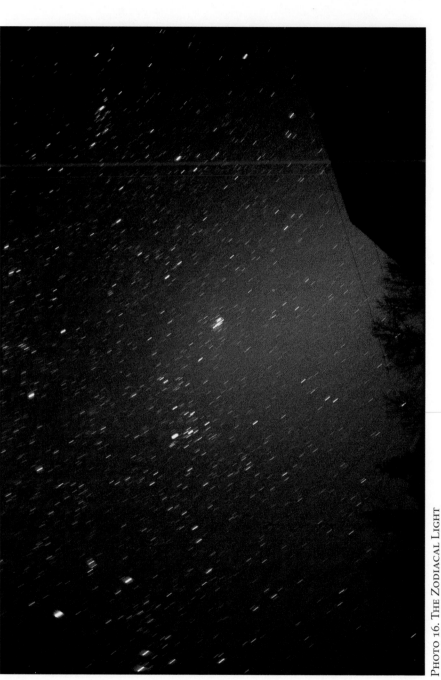

PHOTO 16. THE ZODIACAL LIGHT
After the end of evening twilight in springtime, this large pyramid of light may be seen on clear nights. To photograph it, I used a 28 mm lens, ISO 400 film, and a 200-second exposure, with camera on a tripod.

note particularly the position in the sky and the time when the meteor was seen. (See Photo 4.)

Meteors are most common on certain special "shower" nights during the year, when the Earth encounters a stream of meteoroids or dust particles. We can tell when this is happening because, after observing for a while, we will see that most of these "shower" meteors appear to come from a single location in the sky. We say that they are "radiating" from that point in the sky, and that point is called the "radiant."

"Meteor showers" are usually named after the constellation in which the radiant is found. The constellation name has an "id"-ending. For example, the Leonids radiate from a spot in the constellation Leo. From the list below, it can be seen that two showers are called Aquarids. These are distinguished by naming the stars in Aquarius near which the radiants are found — delta and eta. The Quadrantids are named after a constellation that is no longer recognized; it was located near Bootes.

Here is a list of some of the main "meteor showers" during the year:

The Quadrantids

Early in January each year, the Earth runs into a special stream of meteors, and if we are observing at exactly the right time, we may see up to 50 meteors per hour. However, such a large numbers is usually seen only for several hours on *January 3rd or 4th*. Unless the Moon is out of the sky on that particular night and unless the maximum period occurs at night, instead of during daylight hours, this shower will be missed by most people. Another reason that many people miss this interesting shower is that the weather is often very cold in early January, and also there may be cloudy skies at that time of year.

An April Shower: The Lyrids

We have to wait almost four months for the next good meteor shower to occur — the Lyrids. This shower offers us about 15 meteors per hour when they are observed under good conditions on the night of their maximum, about *April 22* each year.

A May Flower: The Eta Aquarids

This is one of the two annual showers that are believed to originate from dust particles in the path of the famous Halley's Comet. They may sometimes be seen from April 21 to May 25, with the maximum around *May 3 to 5*. These meteors appear as very fast streaks and the brightest of them sometimes leave long-lasting trains (faintly glowing trails that linger in the sky).

The Delta Aquarids

A delight to observe, this shower reaches its maximum about mid-summer (*July 29*) meaning that it is ideal to observe on summer vacation. These meteors are relatively slow and offer an hourly rate of up to 20 under good viewing conditions.

A Midsummer Night's Dream: The Perseids

This shower can be a magnificent spectacle. You may see Perseids coming in rapid succession, followed by slack periods with little activity. You may also see "firework" Perseids, when two or more meteors appear almost simultaneously. Fireballs, bright enough even to cast a shadow, are seen from time to time. (See Photo 4.) They may be seen over a period of many nights but the maximum occurs about *August 12.*

The Orionids of Fall

Like the Eta Aquarids, these meteors come from the stream of dust particles associated with the path of Halley's Comet. Often as many as 25 meteors per hour are seen. They are easily identified, not only from their radiant near Orion, but also from their rapid speed. Maximum activity occurs about *October 22.*

The Taurids

This shower's maximum rate is 15 per hour, *between November 1 and 3.* These are the slowest meteors of all the major showers. Fireballs reported in the months of October, November, and December might belong to this stream.

The Leonids

This moderately active shower has a normal maximum rate of 15 per hour for a person who is observing alone about *November 18* each year. However, every 33 years the Earth crosses the densest concentration of meteors and a real "meteor storm" often occurs, during which the number of meteors is measured, not in meteors per hour, but in meteors per second. In 1966, some observers in some places estimated the number they were seeing to be over 40 per second! On the nights of November 17-18 in the years 1999 to 2002, many observers watched a great increase in the numbers of Leonid meteors, in 1999 especially in Europe, and in 2000 and 2001 in North America and other parts of the world.

Winter's Graceful Geminids

This is now the major shower of the year. The Geminids offer a maximum of as many as 75 per hour, and they stretch out for two and a half days on either side of the maximum, *December 14.* The night before and the night of maximum are often the best nights of the year for high totals. Their relatively slow speeds add to the fun of watching this magnificent shower.

Whether you are observing a specific meteor shower, or just spending part of a night watching for any meteors that might happen to appear, you would be wise to follow a few suggestions in order to make your experience as profitable as possible:

1. *Plan* your observing session as you would other observing sessions, knowing when the Moon will rise or otherwise possibly interfere with your plans. Moonlight greatly reduces the number of meteors you may see in a given period of time.

2. Rather than standing, use a *reclining lawn chair*. Adjust the back of the chair so that you are facing an area of the sky that is 45 to 55 degrees above the horizon.

3. *Dress warmly* so that you will be comfortable while observing. Have an extra sweater or jacket available since the temperature may drop considerably during the night. Observing from a reclining position may mean that you will feel the cold sooner than if you were standing.

4. Do not try to observe the entire sky. If you are observing at a time other than at one of the major meteor showers, choose the darkest area of the sky, that is, the area with the least light pollution. Face in that direction so that you can comfortably see about *a quarter of the sky*, and record the number of meteors that appear in that area over a one-hour or two-hour period. If you are observing at the time of one of the major showers, face, not exactly in the direction of the constellation from which the meteors are radiating, but about 50 to 60 degrees away from that constellation, and if possible, toward the darkest part of the sky.

5. Try to develop *a system of recording* the meteors seen. Some beginning observers merely count the number of meteors seen in a one-hour period. This is the minimum that you should try to do. Other more advanced observers use a tape recorder to record the number of meteors, the brightness or magnitude of each one, and any special features observed, such as "unusually fast" or "with a train that lasted for five seconds." Some observers use a star map to record the meteors by drawing the path of each one. During meteor showers they soon notice that almost all the meteors can be traced back to the "radiant." The problem with drawing while observing is that, unless the path is marked quickly, the observer may miss other meteors. One reason for observing in groups is that one person can act as a recorder while the others continually watch the sky.

6. *Take a break* after the end of each hour's observing. Move around in order to keep warm. A person's concentration drops if he or she tries to observe for a very long period of time. Note carefully the times when you were

observing, so that the numbers of meteors seen can be recorded in one-hour time periods.

It is very easy to enjoy meteor watching. With no special equipment required, no one should miss the chance to observe a meteor shower.

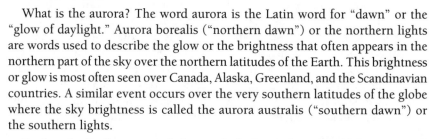

18

Observing the Aurora

People who have never seen a beautiful aurora have missed one of the fabulous spectacles of nature. The dancing, shimmering rays and curtains of the aurora borealis are a thrilling sight to see in the northern sky. Without warning, the sky can suddenly come alive with a flood of red, green, purple, and yellow patterns that are fascinating to watch whether it is for an hour or a whole night.

One of the things that makes the aurora so fascinating is the fact that it is often quite unpredictable. Sometimes when we think a fabulous light show will last all night, it may last for only a few minutes or a half hour. At another time when we think it is a weak show and will soon die away, it bursts into action and lasts for hours, or even the whole night, or longer. During April 1981, there was a huge outburst of auroral activity that lasted for more than a week. Of course, it was not actually seen during daylight hours because of the brightness of the Sun, but night after night, as soon as the sky was dark, the aurora continued.

What is the aurora? The word aurora is the Latin word for "dawn" or the "glow of daylight." Aurora borealis ("northern dawn") or the northern lights are words used to describe the glow or the brightness that often appears in the northern part of the sky over the northern latitudes of the Earth. This brightness or glow is most often seen over Canada, Alaska, Greenland, and the Scandinavian countries. A similar event occurs over the very southern latitudes of the globe where the sky brightness is called the aurora australis ("southern dawn") or the southern lights.

For hundreds of years people have asked what is the cause of these strange, weird, and wonderful lights that frequently filled the northern sky and sometimes covered almost the whole sky. We are still asking the same question, because even yet we do not *completely* understand the operation of the aurora. We do know that the light of the aurora is caused when energy is released as the upper part of the Earth's atmosphere (100 kilometres or more above the Earth) is bombarded by extremely tiny particles in the solar wind. These very minute particles are electrons and protons — much smaller than atoms. It is activity on the Sun that causes the solar wind. An outburst of particles from the Sun, known as a solar flare, and sometimes associated with a large Sunspot or group of sunspots, can cause huge numbers (billions upon billions) of these tiny particles to flood out into space. When this "flood of particles from the Sun" reaches the Earth, there will be increased activity as they interact with the particles in the Earth's magnetosphere. The magnetosphere is a magnetic field that surrounds the Earth. There is always some interaction between the solar wind and the Earth's magnetosphere. This constant interaction causes an auroral ring above the northern part of the Earth and centred over the Arctic islands of northern Canada, but most people in North America have never seen this glow. Observers in southern Canada and northern United States can expect to see the aurora only at times of increased solar activity, such as at those times when a solar flare occurs. At those times, the bright glow of the aurora extends further south. Sometimes after a very large burst of solar activity, the aurora can be seen as far south as Mexico, Cuba, Central America, and the Caribbean, but such events happen only rarely.

What produces the varying colours of the aurora? Scientists who have studied the aurora for many years are able to associate certain colours with the kinds of atoms that have caused the glow in the upper atmosphere. They have learned that red and green colours are produced by atoms of oxygen that have become luminous like the gas in a fluorescent light fixture. Blue is produced by nitrogen molecules.

In auroral displays many different auroral patterns are possible. The most common pattern in mid-northern latitudes is a steady white *glow* in the north. Sometimes over the course of a night, the glow increases in size and brightness, and spreads out from the north until it reaches from east to west and up as high as the North Star or even the zenith, and it may become so bright that it is difficult to see many of the stars in the northern half of the sky. Another common pattern of aurora is called the *arc*. It may look like a slightly flattened arch in the northern sky; sometimes there may be two or three of them, one above the other, and they may be combined with a glow underneath. A third pattern is seen when auroral activity is strong. "*Rays*" or "*spikes*" may shoot up into the sky. They are most commonly seen in the north, from northwest to northeast, but may sometimes be found in other parts of the sky. They sometimes may "shoot up" to the zenith. A fourth pattern, seen at times of increased auroral activity, is the "*band of flame*"; it looks like the flames of a large fire shooting up into the sky. It may appear as a pulsation that spreads quickly upward over a large area of the sky with repeated flaming pulsations following at intervals of a second or less. Another pattern, much less common in southern Canada than northern Canada, is what looks like a great *curtain* or drapery hanging in the sky. Varieties and combinations of these and other patterns can be seen on any one night. (See Photos 5 and 6.)

When can a person expect to see the aurora? Since a person who lives at the latitudes of southern Canada or most of the United States can very rarely be certain of seeing the aurora on any particular night, the best advice for those who want to see this spectacle is just to *check* the sky, particularly the northern sky, *every clear night* for the possibility of seeing it. The next best piece of advice is to join an astronomy club where you can keep in contact with members who are interested in observing and monitoring the activity of the Sun. These people will know when the number of Sunspots is great, and perhaps when solar flares occur. If they know *when a solar flare has occurred*, they may agree to inform you and other members; you then ought to *check the sky* for an aurora *over the next few nights*, because there will be a greatly increased possibility that you will see one then, if the skies are clear.

What are the chances of seeing good displays of the aurora in the years 2003 to 2010? Even though *we cannot predict exactly when there will be an aurora visible at a certain location*, there are a few facts that will help us to understand when we *might expect to see one*. We know that there is the greatest chance of seeing an aurora *at the time when the Sun is very active*. As a result of observing the Sun and studying it over the last two hundred years, astronomers now know that the Sun's activity varies *on about an 11-year cycle*, with the number of Sunspots very low at the beginning and end of the cycle and the Sunspot numbers very high near the middle of the cycle. During the years 1994 and 1995, the number of sunspots and the amount of solar activity were generally low. The previous 11-year cycle was ending. There were few displays of the aurora. During 1996, 1997, and 1998, the amount of solar activity slowly increased from what it was in 1995. It was the beginning of a new 11-year cycle of activity. In those years the aurora was seen on a few occasions from the latitude of southern Canada and northern United States. During 1999 and 2000, there were further increases in solar activity, with the peak of the cycle being reached in late 2000 and 2001, though this peak did not rival the peaks of 1946 and 1957. There were several good auroral displays in those years. In 2002 and 2003, solar activity generally declined, though there were occasionally good auroral displays in those years as well. Based on past experience, we can expect solar activity to decline in 2004 and 2005, and auroral activity to become generally less frequent, though occasional displays may be seen. In 2006, the amount of solar activity may be low, and the end of the cycle may possibly be reached then, with a new cycle beginning at that time, or possibly in 2007. Increasing solar activity in the new cycle may become more evident in 2008, 2009, and 2010. It is possible the peak of the next cycle may be reached in 2011 or 2012 with increasing numbers of auroral displays at that time also. The decline in activity may begin in 2012 or 2013, though there may continue to be active auroral displays into those years as well.

Remember to look for the possibility of an aurora at every observing session in which you participate, and try to check the northern skies every clear night.

Remain alert for reports in the news media about solar flares and for the possibility of an active aurora a couple of days after the event. Above all *enjoy the aurora whenever you see it*. It is one of nature's most beautiful spectacles.

19

Observing Comets

Comets are visitors from the outer reaches of our Solar System. They are large "dirty snowballs" made of frozen gases and dust, and they are often several kilometres in diameter. The frozen materials are water ice, ammonia, methane, and other compounds. Most comets spend their lives at great distances from the Sun, far too distant to be seen from the Earth. Occasionally, a comet never before seen by humans is deflected toward the Sun and begins its long journey on a great looping orbit around the Sun. Only when it is relatively near the Sun is it discovered by a keen-eyed observer and then seen by hundreds or thousands of other amateur astronomers and other interested observers as well.

Some comets are surprise visitors, totally unexpected. Others are familiar visitors that human beings have seen many times before; perhaps their first visit to the inner part of the Solar System was thousands of years ago. By now their orbits are well known and predictable, and we can know precisely when their next appearance will be. Depending on the size of the orbit, it may take from a few years to millions of years for a comet to complete a single journey around the Sun. Those that take less than 200 years are called periodic or short-period comets; others are called long-period comets.

As comets approach the Sun, a change takes place. Their solid icy surfaces are heated and turned to gas. Around the solid inner core, which is known as the *nucleus*, the gas, along with dust rising from the icy surface, forms a cloud. It is only the fuzzy cloud of gas and dust, called the *coma*, not the nucleus, that is seen, when we observe a comet sweeping across the sky. In some cases, enough gas and dust is produced to form a noticeable *tail* which can stretch out into space for millions of kilometres. The tail consists of two parts — the *gas tail* and the *dust tail*. The gas tail, often appearing bluish in photographs, points almost directly away from the Sun. The dust tail, appearing whitish or yellowish because we see Sunlight reflected from the dust particles, presents a slightly curved appearance because it lags behind the rest of the comet in its orbit.

There are several hundred known comets that have been discovered over the centuries of recorded history. Most are named after their discoverer. One exception to this rule is Comet Halley, perhaps the most famous comet of all, one that makes its appearance every 76 years. It is named after Edmond Halley, the first person to predict its reappearance, which he did in the eighteenth century. It was last visible in 1985, 1986, and 1987 when it was close enough to the Earth to be seen in binoculars and telescopes; it was also seen with the naked eye for a much shorter period of time. In about the year 2060 and 2061, amateur astronomers will again be excitedly viewing its return to the region of the inner Solar System.

Previously unknown comets can appear at any time and from any direction in the sky. In fact, in the last few years there have been many more new comet discoveries than would have been predicted from the number of discoveries in previous years. Many of these comets have remained close enough to the Sun and Earth to be seen by observers for several months; in a few cases they could be seen for almost a year. Most comet discoveries are made by amateur astronomers because professionals do not have the time to spend long hours patiently searching the sky. A few of the comets discovered in recent years, though originally seen in fairly large telescopes, became bright enough within several months to be easily seen in binoculars. A few of them could be seen with the naked eye. One example was Comet Levy 1990c. It was a beautiful naked-eye sight during August 1990 when it was seen in the constellations Delphinus and Aquarius. As the letter "c" in its name indicates, it was the third comet discovered in 1990; it was discovered by a noted Canadian, David Levy, who has by now discovered a total of 21 comets. His many long hours spent searching the sky have been duly rewarded. Two other examples of comets that became very bright are Comet Hyakutake (See cover photo.) and Comet Hale-Bopp.

What comets can we expect to observe during the coming years? Several comets are predicted to be in the region of the Sun and Earth, and to be bright enough to be seen in amateur telescopes. More information about comets may be found in the *Observer's Handbook* and in astronomy magazines.

Another way of naming comets, other than the one mentioned above, has come into use. Under the new system, Comet Hale-Bopp is called C/1995 O1. More information about this new method of naming comets may be found in the *Observer's Handbook*.

There is a possibility that one or several other "new" comets will be discovered, which will become bright enough to be seen in binoculars or with the unaided eye. The news of such events is known by members of most astronomy clubs soon after such discoveries are made.

20

Observing the Zodiacal Light

On the clear moonless nights in late winter and early spring there is a strange light that can be seen in the western sky about an hour and a half after sunset.

It is much larger and sometimes much brighter than most people realize; yet few people have seen this strange large light. Many people also do not know that it is really very easy to see, if they are away from city light pollution and have a good view of the western horizon.

What is this strange light that makes its appearance on clear spring nights in the western sky? It is a phenomenon known as the *zodiacal light*, and it actually appears, not just in the western sky after twilight in the springtime, but also before dawn in the morning sky during the late summer and autumn. This very large area of sky brightness is caused by tiny dust particles orbiting the Sun. Our Solar System has not just planets and comets and asteroids, but also a great ring of dust in the region of the inner planets. When sunlight strikes these trillions of tiny dust particles, it is reflected from them just as it is when it strikes the Moon or the planets. And just as the sunlight striking the Moon (three or four days after New Moon allows us to see it as a crescent) in the western sky, so also the sunlight striking the ring of dust allows us to see it.

Exactly when and where should I look for the zodiacal light? The answer is you should look for the evening zodiacal light *in the western sky from 1 1/2 to 2 1/2 hours after sunset* during the months of February and March at times when there is not a bright Moon in the sky. The morning zodiacal light may be seen *from 2 1/2 to 1 1/2 hours before sunrise in the eastern sky* during the months of September and October at times when the sky is clear and moonless. The reason you do not observe it within 1 1/2 hours of sunset or sunrise is that a glow seen at that time above the horizon is indistinguishable from the glow of twilight. A bright Moon in the sky also prevents us from seeing the zodiacal light, just as it hinders a good view of the Milky Way. (See Photo 16.)

What should we expect to see? If the sky is clear, you can expect to see a large triangle or pyramid of light whose base is about 60 degrees wide along the western horizon (if it is the evening zodiacal light) and whose upper point is about 60 degrees above the western horizon. In other words, during February, it extends upward about as high as the Pleiades 1 1/2 hours after sunset. The upper point is not exactly above the centre of the base of the triangle, but somewhat to the left, so that the triangle seems to be slightly tilted to the south. The triangle of light observed as the morning zodiacal light is similarly tilted to the right or to the south. Within this large area you will see a glow or brightness that may occasionally be as bright as the Milky Way, depending on the observing conditions, though usually it is not that bright. However, under some superb viewing conditions, I have actually seen it considerably brighter than the Milky Way. This glow or brightness may last for a couple of hours, depending on the observing conditions, but usually after an hour or so it becomes more difficult to see.

After you have learned to recognize the zodiacal light at the appropriate time of year, you will wonder why you did not notice this strange, fascinating glow in the sky long before you did.

21

Observing the Sun Safely

Many people think that astronomers study only the stars, planets, and other objects in the night sky. In fact, many observers regularly study the Sun during daylight hours.

The Sun is our nearest star. It is the centre of the Solar System to which our Earth belongs. It has produced the light and energy that have enabled life to emerge on Earth. It makes possible the production of our food and everything else that we see on Earth. Therefore, it is certainly reasonable to study the Sun and learn as much as we can about it.

Before anything else, several warnings must be given about observing the Sun.

1. NEVER look directly at the Sun with the unaided eye.

2. NEVER look at the Sun when using binoculars or a telescope, unless you are absolutely certain that you are using the correct kind of solar filter.

    The Sun must be treated with great respect. Even the briefest glimpse at the Sun, when using any kind of optical aid without the proper filter, can focus enough heat and light into the eye to cause permanent eye damage or permanent blindness. It is not just at times of a solar eclipse that viewing the Sun can be dangerous; such an idea is nonsense. Looking at the Sun, without the protection of a proper filter, is ALWAYS DANGEROUS.

Safe viewing of the Sun can be done in a limited number of ways:

1. For direct viewing of the Sun, you may use an arc welder's glass #14. This very dark glass may be purchased at welding supply outlets. Welder's glass with numbers other than 14 is not suitable. When using it, be sure that it is properly in place over your eyes before looking in the direction of the Sun.

2. You may construct a simple pin-hole camera, to project an image of the Sun.

Constructing a pin-hole camera is quite simple. Obtain a shoe box or one of similar size. Using a pencil, punch a small hole in the middle of one end of the box. Put a piece of white paper on the inside of the opposite end of the box. Turn the box upside down, and hold the box up so that the end with the pinhole is pointing toward the Sun. DO NOT LOOK THROUGH THE PINHOLE. Let the sunlight enter the box through the pinhole, and let the image fall on the white paper on the opposite end of the box. With your back to the Sun, you can now observe the image of the Sun. You may possibly notice that the image shows one or several sunspots, if there are large ones on the Sun at the time of your observation.

3. You may use a mirror to project an image of the Sun.

    Obtain a small mirror and a piece of cardboard the same size as the mirror. Make a hole 3 to 5 mm in diameter in the centre of the cardboard, and tape the cardboard over the mirror. Put the mirror in sunlight so that the light is reflected from the mirror onto a wall or flat surface. You will see an image of the Sun. DO NOT LOOK INTO THE PATH OF SUNLIGHT REFLECTED FROM THE MIRROR. The quality of the image will be better if you project it onto a white wall or screen and if the surrounding area is dark. This method works well if the mirror is located in a window and the image of the Sun is projected onto a white screen in a darkened room. The image may not be sharp, but it may be good enough to allow you to see sunspots if there are large ones on the Sun at the time.

4. When using a telescope, one kind of solar viewing that is safe is through a commercially produced solar filter designed to fit over the front end of the telescope. These very reflective metallic-coated glass filters reflect almost all of the Sun's light back into space, and allow only a very tiny amount to enter the telescope. Such filters may be expensive, but the assurance of safety is worth the cost. If you use a filter of this kind, you should check it frequently to be sure that very tiny pin-holes do not appear in the metallic coating.

    Solar filters that are designed to be used at the eyepiece end of the telescope *must not* be used. They are very unsafe because heating could cause them to crack or shatter, and instant and permanent eye damage could result. A few years ago this type of filter was sold with some telescopes. Anyone who owns such a filter should destroy it, and not use the telescope for solar viewing, unless a proper kind of filter can be obtained.

Observing the Sun Safely

What can one see when observing the Sun? There are a number of things that you will notice:

1. The image of the Sun appears perfectly round. You will notice that this is true even if the hole in the pin-hole camera or in the cardboard over the mirror is not perfectly round. The Sun is actually a giant sphere which is much closer to being a perfect sphere than the Earth is; the Earth, in fact, is larger around its equator than around the poles.

2. The image of the Sun appears slightly darker near the edge of the disk than at the centre. This is called "limb-darkening." There is a reason for this. When we look at the centre of the disk, we are looking more directly into various layers of the very hot gases in the outer parts of the Sun, but when we look at the edge of the disk, we are looking across only the outermost layers that are not as hot and bright as the layers of gases further inside

3. There may be a small dark spot or spots visible on the disk of the Sun. Do not expect to see very many spots, certainly not as many as you may have seen on pictures of the Sun taken at large observatories, but you may see one or two, or even more depending on your method of observing. If you see any sunspots at all, you should repeat the observation the next day or on several following days, and record any changes you notice. Perhaps you will soon begin to learn something about the rotation period of the Sun and about the "life-cycle" of sunspots.

Many amateur astronomers observe the Sun every clear day and carefully record the number of sunspots and sunspot groups that they see. Over the years observers have noticed that there is an 11-year cycle, with few sunspots at the beginning and end of the cycle and large numbers near the middle of the cycle. Scientists have also learned that there is a relationship between solar activity and certain things that happen on Earth, such as the appearance of the aurora or northern lights. Observations of the Sun made by amateur astronomers with simple equipment have helped us to gain a better understanding of what is happening in the Sun. However, there is still a great deal to learn even about our nearest star.

Several excellent books are available to help you understand the activity of the Sun, the 11-year sunspot cycle, and other features that you may begin to observe on the Sun. Above all, exercise caution and follow the rules of safe observing when you study the Sun. In that way you can enjoy the experience.

22

The Problem of Light Pollution

When they are introduced to the wonders of amateur astronomy, many people become aware for the first time of the existence of something called "light pollution." Usually they then begin to see its annoying and devastating effects upon the astronomical community and upon astronomy in general.

"Light pollution" is an artificial nighttime glow in the atmosphere above many communities, a glow that adversely affects the environment in several ways. It originates usually from excessive man-made lighting, generally from lighting fixtures that are poorly designed. Prime examples are lights that glare into the eyes of homeowners and motorists, often severely compromising the vision, safety, and security that some people may think is being improved. Light pollution has become, in the past few decades, a matter of economics as well as aesthetics. In North America, well over a billion dollars are spent each year in the production of light that is totally wasted, the light that produces that useless nighttime glow over our cities, towns, and villages.

A number of years ago, a noted Canadian, Dr. Helen Sawyer-Hogg, pointed out in one of her books, that in the 1940s people could see the Milky Way from downtown Toronto. Instead of seeing a myriad of stars, Torontonians now, even on the clearest of nights, are fortunate to be able to see a half-dozen of the brightest stars and planets. In the past, generation upon generation of young people grew up having a familiarity with the night sky. Now, that priceless heritage of thousands of years is lost in a single generation, lost amid the blazing glare of excess light that fills the sky. What a shame it is! In the past decade, while Comets Hyakutake and Hale-Bopp were truly and totally awesome sights from unpolluted, rural skies, the citizens of our big cities were unimpressed, lucky if they could even see the faint objects. Friends of mine who happen to live in a big city, routinely have to drive for several hours each way simply to get away from the urban glow each and every time they wish to explore the wonders of the heavens, and every year or two, their trips get longer and longer.

Light pollution poses several problems for, not just the views and appreciation of the night sky, but also for the serious study of the heavens, for the science of astronomy. Whereas once, in the 1930s and 1940s, serious astronomy could be pursued at the David Dunlap Observatory in Richmond Hill, one of the northern suburbs of Toronto, such pursuit of science has not been possible for several decades simply because of the growth of outdoor lighting and its skyglow in the surrounding area. The generation after the astronomers who once did observations there on the finest instrument in Canada now must journey, at

> **Light pollution presents severe problems, not just for the enjoyment of our views of the night sky, but also for the serious study of the heavens by professional astronomers, that is, for the study of astronomy at every level.**

considerable cost, to an unpolluted mountaintop in northern Chile to use a much smaller instrument in order to make their similarly important observations.

The career of my own personal friend, David Levy, now perhaps the world's most famous amateur astronomer, provides another example of the effects of light pollution. For over 19 years while living in, and near, two light-polluted cities, namely Montreal and later Kingston, he persistently and faithfully practised a systematic comet-search program. Results: 0 discoveries over the 19 years. In 1980 David moved to the suburbs of Tucson, Arizona. Within a very short while, he discovered his first comet. Later over several years he discovered 8 comets from his backyard. Now there are 21 comets that have had his name attached to them, some discovered from his backyard observatory and some from a search program with other comet-hunters. He is ranked third on the list of comet-discoverers in all of human history. Why the difference? Certainly one most important difference is the fact that the city of Tucson has taken the problem of light pollution very seriously, because of the number of large astronomical observatories located nearby. Outdoor lighting ordinances are strict and they are enforced. They are aimed at eliminating the totally wasted glow above the city at night. Other places could control this serious problem by following the example of Tucson.

Some people are well aware of the problems that light pollution causes in the animal kingdom. Hundreds of thousands, if not millions, of migratory birds are killed each year from flying into "overlit" office buildings, though some of them are no longer "overlit" to the extent they once were. In addition, light pollution interferes with our migratory birds' sense of their traditional flight lanes. Sea turtles, and other sea creatures along the coastlines, such as those in Florida, have their lives and their behaviour patterns severely disrupted by the light pollution of the coastal cities. Those who study circadian rhythms and sleep patterns in all living creatures, including humans, can probably verify that light pollution interferes in ways that we do not even fully understand.

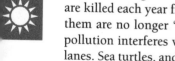

What is the solution for this pollution problem? The main solution is eliminating unnecessary outdoor lighting, and using only outdoor and street lighting that uses "full-cutoff fixtures," which direct all of their light *below the horizontal*, such that the light source itself is *NOT* seen from the side. (Being seen from the side is the common and universal fault of all the older "cobra-head" type of street lights.) Since "full-cutoff fixtures" direct their light downward, to where it is needed, and *NOT* upward and to the side, there is less light required and less energy used.

Additionally, more efficient light sources can provide better and safer lighting at a fraction of the cost of the older "light polluting" types. Incandescent lights, mercury vapour, metal halide, and high-pressure sodium fixtures are costly and inefficient. Low-pressure sodium lights, such as those now found in some cities, are much more efficient and inexpensive. "Full-cutoff fixtures" with low-pressure sodium lighting provide the same amount of illumination, and where it is needed, at about 10% of the cost of using the older fixtures and types of illumination. Cities such as Tucson and San Diego in the US, which have followed this path for their street lighting, have realized savings in the millions of tax dollars. To be specific, and to address the issue at the private-property level: a grossly obnoxious 175-watt mercury vapour "security" light can be replaced with a properly-shielded (i.e., full-cutoff) 35-watt low-pressure sodium light, giving the same amount of illumination, with no glare and no light trespass on a neighbour's property, and with enormous savings in energy cost.

There is no credible statistical evidence that the traditional "security" lights ever provided real security. However, in the cities where they were promoted, there is plenty of real statistical evidence that crime rates have soared, as criminals learned to take advantage of the shadows and the glare that such lights created. In rural areas, they simply pointed out, for the potential criminals, the properties that would be worth their attention. How many of the owners of rural properties with the old poorly designed "security" lights ever realized how much glare, pollution, and *little security* they really provided? If rural property owners wanted real security, they would use properly shielded, motion-activated lights, that come on only when nearby motion is detected, the kind of light that really does alert others that there is a potential problem and provide glare-free visibility when necessary. The savings to the owner would also be very significant.

The biggest cause of light pollution is the lack of awareness of the problem and of the solutions. Once there is an awareness of such a problem, most people are willing to try to solve it, especially when they understand the effects that it is having on their neighbours and the monetary cost to themselves. (Remember: An outdoor neighbourhood light should not, itself, be seen; if a neighbour wants his or her property illuminated, only the ground under the light should be seen, NOT THE LIGHT ITSELF. If the light is seen, it produces a "veiling glare," which can hide criminal activity, and it may be a source of "trespass" against a neighbour.) One person has well summarized the lack of awareness of some people: "It surprises me that someone, who would never think of leaving a plastic bottle on the ground at a picnic site, would pay extra money each month to illuminate the neighbourhood with unnecessary, distracting light." Such people should know that the concept of "light trespass" has entered into law, and lawsuits have actually been won over the matter. They should also know that almost all the solutions to light-pollution problems involve saving money, sometimes very large amounts of money – a fact that is so vastly different from the solutions proposed for other kinds of modern pollution. Moreover, everyone benefits in applying these solutions for light pollution.

Although, in the province of Ontario, the residents may be far from having the laws that regulate light pollution in Tucson, Arizona, an important first step in the right direction was taken in 1999 with the declaration of Torrance Barrens Nature Reserve, near Gravenhurst, as a protected, light-pollution-free environment. May it be the first of many such parks both in Ontario and in other provinces! And may we all do our part to fight light pollution in our own neighbourhoods, and throughout our province and country, so that we and our children can enjoy the splendour and the countless wonders of the nighttime sky!

Additional information on this topic may be obtained by contacting the Royal Astronomical Society of Canada's National Light Pollution Abatement Committee (by mail to the Society's address given elsewhere in this book, or through the Society's Web site: www.rasc.ca). Many Centres of the Society throughout the country have a committee that is actively dedicated to addressing poor lighting practices in the local area, and they also should be contacted for information (by mail to a Centre's address given elsewhere in this book, or through a Centre's Web site that may be reached through the Society's Web site).

The International Dark-Sky Association (IDA) is a large organization whose aims are concerned with preserving dark and unpolluted skies on this planet. Information about joining this highly recommended organization, or about obtaining its "information sheets," may be obtained at its Web site: www.darksky.org or by mail to the International Dark-Sky Association, 3225 N First Avenue, Tucson AZ USA 85719-2103.

By acting both as individuals and as part of a group, whether it is a local, national, or international group, amateur astronomers have been able to achieve important victories in the ongoing struggle against the light pollution of our precious night skies.

23

Where to Get More Information

This book is intended only as a very basic introduction to astronomy and the study of the night sky. As you become more familiar with the stars, planets, and other objects of interest, you will want to gain more knowledge about all of these things. Luckily there are many resources that you can turn to, in order to satisfy your curiosity.

(a) From Joining an Astronomy Club

There are many advantages to joining an astronomy club. You will meet people who will be able to assist you in finding the information you want. Most of the people you will meet have already been through the stages you are now going through, and they know how it feels to be unsure about where to get answers to certain questions.

In Canada, the largest organization of people who are interested in astronomy is the Royal Astronomical Society of Canada. This organization is over a hundred years old and it has over 4500 members. It has 27 clubs called "Centres" in the major cities all across Canada.

Here are some of the many advantages to joining the local club or Centre of the Royal Astronomical Society of Canada (RASC):

1. When you join, you will receive two publications mailed to you six times a year. The *Journal of the Royal Astronomical Society of Canada* contains articles about astronomical discoveries, and about important people and events in the history of Canadian astronomy. *SkyNews* is an astronomical newsmagazine which reports happenings of interest to Canadian amateur astronomers. It contains information about sky events for the next two months and reports on news from the amateur astronomical community.

2. You will receive a copy of the *Observer's Handbook*. This is a very high-quality observing guide, loaded with many kinds of information, including star maps and many lists of interesting objects to observe. (Remember that the cost to non-members of this book alone is $23.95 per year, but you will have it included in your membership.)

3. You will receive your club or Centre's newsletter. It will tell you about the interesting things happening in your own area. The members of the club have a chance to write about what they have been observing lately. They

may also write about what equipment they have bought or have built, and they may discuss whether they are satisfied with it.

4.   By being a member of the RASC, you may receive discounts at certain retailers when you buy things that interest amateur astronomers. You will hear of items that are for sale much sooner than if you did not belong to a club. Several members of a club may wish to share in the purchase of a large or expensive item, and thus they may be able to save money. Some members have actually saved hundreds of dollars when they bought their equipment – because they belonged to a Centre.

5.   You will have a chance to attend a regular organized program of free talks or lectures by both professional and amateur astronomers. Most of the Centres have at least one talk or lecture a month on some topic that interests the members. There are usually monthly meetings also, at which members discuss their recent and planned observations.

6.   You will be able to share in the use of the Centre's telescope, or telescopes, or observatory, depending on the equipment owned by the Centre. Some of the Centres own beautiful observatories that the members have worked hard to build. They are happy to have interested beginners join in their observing programs.

7.   You will have access to the RASC's library resources and the Centre's library. Many Centres have a very good libraries. Borrowing some of the books or other materials may save you from having to make costly purchases.

8.   You will have access to the back-issues of the Centre's newsletters and to the newsletters from the other Centres across Canada. Many of these other newsletters contain a great deal of important information. Most Centres receive the newsletters from the other Centres across Canada.

9.   You will be able to receive the advice of experienced amateur astronomers on observing, astrophotography, and many other aspects of astronomy. Some members of the Centres are experts in certain areas because they have been interested in astronomy for many years. Their advice can be very helpful.

10.   You will have the chance to attend and to vote at the RASC's annual General Assembly. This large three-day event is held in a different city across Canada every year. You will be able to hear talks and see projects and displays that have been prepared. The Society's annual awards are also presented. It is an opportunity to meet astronomers from all across the country, and to have some fun, too; there is even a humorous song contest.

11. There is the general opportunity for the exchange of ideas and friendship with many people who share an interest in astronomy. Within some Centres there are groups of members who are interested in observing certain kinds of objects, or in building telescopes, for example.

12. There is the chance for outings, field trips, and observing sessions with knowledgeable amateur astronomers. Many Centres have regular programs for observing at an observatory or "dark-sky" site away from the light pollution of a large city. These events include sessions for members, as well as sessions open to the public.

Certainly there are many benefits of joining the R.A.S.C. and they far outweigh the inexpensive fees. Current membership fees are $44 per year, or $27.50 for persons under 21 years of age. Some of the Centres levy a small surcharge to cover the cost of maintaining their equipment.

The following is a list of the Centres of the R.A.S.C. and addresses:

Belleville Centre	c/o Joe Shields, 9 South Park St., Belleville, ON K8P 2W8
Calgary Centre	c/o Calgary Science Centre, P.O. Box 2100, Station M, Loc. #73, Calgary, AB T2P 2M5
Charlottetown Centre	39 Mt. Edward Rd., Charlottetown, PE C1A 5S2
Edmonton Centre	Edmonton Space & Science Centre, 11211 - 142 St., Edmonton, AB T5M 4A1
Halifax Centre	P.O. Box 31011, Halifax, NS B3K 5T9
Hamilton Centre	P.O. Box 1223, Waterdown, ON L0R 2H0
Kingston Centre	P.O. Box 1793, Kingston, ON K7L 5J6
Kitchener-Waterloo Centre	c/o Peter Daniel, 36 Talbot St., Apt. 101, Kitchener, ON N2M 2A9
London Centre	P.O. Box 842, Station B, London, ON N6A 4Z3
Moncton Centre	c/o Dr. Francis LeBlanc, Département de physique et d'astronomie, Université de Moncton, Moncton, NB E1A 3E9
Société d'Astronomie de Montréal	C.P. 206, St. Michel, Montréal, QC H2A 3L9
Montreal Centre	P.O. Box 1752, Station B, Montréal, QC H3B 3L3
Niagara Centre	P.O. Box 4040, St. Catharines, ON L2R 7S3

Okanagan Centre	P.O. Box 20119 TCM, Kelowna, BC V1Y 9H2
Ottawa Centre	P.O. Box 33012, 1974 Baseline Rd., Nepean, ON K2C 0E0
Prince George Centre	7365 Tedford Rd., Prince George, BC V2N 6S2
Quebec Centre	2000 boulevard Montmorency, Quebec, PQ G1J 5E7
Regina Centre	P.O. Box 20014, Cornwall Centre, Regina, SK S4P 4J7
St. John's Centre	c/o 206 Frecker Drive, St. John's, NF A1E 5H9
Sarnia Centre	c/o Jim Selinger, 160 George St., Sarnia, ON N7T 7V4
Saskatoon Centre	P.O. Box 317, RPO University, Saskatoon, SK S7N 4J8
Toronto Centre	c/o Ontario Science Centre, 770 Don Mills Rd., Don Mills, ON M3C 1T3
Thunder Bay Centre	286 Trinity Cres., Thunder Bay, ON P7C 5V6
Vancouver Centre	c/o Gordon Southam Observatory, 1100 Chestnut St., Vancouver, BC V6J 3J9
Victoria Centre	764 Mapleton Place, Victoria, BC V8Z 6W2
Windsor Centre	c/o Frank Shepley, 671 Inman Sideroad, R.R. #2, Ruthven, ON N0P 2G0
Winnipeg Centre	P.O. Box 2694, Winnipeg, MB R3C 4B3

People who do not live near any of the above Centres, or who do not wish to attach themselves to one of the Centres, may join as "unattached" members by contacting the National Office at this address:

> The Royal Astronomical Society of Canada,
> 136 Dupont Street,
> Toronto, ON M5R 1V2

(b) From Books

There are many books which can continue to provide a good introduction to the night sky. Here is a list of those that are recommended.

Dickinson, Terence. *Exploring The Night Sky: The Equinox Astronomy Guide For Beginners.* Camden House Publishing Ltd., Camden East, ON 1987. This short and well-illustrated guide to the sky is particularly suitable for young people and beginners.

Dickinson, Terence. *Nightwatch: A Practical Guide To Viewing The Universe.* Third Edition. Firefly Books, Toronto, ON 1998. This is a superb introduction to the art of observing the night sky. Its various chapters deal with many aspects of amateur astronomy. You will be proud to own and use this book.

Dickinson, Terence. *Summer Stargazing: A Practical Guide For Recreational Astronomers.* Firefly Books, Toronto, ON 1999. The star charts in this book assist the beginner in learning where to locate many objects in the summer constellations.

Gupta, Rajiv (Editor). *Observer's Handbook.* The Royal Astronomical Society of Canada. Toronto, ON This is one of the world's best annual guides to observing the night sky. It contains many lists of objects that can be used in planning observing projects, and a vast wealth of information about many aspects of astronomy.

Levy, David H. *Cosmic Discoveries: The Wonders of Astronomy.* Prometheus Books, Amherst, N.Y. 232 pages. This book tells many of the stories behind the great discoveries in the science of astronomy.

Levy, David H. *David Levy's Guide to the Night Sky.* Cambridge University Press. 2001. 368 pages. This book is full of good advice for observing the night sky, whether one is using the unaided eye, binoculars, or a small telescope.

Levy, David H. *Making Friends With The Stars.* Ken Press, Tucson, AZ. 2001. 126 pages. This book contains many ideas about introducing the sky to young people.

Levy, David H. *Observing Variable Stars: A Guide for the Beginner.* Cambridge University Press. 1998. paperback. 198 pages. For those who wish to learn about variable stars and how to observe them, this is one of the very finest introductions available anywhere.

Peltier, Leslie C. *Starlight Nights: The Adventures of a Star-Gazer.* Sky Publishing Corp. Cambridge, Mass. This is a most interesting autobiography of a person who truly loved the stars, and joyfully observed the night sky for over sixty years.

Books for the Binocular Observer:

There are several excellent books that have been written especially for those who observe the night sky with binoculars. The following three are especially recommended. Each one of them could assist the observer in planning his or her binocular observing sessions. All of them can be ordered from Sky Publishing, whose address is given below in the magazines section.

Cherrington, Ernest H. *Exploring the Moon Through Binoculars and Small Telescopes.* 229 pages.

Crossen, Craig, and Tirion Wil. *Binocular Astronomy.* 224 pages.

Harrington, Philip S. *Touring The Universe Through Binoculars. A Complete Astronomer's Guidebook.* 294 pages.

Star Atlases:

Every observer eventually wants to own a good star atlas. It provides the "roadmaps of the night sky." A good basic star atlas usually also provides lists of interesting objects to observe, as shown on each of its star maps. There are many star atlases available, some good and some not very good. The following is a list of four of the best available.

Bright Star Atlas 2000.0 by Wil Tirion. This inexpensive, excellent star atlas contains easy-to-read star charts and very useful lists of interesting objects accompanying each of the 10 star charts. These charts, covering the whole sky, show over 9 000 stars and 600 deep-sky objects (star clusters, nebulae, and galaxies). This atlas is strongly recommended as a beginner's atlas.

Norton's 2000.0 Star Atlas And Reference Handbook. ed. by Ian Ridpath. This is an updated version, the 18th edition, in fact, of a classic star atlas that has been a favorite for over 80 years. It is an ideal star atlas for a beginning observer and one that he or she can use for many years. The entire sky is shown on 8 charts. Over 8 700 stars, to the faintest discernible with the unaided eye under the very best sky conditions (magnitude 6.5) are shown, as well as over 500 variable stars and over 800 deep-sky objects (star clusters, nebulae, and galaxies).

SkyAtlas 2000.0 by Wil Tirion. This is a more advanced star atlas, and is the kind that will be needed as you begin to observe fainter objects. There are 26 large-format charts that show the entire sky. This atlas is available in three versions. The Deluxe bound version has large folded charts that are colour-coded for different kinds of objects in the sky. The Desk Edition has unbound charts showing black stars on a white sky background. The Field Edition has white stars on a black sky background. All three editions show about 43 000 stars and 2 500 other deep-sky objects (star clusters, nebulae, and galaxies). The Field Edition is recommended for those who wish to take their star maps out to the observing site. The black sky background means that there will be less glare when you shine a flashlight on it. Some observers have found also that it is best to have the charts laminated, especially the ones that are frequently used. The laminated plastic coating prevents dew and frost from damaging the paper.

Planispheres:

Many amateur astronomers find it helpful to own a planisphere, which is a "star wheel" that shows the bright stars and constellations visible throughout the year from certain latitudes. Most planispheres are more durable than the star maps found in many astronomy books, such as this one, or the star maps found in astronomy magazines, and so they are often preferred for use at an observing site when the weather is damp and dew is a problem. They are available in several sizes. Larger ones are recommended (over the very small 'miniplanispheres') since they are easier to read, especially when one is using a flashlight outdoors at night. Both of the following planispheres are available from Sky Publishing:

David H. Levy's Guide to the Stars Planisphere by David H. Levy.

The Night Sky Planisphere by David Chandler.

(c) From Using the Internet

Many beginning astronomers use the World Wide Web to obtain information about observing and astronomy. There are, in fact, numerous Web sites which are excellent sources of information for the beginner, intermediate, and advanced astronomer. However, unfortunately, there are also many Web sites that cannot be recommended for a variety of reasons, such as their promotion of a personal agenda, their desire to advance the cause of a discredited theory, or their enthusiasm for the tenets of astrology at the expense of astronomy. The following list contains Web sites that are recommended:

www.aavso.org	The American Association of Variable Star Observers
www.darksky.org	The International Dark-Sky Association
www.jpl.nasa.gov	The Jet Propulsion Laboratory, which is part of the National Aeronautics and Space Administration
www.rasc.ca	The Royal Astronomical Society of Canada, a very highly recommended site with links to many Centres (astronomy clubs) in Canada, and to an amazing wealth of information and activities for astronomers of all ages, all levels, and all interests.
www.rasc.ca/observing	The RASC's Observing Committee's site containing information about its observing programs and about the

certificates to reward those who have completed the various observing programs. This site is strongly recommended for beginning, intermediate, and advanced observers.

www.skyandtelescope.com   Sky and Telescope magazine and Sky Publishing Corporation (a site that is highly recommended for its "astronomy news," its observing information, and its links to other reputable sites).

www.skynewsmagazine.com   SkyNews magazine, an excellent Canadian amateur astronomy periodical and a very good Web site.

www.spaceweather.com   a source of reliable information about current solar and geomagnetic activity that can cause the Aurora to become active.

www.starlight-theatre.ca   an outlet for purchasing videotapes, star maps, and other astronomy products, including the video, *The Celestial Sphere, A Narrated Tour of the Night Sky*.

(d) From Magazines

One of the best ways to introduce yourself to the regular practice of observing the night sky and, certainly a great way to keep in touch with current developments in amateur astronomy is to make use of the monthly magazines that are available. They may be found in local libraries or bought at many newsstands or ordered through subscription. In Canada the major English language magazine is *SkyNews*. Two magazines *Astronomy* and *Sky and Telescope* are published in the United States and are sold internationally.

SkyNews is called "the Canadian magazine of astronomy and stargazing." It is published bi-monthly by the National Museum of Science and Technology and is edited by Terence Dickinson. In the centre of the magazine are an uncluttered, user-friendly star map and a list of easy-to-follow information about upcoming events that can be observed by most beginning stargazers. The articles are the latest topics of interest to astronomers and are always well illustrated. The annual subscription price is currently $24.00 in Canada. The address is SkyNews, R.R. #1, Cedar Valley, ON L0G 1E0. (Telephone 1-866-759-0005.)

Astronomy is a non-technical, popular monthly magazine that is quite easily understood by the beginning observer. It has articles about the latest developments in astronomy and space exploration, and is filled with beautiful photographs. In the centre of the magazine is a star map for the early-night sky of the current month and on it are marked the bright planets in their proper position for the current month. Following the map are about ten or twelve pages explaining objects that may be observed with binoculars or telescope during the current month. These include planets, asteroids, meteor showers, and comets. There are usually articles about ways to improve your observing, and articles reviewing the latest equipment that astronomers might want to spend their money on. The annual subscription price is currently $39.95 in the United States and $50.00US (including GST) for subscriptions in Canada. The address is Astronomy, P.O. Box 1612, Waukesha, WI USA 53187-1612. (Telephone 1-800-533-6644.)

Sky and Telescope is a more technical monthly magazine that is highly respected by many serious amateur astronomers. It contains excellent articles about current happenings in astronomy and space science. It also has a map of the night sky for the current month and detailed information about the interesting objects to observe in the night sky. All of the information, whether book reviews, historical articles, or reports on the latest discoveries are carefully and accurately written. The annual subscription price is currently $39 in the United States and $47.95US (including GST) for subscriptions in Canada. The address is Sky Publishing Corporation, 49 Bay State Road, Cambridge, MA USA 02138-1200. (Telephone 1-800-253-0245.)

(e) From Visiting an Observatory or Planetarium

(i) Observatories:

Several astronomical observatories in Canada are open to the public at certain times. Some of these observatories receive visitors during the day at certain

> **Some observatories are open to the public at certain hours and even provide guided tours. Some also provide a limited amount of night time observing.**

times of the year. For such occasions, guided tours may be available or may be arranged. *Some* observatories also are open to the public for a limited amount of nighttime viewing with a telescope. Such observing sessions may last for two or three hours, one night per week during the summer months. Always check with the individual observatory to find out if and when public observing times are scheduled.

The following is a list of some Canadian observatories (east to west across the country) with their addresses and phone numbers for obtaining information about tours, visits, or possible public observing sessions.

Burke-Gaffney Observatory, Saint Mary's University, Halifax, NS B3H 3C3 Telephone(902) 420-5633

ASTROLab du Mont-Mégantic Notre-Dame-des-Bois, QC J0B 2E0 Telephone (819) 888-2941 or (866) 888-2941.

Helen Hogg Observatory, National Museum of Science and Technology, 1867 St. Laurent Blvd., Ottawa, ON Telephone (613) 991-9219 Mailing Address: P.O. Box 9724, Terminal T, Ottawa, ON K1G 5A3

David Dunlap Observatory, Box 360, Richmond Hill, ON L4C 4Y5 Telephone (416) 884-2112

York University Observatory, Department of Physics and Astronomy, 4700 Keele St., Toronto, ON M3J 1P3 Telephone (416) 736-2199, Ext. 77773.

Hume Cronyn Observatory, University of Western Ontario, London, ON N6A 3K7 Telephone (519) 661-3183

Science North Solar Observatory, 100 Ramsey Lake Rd., Sudbury, ON P3E 5S9 Telephone (705) 522-3701

University of Saskatchewan Observatory, c/o Department of Physics and Engineering Physics, 116 Science Place, Saskatoon, SK S7N 5E2. Telphone (306) 966-6429.

Dominion Radio Astrophysical Observatory, Penticton, BC V2A 6K3 Telephone (250) 490-4355.

Gordon MacMillan Southam Observatory, 1100 Chestnut St., Vancouver, BC V6J 3J9 Telephone (604) 738-STAR

University of British Columbia Observatory, 2219 Main Mall, Vancouver, BC V6T 1Z4 Telephone (604) 822-6186

Climenhaga Observatory, Department of Physics and Astronomy, University of Victoria, Victoria, BC V8W 3P6 Telephone (250) 721-7750.

Well equipped amateur observatories are operated by many of the Centres of The Royal Astronomical Society of Canada. These observatories are generally open to the members of the individual Centre. (In some cases, a small annual fee, in addition to the membership fee, may be charged for the use of the equipment.) Belonging to an RASC Centre and sharing in the use of the Centre's equipment is a great way to become acquainted with the fine equipment that the advanced amateur astronomers in some of the Centres are using. The best way to learn how to use such equipment properly is to share in an observing project when the equipment is being used by experienced amateur astronomers. Such people will probably have used the equipment many times to pursue their interest in the study of the heavens. Information about joining a Centre of the Royal Astronomical Society of Canada has already been given in a previous section of this chapter.

In most Centres new members may also make arrangements to see equipment that is privately owned and used by the more experienced members of the group, but such arrangements must be obtained on an individual basis, when a new member wishes to do this.

(ii) Planetaria:

A visit to a planetarium can be an exciting educational adventure. Most

> # A planetarium visit can be an enjoyable and educational experience.

planetaria (the proper plural of the word "planetarium") are able to use their special projectors to project a large map of the nighttime sky, with all of the visible stars and planets, on their dome-like ceilings. These large star maps projected on the huge domes give a very real picture of the nighttime sky. This method is much better than holding up a large instructional star map, even a very large one. It is also much better than using an ordinary home or school projector to give a picture of stars and constellations. A planetarium's special projectors can show the whole visible sky as it appears at any time of the year

> # The special projectors in a planetarium can show the whole visible sky as it appears at any time of year, any time of day or night, and from anywhere on Earth.

and from any place on Earth. These projectors are also used to present shows that demonstrate many things relating to the study of the stars, the planets, and space.

Here is a list of some of the planetaria in Canada (arranged from east to west across the country) along with their addresses and telephone numbers which may be used to obtain information about shows that are being presented.

Planetarium De Montréal, 1000 St. Jacques St. W., Montreal, QC H3C 1G7 Telephone (514) 872-4530

Ontario Science Centre, 770 Don Mills Rd., Don Mills, ON M3C 1T3 Telephone (416) 696-3127

W.J. McCallion Planetarium, Department of Physics and Astronomy, McMaster University, 1280 Main St. W., Hamilton, ON L8S 4M1 Telephone (905) 525-9140 Ext. 27777

Doran Planetarium, Laurentian University, Ramsey Lake Rd., Sudbury, ON P3E 2C6 Telephone (705) 675-1151 Ext. 2271

Manitoba Planetarium, 190 Rupert Ave., Winnipeg, MB R3B 0N2 Telephone (204) 943-3139

The Lockhart Planetarium, 394 University College, 500 Dysart Rd., The University of Manitoba, Winnipeg, MB R3T 2M8 Telephone (204) 474-9785

Calgary Science Centre, 701 – 11 St. S.W., P.O. Box 2100, Stn. M, Calgary, AB T2P 2M5 Telephone (403) 268-8300

Odyssium, Edmonton's space and science centre, Coronation Park, 11211 - 142 St., Edmonton, AB T5M 4A1 Telephone (780-451-3344)

H.R. MacMillan Planetarium, 1100 Chestnut St., Vancouver, BC V6J 3J9 Telephone (604) 738-7827

Centre of the Universe, Herzberg Institute of Astrophysics, 5071 West Saanich Rd., Victoria, BC V9E 2E7 Telephone (250) 363-8262

Most people enjoy a visit to an observatory or a planetarium. If there is one in your area of the country, plan to visit it soon. You will be glad that you did.

24

Questions I Always Wanted to Ask About Astronomy

There are many questions that come to the minds of people when they begin to become interested in astronomy. Some of them are presented here along with suitable answers.

Q.: *Why does a Full Moon look so large when it is rising and much smaller when it is high in the sky?*

A.: This strange fact — that the Moon looks very large when near the horizon — is called the "Moon illusion." The Moon near the horizon is definitely not nearer to us than when it is high in the sky. In fact, our brain plays a trick on us. When we look toward the horizon we see trees and hills and houses and many objects spread over the landscape. Our mind must know that the Moon is really the same size whether high overhead or near the horizon. Because of the objects on the landscape, there is a suggestion of great distance to the Moon on the horizon. The mind then makes the Moon on the horizon appear larger in order to be like the one it remembers seeing high in the sky.

Yes, it is an illusion; the brain makes the Moon look larger! All extended objects look larger when near the horizon. Compare the appearance of the Big Dipper and Orion when near the horizon and when high in the sky. They too appear much larger when near the horizon. Try looking at the rising Full Moon through a long hollow tube; it will suddenly look smaller and just as it does when overhead, because with the tube you have cut off your view of objects on the landscape that cause the illusion.

Q.: *What is the Harvest Moon?*

A.: The Harvest Moon is the name given to the Full Moon nearest to the autumn equinox, which occurs about September 21 or 22. This Full Moon, then, is in either September or early October. For several nights after this Full Moon, the Moon rises only 20 to 30 minutes later from night to night. (At most other times during the year the Moon rises an average of 50 minutes later each day.) At this time of year, the path of the Moon's orbit around the Earth makes a different (smaller) angle with the line of the eastern horizon than at any other time in the year. This fact allows the Moon, for several nights, to rise sooner than we would expect it. Long

FMS / **FMA**

E

H

A1

A2

A3

S1

S2

S3

Harvest Moon Explained

The double line, EH, represents the Eastern Horizon, as viewed from southern Canada, at about the time of Sunset. The dashed lines represent the Moon's orbit in autumn and in spring. The circles, FMA, A1, A2, and A3, represent the rising Full Moon in autumn, and the Moon 1, 2, and 3 days later. The circles, FMS, S1, S2 and S3, represent the rising Full Moon in spring and the Moon 1, 2, and 3 days later. The autumn Moon rises more quickly from day to day because its path is closer to the horizon.

ago farmers said that these "quickly rising" Moons in the early autumn gave them extra light when they needed it to finish harvesting their crops.

Q.: *What is the Hunter's Moon?*

A.: The Hunter's Moon is the name given to the Full Moon that occurs one month after the Harvest Moon. For the same reason as mentioned on the previous page, the Moon rises only 25 to 35 minutes later from night to night for several days after the date of this Full Moon. Hunters, as well as farmers, are thankful that these "quickly rising" Moons in October and November give them some extra light after sunset.

Q.: *Why do stars twinkle?*

A.: Stars twinkle because the light we see coming from the stars travels through the atmosphere around the Earth and there is turbulence in the Earth's atmosphere. Stars are enormously large compared to the Earth; many stars are much bigger even than our own Sun. However, all stars are very, very far away from us. They are so far away that they appear as tiny dots or tiny points of light. As this light from the stars moves down through our Earth's atmosphere it meets turbulence that causes it to appear to "jiggle," just as light coming up through a rippling swimming pool on a hot day seems to jiggle. Some people have noticed that planets usually do not twinkle. The reason is that they are much nearer to us than any star. The planets, though they may seem to be just tiny dots to the unaided eye, are really little disks of light. Even though the little disk may jiggle because of turbulence, there is still one spot on the disk from which light is always coming. Many people have said that it would be great to observe the sky from the Moon, which has no atmosphere. Then there would be no twinkling at all.

Q.: *What is a black hole?*

A.: Many astronomers believe that there are very dense objects in the universe, objects that are called black holes. An object is very dense if it is very massive or heavy for the volume of space that it occupies. (We would say that air is not very dense but marble and lead are dense.) Black holes may have been formed at the very early stages in the history of the universe, or when large stars go through a supernova explosion, or when an object like a star gathers into itself a great deal of mass from other stars. A black hole is so very massive that it has enormous gravity associated with it. (We know that the Earth, which is more massive than the Moon, has more gravity associated with it than the Moon does.) The gravity of a black hole is so great that *everything* in space around it is pulled into it, and is never seen again. In fact, the force of gravity is so great that even light itself cannot escape from the black hole. We can never "see" a black hole, as we can see a star like our Sun, if there is no light escaping from it. That is why it is "black," and why it is like a "hole in space." Astronomers must use other methods (other than direct optical viewing) to determine that a black hole exists; they must examine what is happening in the area around where it may exist. There is still a great deal to be learned about strange objects like black holes, and they will be discussed by astronomers for many years as we find out more and more about them.

Q.: *How far away is the nearest star? How long would it take to get there?*

A.: The nearest star to the Earth is our own Sun. Our Earth is part of the system of nine planets that travel around this great star. It takes light over

8 minutes to travel from the Sun to the Earth. The speed of light is 300 000 kilometres per second. The distance between the Sun and the Earth is about 149 600 000 kilometres. If we could travel in a space ship at a speed of 50 000 kilometres per hour, it would take us 125 days to reach the Sun.

Perhaps in your question you wanted to ask how far away was the nearest star beyond our Sun, and how long it would take to get there? The star that is nearest to our Sun is the star that is called Proxima Centauri. It is 4.2 light-years away. That means that it takes light, travelling at 300 000 kilometres per second, *over 4 years* to travel from that star to our Earth. If we could travel in a space ship at a speed of 50 000 kilometres per hour, it would take us over 88 000 *years* to reach this star which is the *nearest* star of all to our Sun.

Q.: *What are "deep sky objects"?*

A.: "Deep sky objects" is a term used by amateur astronomers to describe many kinds of objects that they observe in the night sky. The objects are all very far away and most of them are faint and challenging to see in binoculars or a telescope. The term includes star clusters, nebulae, and galaxies. Many of these objects are best seen with rather large telescopes, which have greater light-gathering ability than smaller telescopes.

Q.: *What is the difference between a reflection nebula, an emission nebula, and a dark nebula?*

A.: Reflection nebulae are huge clouds of gas and dust that are located near stars. The gas and dust shine because they reflect the light from the nearby stars. An example is the nebulosity near the stars of the Pleiades; this can be seen in large binoculars or a wide-field telescopes used at low power.

Emission nebulae are clouds of gas and dust located near hot stars; the light from the stars energizes the gas and causes it to glow by fluorescence, as the gas in a fluorescent light glows. An example is the Orion Nebula; this can be seen with the unaided eye or in binoculars and is a very interesting object.

Dark nebulae are clouds of gas and dust that block the light coming to us from distant stars. The area of the sky looks dark only because we see stars from the surrounding area, but do not see the light from stars in the area of the gas and dust cloud. An example is the dark lane in the constellation Cygnus. Under good conditions it can be seen with the unaided eye.

Q.: *What are the meanings of the terms "Right Ascension" and "Declination," which I often hear experienced amateur astronomers using?*

A.: These terms "right ascension" and "declination" are used when stating the position of an object in the sky. In Chapter 4 we learned about a simple system of stating the location of an object in the sky; we used the horizon as a reference and gave the position of an object by saying it was in a certain direction as measured around the horizon (azimuth) and at a certain distance in degrees above the horizon (altitude). Another and more commonly used method of stating the location of an object in the sky is to use the equator as the reference. The equator of the sky, usually called the "celestial equator," is directly above the Earth's equator, just as the celestial poles are above the Earth's poles. Declination is the distance, in degrees, of an object either north or south of the celestial equator. A declination of 45°N means that the object is 45° north of the celestial equator. When looking south in the winter sky we can visualize where the celestial equator is if we know that it runs approxiately through the belt of Orion. Right Ascension is the distance of an object, measured eastward along the equator, from the point called the Vernal Equinox, which is the apparent position of the Sun on the celestial equator on March 21 each year. Rather than measuring in degrees, as rarely happens, Right Ascension is more commonly measured in hours and minutes, with 24 hours being the complete distance around the celestial equator. An object at 6 hours and 30 minutes would be 6 1/2 hours east of the Vernal Equinox, or a little over a quarter of the distance around the sky from the Vernal Equinox.

Q.: *How far can you see in a telescope?*

A.: This is a question that amateur astronomers are often asked. It is very difficult to answer precisely, and most amateurs prefer not to have to try to answer questions like this one. One way (and this is only *one* way) in which it could be answered would be to say that many amateur astronomers regularly observe galaxies, for example, that are extremely distant from our galaxy, the Milky Way. A few amateur astronomers also observe some of the quasars, which are much more remote that most galaxies. As an example of the enormous distance of some galaxies, we may use the Virgo Cluster of Galaxies, which are thought to be at least 40 million light-years away. An example of a quasar that can be seen in amateur telescopes is the one called 3C273, which is thought to be about 3 billion light years away, and it is probably one of the nearer quasars! Remember that a light year is the distance that light travels in one year, and that the speed of light is 300 000 kilometres per second. To express the distance to one of the Virgo galaxies in kilometres (which will make a ridiculously huge number — which astronomers try not to use), (1) you might find the number of seconds in a year (60 X 60 X 24 X 365), (2) multiply that number by 300 000 to obtain the speed of light in kilometres per year, and (3) multiply that number by 40 000 000 to obtain the approximate distance in kilometres to one of the galaxies that can be seen in Virgo. (The answer, a number with 21 digits, would be extremely cumbersome to use.) Perhaps we can now understand why astronomers use "light-years" rather than "kilometres" to describe the distances to galaxies.

Some astronomers would prefer to answer this question by saying that whether you can see a very distant object depends entirely on the brightness of the object. In some telescopes you may see a bright galaxy that is dozens of millions of light-years away, but a faint galaxy at only a fraction of that distance may not be detected at all.

Q.: *Can I observe any of those planets that astronomers have discovered orbiting stars beyond our Solar System?*

A.: In the past few years there have been many reports in the news about the discovery of planets orbiting several stars in our galaxy. These planets can *not* be seen in the telescopes of amateur astronomers. In fact, no

> **Since the discovery in 1995 that the sun-like star, 51 Pegasi, had a planet orbiting it, dozens of other planets have been discovered orbiting other stars, but none of these "extra-solar" planets has been "seen" in the way we observe the planets in our Solar System.**

telescope on the surface of the Earth, even the very largest, is able to give a view of any of these planets. These planets are far too distant, too faint and too close to the glare of their stars to be seen. They were discovered only because very sensitive telescope equipment was able to detect very slight movements of the stars, caused by the orbits of the planets.

The first *sun-like* star known to have a planet orbiting it was the star called *51 Pegasi*. (See Chapter 5, Section 3 – The Flamsteed Number System) This star is in the constellation Pegasus. In early October 1995, astronomers Michel Mayor and Didier Queloz announced that, after using the telescope and other equipment at the Haute Provence Observatory in France, they had detected slight movements in this star. Calculations showed that the planet must be at least half as massive as Jupiter, be only seven million kilometres from the star, and have an orbital period of only about four and a quarter days. The reported observations were soon confirmed by others, including a team of astronomers at Lick Observatory in California. At no time was the planet itself "seen."

The star *51 Pegasi* can be easily found near the Great Square in the constellation Pegasus. It is about half-way between the two bright stars on the *western side* of the large square. (See Star Maps 4, 5, and 6.) In fact, on Maps 4 and 5, it is located just to the left of the letter P in the word "Pegasus."

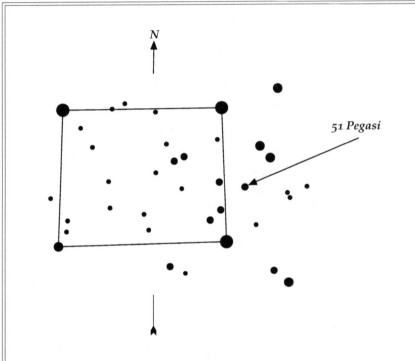

Locating the Star *51 Pegasi*

This map shows the stars visible to the naked eye under excellent "dark sky" conditions, that is, stars of magnitude 6 or brighter, in, and just west of, the Great Square of Pegasus. (For the region of the sky, see Star Maps 4, 5, and 6.) *51 Pegasi*, a star of magnitude 5.5, is marked with the arrow. Under most observing conditions, binoculars should be used to see it.

25

A Glossary of Astronomical Terms

Rather than being precise and technical definitions, the following explanations are intended to be practical and helpful to a beginning amateur astronomer who may have encountered these words for the first time without knowing how they are usually understood in the amateur astronomical community.

albedo: the ability of a planet, or other body in the Solar System, to reflect sunlight. Albedo is usually given by a number between 0 and 1. If an object has an albedo of 0, it reflects none of the light striking it; at the opposite extreme, if it has an albedo of 1, it reflects all of the light striking it. As examples, the "poorly reflective" Mercury has a low albedo of 0.11, whereas the "brilliantly reflective" Venus has high albedo of 0.65.

altitude: measure of the angular distance of an object above the horizon. An object at the horizon has an altitude of 0 degrees. An object at the zenith (directly overhead) has an altitude of 90 degrees.

aphelion: that point in the orbit of a Solar System body at which it is farthest from the Sun.

apogee: that point in the orbit of an object, such as the Moon, at which it is farthest from the Earth. In addition to describing a point on the Moon's orbit, the word can also describe a point on the orbits of all artificial Earth satellites.

asterism: a recognizable group, or grouping, of stars, either within a recognized constellation or involving stars of several constellations. Examples of asterisms within a single constellation are the Big Dipper within Ursa Major, and the Pleiades and the Hyades, both within the constellation Taurus. Examples of asterisms involving stars of several constellations are the Summer Triangle and the Winter Hexagon.

asteroid: a Solar System object smaller than a planet and orbiting the Sun. Most (but not all) asteroids are found within the asteroid belt, which is located between the orbits of the planets Mars and Jupiter.

astronomical unit (a. u.): the mean ("average") distance between the Sun and the Earth, approximately 149.6 million kilometres or 8 1/3 light minutes.

aurora: the glow produced in the upper atmosphere when billions of sub-atomic particles from the Sun are captured by the Earth's magnetic field, and then interact with molecules of various gases in the upper atmosphere. (See Chapter 18, concerning the aurora.) The aurora of the regions surrounding the Earth's North Magnetic Pole is called the Aurora Borealis (Latin: the Northern Dawn); that of the regions surrounding the South Magnetic Pole is called the Aurora Australis (Latin: the Southern Dawn). The popular terms are "the Northern Lights" and "the Southern Lights."

averted vision: a "looking slightly away" from the object one is viewing, or attempting to view, in order that its light may fall on a more light-sensitive part of the eye. This practice often greatly improves the chance of seeing or recognizing very faint objects.

azimuth: the angular distance of an object along the horizon, measured from the north point on the horizon. An object at the East point on the horizon has an azimuth of 90 degrees, at the South point 180 degrees, and at the West point 270 degrees. The position of any star, planet, or celestial object can be defined by numbers giving its azimuth and altitude at any given time. However, because of the Earth's constant rotation on its axis and the constant change in the azimuth and altitude of any object in the sky, it is essential to state the time whenever this system is used. Most astronomers prefer to use a "sky-based" system, rather than this "horizon-based" system. (See **Right Ascension** and **Declination**.)

binoculars: a viewing device composed of aligned lenses, and often prisms, attached side-by-side, like a pair of refracting telescopes, in order to allow viewing with both eyes.

black hole: a massive collapsed star whose gravitational field is so enormously strong that nothing, not even light, is able to escape from it.

bolide: a name for an extremely bright meteor, one that is brighter than Venus, which can be magnitude - 4.6, and one that is often seen exploding in the atmosphere.

cataclysmic variable (or cataclysmic variable star): a type of variable star that suddenly and dramatically changes its brightness. "Flare stars" and "novae" are examples of cataclysmic variable stars.

celestial equator: the line that divides the celestial sphere in half. The celestial equator is directly above the Earth's equator, and has the same purpose in the sky as the Earth's equator has for the Earth. Just as latitude on Earth is measured in degrees, 0 degrees to 90 degrees, north and south of the equator, so also on the sky, declination is measured in degrees, 0 degrees to 90 degrees, north and south of the celestial equator.

celestial pole: a point on the sky that is 90 degrees north and 90 degrees south declination, measured from the celestial equator. The imaginary line between the Earth's north pole and its south pole is the axis of rotation of the Earth; the extension of this line into space meets the celestial sphere at the north celestial pole and the south celestial pole, the only two points on the celestial sphere where there is no apparent movement of celestial objects because of the Earth's rotation. The celestial poles are precisely above the Earth's poles.

celestial sphere: the sky above the Earth. It is represented as a great sphere that we can view from the inside. For convenience, when we study this sphere, we temporarily assume that all celestial objects are at the same distance. Like the Earth, which is at its centre, the celestial sphere is divided in half by an equator (the celestial equator) and has two poles (the north and south celestial poles).

circumpolar: a word describing stars and constellations that are visible at any time of night throughout the whole year, because of the fact that they are located close enough to the celestial pole always to be seen above the horizon, as viewed from a certain latitude on Earth.

clock drive: a mechanical device that is part of some telescopes, in order that the telescope may move in a certain direction and continue to point to a certain object, to compensate for the Earth's rotation on its axis.

comet: a class of objects within our Solar System, any one of which is composed of ices, dust, and rocky material, and usually has an orbit that is more eccentric (elongated) than that of a planet or asteroid.

conjunction: the position of a planet or other Solar System object at the time when it appears in the sky to be close to the Sun, or to another planet, or to another Solar System object. (The planets Mercury and Venus, which are called inferior planets, because their orbits lie inside the orbit of the Earth, have two kinds of conjunctions (with the Sun): (1) an **inferior conjunction**, when the planet appears closest to the Sun, and is on the "near" side of its orbit, and (2) a **superior conjunction**, when the planet appears closest to the Sun and is on the far side of its orbit. (See also **transit**.)

constellation: any one of 88 areas into which the sky has been divided. The number of constellations has varied throughout history. (The boundaries of the current 88 constellations were established by the International Astronomical Union in 1930, and that number has been the standard since then.) In popular culture, and in times past, a constellation has usually meant an imaginary figure of a hero, an animal, or an object, often taken from an ancient myth and formed by an imaginary connection of the bright stars in one of these areas.

corona: the outer region of the Sun's atmosphere, an extremely hot part of its atmosphere. This is what provides the spectacular sight at the time of a total solar eclipse for those who are able to view it from within the path of totality.

culmination: the highest point in the sky reached by a star or other celestial object; it occurs when the star or other object crosses the **meridian**.

dark adaptation: the process of having the eye become sensitive to low or faint levels of light. When a person remains in a dark environment for 15 to 30 minutes, (s)he becomes "dark adapted," that is, is better able to distinguish faint objects.

declination: a measure of the distance of an object in the sky from the **celestial equator**. North of the celestial equator, the distance is measured in degrees, from 0 degrees to 90 degrees, from the celestial equator to the North Celestial Pole, and is designated by a plus sign (+) or by the letter "N." South of the celestial equator, the distance is measured in degrees, from 0 degrees to 90 degrees, from the celestial equator to the South Celestial Pole, and is designated by a minus sign (-) or by the letter "S."

degree: the standard unit of measurement to indicate angular distance on the sky. By convention, a complete circle going all the way around the sky is 360 degrees. A quarter-circle, such as the angular distance between the horizon and the zenith is 90 degrees. Two stars that appear to be separated by the width of a fist held at arm's length are said to be about 10 degrees apart. The width of a fingernail at arm's length indicates about one degree. For smaller units of measurement, a degree is divided into 60 arc minutes, and for even smaller units, an arc minute may be divided into 60 arc seconds.

eccentricity: in describing the orbit of a Solar System body: the amount by which that elliptical orbit differs from a perfect circular orbit. (See definition of a **comet**.) The degree of eccentricity is designated by a number between 0 and 1. A perfectly circular orbit would have an eccentricity of 0. The more elongated or "squeezed" an orbit is, the more its eccentricity approaches the number 1. A perfect circle has one centre or focus. An ellipse of slight eccentricity has two foci (the plural of the word "focus") that are relatively close to each other, but an ellipse of greater eccentricity has two foci that are relatively farther apart. As examples, the orbit of Earth, which is close to being circular, has an eccentricity of 0.0167, whereas the orbit of Pluto, which is much more elliptical, has an eccentricity of 0.2491.

eclipse: (lunar eclipse): the phenomena (events) that occur when the Full Moon passes through the Earth's shadow or a part of the Earth's shadow. If the disk of the Moon, as seen from the Earth, does not completely enter, but only partially enters, the Earth's shadow or umbra, the event is called a *Partial Lunar Eclipse*. If the disk of the Moon enters and passes through only the penumbra, or the tenuous, outer shadow of the Earth, the event is called a *Penumbral Lunar Eclipse*. If the disk of the Moon, as seen from the Earth, completely enters the umbra, or the darker central core of the Earth's shadow, the event is called a *Total Lunar Eclipse*.

eclipse: (solar eclipse): the phenomena (events) which occur when the New Moon passes between the Sun and the Earth so that the Moon's shadow falls on some part of the Earth. If the disk of the Moon completely covers the Sun's disk, as seen from certain places on the Earth, the event is called a *Total Solar Eclipse*. If the disk of the Moon covers only part of the Sun's disk, as seen from certain places on Earth, the event is called a *Partial Solar Eclipse*. If the New Moon occurs near the time when it appears slightly smaller than usual

(See apogee.), or if the event occurs near the time when the Earth is nearer the Sun than usual making the Sun appear larger than usual (See perihelion.), the event may be called an *Annular Solar Eclipse*, meaning that, as seen from the path of the eclipse, the Sun will appear as a ring when the disk of the Moon passes in front of it.

eclipse season: the two (occasionally three) periods of time each year within which all solar and lunar eclipses occur. Each eclipse season lasts slightly more than a month. A second one begins about 173 days after the year's first one begins. A third eclipse season begins about 346 days after the beginning of the year's first one; and so, if the first eclipse season of the year begins in early January, then a third one begins in December of the same year. In each eclipse season, there are always two, and sometimes three, eclipses. In each eclipse season, there is at least one solar eclipse and at least one lunar eclipse. If a "major eclipse," such as a total solar eclipse of long duration, occurs in the central part of an eclipse season, then there are usually two "minor eclipses" in the early and late parts of that season — such as a penumbral lunar eclipse both two weeks before, and two weeks after, the date of the major solar eclipse. In short, whenever a solar eclipse occurs, there is always a lunar eclipse either two weeks before, or two weeks later, or both. Similarly whenever a lunar eclipse occurs, there is always a solar eclipse either two weeks before, or two weeks later, or both. Of course, popularly, the frequency of eclipses is not appreciated because most solar eclipses are seen over a smaller area of the Earth's surface than are most lunar eclipses.

eclipsing binary: a double star system (or multiple star system) in which one star passes in front of the other one, as seen from the Earth, causing the system to appear to be a variable star. As the two stars orbit their common centre of gravity, they produce a very regular pattern of varying brightness.

ecliptic: the apparent path of the Sun around the sky. It is really the projection on the sky of the Earth's orbit around the Sun. Since, in our Solar System, the plane of each planet's orbit around the Sun is fairly close to the plane of the Earth's orbit (with the exception of Pluto), the planets also appear near the Sun's apparent path in the sky, that is, near the ecliptic. (See also **zodiac**.)

epoch: the period of time for which the positional coordinates of objects on a star chart are intended. Because of the very slow process known to astronomers as the "precession of the equinoxes," which results in a very gradual change in the celestial coordinates (See **Right Ascension** and **Declination**.) of objects in the sky, the epoch of many star maps and atlases has been revised every 50 years. Traditional atlases in our time have been, for example, for Epoch 1900, Epoch 1950, or Epoch 2000. For practical purposes, most amateur astronomers need not worry at all about the small differences between a star's coordinates given on an Epoch 1950 map and those given on an Epoch 2000 map. Beginning astronomers must understand that this gradual change is NOT an actual change in any star's position, but only a slight and very slow shifting in the coordinate system that we impose on the sky in order to recognize the shifting caused by the Earth's "wobble" as it spins on its axis over a period of over 26 000 years, a "wobble" that causes the celestial poles to move about in a circle over that same period.

equation of time: the difference between the time shown by a sundial and the time shown by a clock. "Sundial time" is apparent solar time. "Clock time" is mean solar time. The difference is due to the fact that the Earth's orbit is not a circle, but an ellipse. If the Earth's orbit were a circle, the two would always be the same. As it is, apparent solar time may vary from mean solar time by as much as 16 to 17 minutes at certain regular times during the year.

equatorial mount: the mounting or the "controlling and pointing" structure of a telescope designed so that the "polar axis" is parallel to the axis of rotation of the Earth and the "declination axis" is perpendicular to it, or in other words, parallel to the celestial equator. With such a system, a telescope can be pointed at celestial object or at the celestial position representing the coordinates of a known object, enabling the desired object to be located more easily than otherwise.

equinox: (1) one of two points in the sky at which the **ecliptic** crosses the **celestial equator**. The *vernal equinox* is designated 0 hours Right Ascension, 0 degrees Declination. The *autumnal equinox* is designated 12 hours Right Ascension, 0 degrees Declination.

(2) one of two times in the year at which the Sun, in its annual apparent path around the sky, crosses the celestial equator. The first such date in the year, the one traditionally called "*the spring equinox*" in the Northern Hemisphere, occurs about March 21. The second one in the year, the one traditionally called "*the autumnal equinox*" in the Northern Hemisphere, occurs about September 21 or 22.

extinction (also called *atmospheric extinction*): a reduction in the usual brightness of a star, planet, or other celestial object, when it is seen near the horizon. This fading is caused by the fact that the light from the object must pass through more atmosphere than when the object is seen overhead or near the zenith. (Light from an object near the horizon is also affected by **refraction**.)

eyepiece (also called *ocular*): a small device composed of one or several lenses and placed at the focal point of a telescope's lens or mirror, in order to magnify the image. If the **focal lengths** of both the telescope and the eyepiece are known, the magnification (power) of the system may be calculated simply be dividing the telescope's focal length by the eyepiece's focal length. For example, an eyepiece of focal length 40mm used in a telescope whose focal length is 2000mm gives 50 power. (2000mm / 40mm = 50 X)

finder scope (also called a '*finder*'): a relatively small, low-power telescope attached to a larger telescope and used to assist an observer in bringing a celestial object into the larger telescope's field of view. If the "**finder**" is properly mounted and precisely aligned with the larger telescope, the "centring" of an object in the finder will ensure that it is within the field of view of the main telescope.

fireball (also called *bolide*): an extremely bright meteor, often one that is much brighter than the planet Venus.

flare: a short-lived and very bright eruption in the atmosphere of the Sun, and sometimes in the atmospheres of other stars.

focal length: in a telescope, the distance between the main lens or mirror and the point at which the light rays converge or reach a focal point. In an eyepiece, it is the distance from the centre of the lens (or the primary lens, if there are several) and the point at which the light rays converge or reach a focal point.

focal point (or focus): in a telescope, the point at which the rays of light, passing through the main (or objective) lens or reflected from the main (or primary) mirror, converge or meet.

galaxy: a very large grouping or collection of stars, much more massive than a globular star cluster. At one time **galaxies** were called "*nebulae*," a term now used for massive conglomerations of gas and dust.

gibbous: in regard to the Moon: the phase in which the visible disk is seen to be more than half, but less than completely, illuminated.

globular cluster: a large, massive, densely populated and very old group of stars that are gravitationally associated with each other. (Compare **open cluster**.)

gravitation (or gravity): the mutual attraction of all objects in the universe. This force of attraction of two objects is defined by Newton's Law of Gravity as being proportional to their masses and inversely proportional to the square of the distance between them.

heliacal rising: the rising of star, planet, or other celestial object with the rising of the Sun, or at the same time as the Sun rises. In practice, and historically, it has meant the first occasion on which a star, planet, or other heavenly object can be seen rising before the Sun rises.

H - R diagram (Hertzsprung-Russel diagram): a well-known graph on which stars are plotted on one axis according to their colour or temperature and on the other axis according to their luminosity or absolute magnitude. During the life-cycle of a star, it may appear in the "main sequence" or central region of the graph, and later in its life-cycle, it may appear in what is called the "red giant branch," and still later, in what is called the "white dwarf region." The diagram is named after two scientists who first used its ideas to explain stellar evolution.

hour: astronomically, in stating the position or the coordinates of a star or celestial object, either in the sky or on a star map: the primary unit of measurement in Right Ascension, measured around the celestial equator. There are 24 hours, just as there are 360 degrees measured around the Earth's equator. Each hour may be divided into 60 minutes of Right Ascension, and each minute may be divided into 60 seconds.

IC (Index Catalogue): designation for the deep sky objects, such as galaxies, nebulae, and star clusters, listed in this catalogue, which was originally published in 1895 and 1908 as a supplement to the NGC. (See NGC.)

inferior planet: a planet whose orbit is inside the orbit of Earth. Mercury and Venus are the inferior planets of our Solar System.

interstellar: referring to gas, dust, or any material lying in the regions between the stars.

Jovian: relating to, comparable to, or classified with, Jupiter, the largest and most massive planet in our Solar System.

Kuiper Belt: the region, in the outer Solar System beyond the orbit of Neptune, within which large numbers of icy objects are found. These objects, which are much smaller than the major planets, are often called TNO's (TransNeptunian Objects).

libration: a change in the Moon's orientation, because of which we are able to see from the Earth, over the course of a month, more than one half of the lunar surface. In fact, it has been possible to see up to 59% of the Moon's surface simply because of libration, which is caused by the fact that the Moon's rotation is not in perfect harmony with its revolution around the Earth and from the fact that its orbit is slightly elliptical, rather than perfectly circular.

light year: the distance that light travels in a vacuum in one year. At a speed of about 300 000 kilometres per second, light travels over 6 trillion kilometres per year. (Note that this is a unit of distance, not of time.)

limb: the edge of the apparent disk of the Sun, Moon, or a planet.

Local Group: the group of galaxies to which our Milky Way Galaxy and the Andromeda Galaxy and more than a dozen other galaxies belong. (A recent listing of the Local Group of Galaxies, that includes the Large and Small Magellanic Clouds, that are satellites of the Milky Way, has a total of 25 members.)

luminosity: the actual or intrinsic brightness (or absolute magnitude) of a star or other celestial object.

lunar month (also called "*the synodic month*"): the time between two successive New Moons or two successive Full Moons. It is 29.530589 days. It is to be noted that the lunar phases are determined by the relative positions of Sun, Moon, and Earth, and with the Earth-Moon system in annual orbit around the Sun, those relative positions will change over a period of a month. The Moon's real orbital period, that is, the time between its twice appearing within the same group of background stars (also called "*the sidereal month*") is different from, and shorter than, the lunar month. This real orbital period (or sidereal month) is 27.321662 days. With the Moon always having virtually the same side facing the Earth, we could say that the Moon's rotation period, or the lunar day, is the same as its true orbital period around the Earth, that is, about 27 1/3 days. In this sense, the "lunar day" is shorter than the "lunar month" by only about 2 "Earth days."

M (or M objects): belonging to the famous list of over 100 objects, mainly galaxies, nebulae, and star clusters, compiled by the seventeenth century comet-hunter, Charles Messier. The list is usually called The Messier Catalogue, and its objects are among the finest and most interesting objects that a beginning amateur astronomer can observe.

Messier Marathon: an attempt to observe in one night all of the objects of the Messier Catalogue, such as those 110 Messier objects recognized by the RASC and listed in the Observer's Handbook. The best time for completing such a "marathon" is a clear, moonless night near the Vernal Equinox.

mare (Latin: "sea"): the term used to designate one of the large, dark plains where lava once flowed over certain areas of the Moon. The term "**mare**" was a mistake; these areas may once have looked like watery oceans and lakes to eyes unaided by telescopes, but the Moon has no seas!

Mars: the fourth planet of our Solar System. It is smaller and colder than Earth, but Earth-like in many ways, has polar caps, seasons, and a tenuous atmosphere.

Mercury: the Solar System's innermost planet. It is smaller, much hotter, and much more cratered than planet Earth.

meridian: an imaginary line through the sky from the North point on the horizon through the zenith to the South point on the horizon. Stars, planets, and other celestial objects, including the Sun during the daytime, are at their highest point in the sky when they cross the meridian. This *"crossing of the meridian"* is also known as the *"culmination"* of these objects. (See **culmination**.)

meteor: one of the many particles from space, composed of pieces of rock, dust, and ice, that enter the Earth's atmosphere and are seen streaking across the sky. If such particles actually hit the Earth, either land or ocean, they are called *"meteorites."*

Milky Way: the large spiral galaxy to which our Sun and its system of planets, along with over 200 billion other stars, belong. Observationally, the name is also used for the night sky's great band of light produced by the stars, nebulae, clusters, and integrated starlight in the disk and arms of the galaxy.

mount (or mounting): the structure that supports a telescope and permits it to be pointed at a certain region of the sky. Since its invention, the telescope, when being used, has been placed on a mount of some kind, to provide stability. Galileo's telescope had a simple "ball and socket" mount, a kind of mount that easily allowed it to be pointed in any direction. Modern telescope mounts used by amateur astronomer are usually of two kinds: (1) the *alt-azimuth mount*, which, in a simple fashion, allows the telescope to be directed toward an object in any direction around the horizon, and up to any altitude above the horizon, right up to the zenith, and (2) the *equatorial mount*, which, in a more complicated fashion and because of an axis that must be aligned to the Celestial Pole, allows the telescope to rotate about that axis and follow celestial objects as the Earth rotates. With a battery-powered or electrically-powered "clock drive" incorporated in such a mount, the telescope can automatically follow a celestial object for prolonged periods of time. (See **telescope design**.)

multiple star: two or more stars which are gravitationally bound, or connected, with each of them orbiting their common centre of gravity. If there are only two stars, they may also be called a *"binary," "binary system,"* or *"double star."*

nadir: on the celestial sphere: a point that is below the observer and directly opposite, or 180 degrees from, the zenith. The point is unseen because it is in the direction of the centre of the Earth, but beyond the Earth.

N.E.O. (Near Earth Object): an asteroid or comet whose orbit causes it to pass close to Earth.

nebula: a diffuse structure composed of interstellar gas and dust. There are several types of nebulae. **Emission nebulae** (also called *"bright nebulae"*) glow somewhat as do neon lights, as they re-emit energy originally produced by nearby stars. **Absorption nebulae** (also called *"dark nebulae"*) appear dark as they block the light from stars behind them. *Reflection nebulae* are dark clouds of gas and dust that have been illuminated by reflected, rather than absorbed and re-emitted light, from nearby stars. *Planetary nebulae* are the glowing shells of gas that have been ejected from an unstable star at a certain stage in its evolution. In the past, the disk-like appearance of such nebulae reminded astronomers of planets, when they were seen in their telescopes, though they are not planets in any way.

Neptune: the eighth major planet in our Solar System. It is the most distant of the four "giant gas planets."

neutron star: an extremely dense spherical object that has had the electrons stripped from its atoms, and thus it is composed of extremely densely packed neutrons.

N.G.C. (New General Catalogue): the designation used for any one of the objects listed in this large catalogue of nebulae, galaxies, and star clusters — originally composed by J. L. E. Dreyer in 1888. There are 7840 objects listed in the catalogue.

node: one of the two points at which the orbit of a Solar System object (usually either the Moon or a planet) intersects the ecliptic (which is the Sun's apparent path around the sky, resulting from the Earth's actual orbit around the Sun). (See **ecliptic**.) The point at which the Moon or planet crosses the ecliptic going from south to north is called the *ascending node*. The point at which the object crosses the ecliptic going from north to south is called the *descending node*.

nova (from Latin "*stella nova*," i.e., "new star"): a star that appears quite suddenly and usually brightens very rapidly.

nucleus: (1) the central core of an atom, composed of protons and neutrons, and around which the electrons revolve.

(2) the solid core of a comet, the part that releases gas and dust to form a coma and a tail, as the comet travels in the inner part of the Solar System.

(3) the bright central core of a spiral galaxy.

objective lens (or **objective**): in a refracting telescope or binoculars: the larger lens, i.e., the one that gathers the light and brings it to a focus.

oblateness: the degree to which a planet is "flattened;" it is mathematically expressed by a number that is the ratio of the planet's equatorial diameter to its polar diameter. Rapidly rotating gaseous planets, such as Jupiter, are more oblate than more slowly rotating, solid planets, such as Earth.

obliquity (of the ecliptic): the angle between the plane of a planet's equator and the plane of its orbit around the Sun. This is the same angle as the one between the planet's axis of rotation and a line perpendicular to its orbit. In the case of Earth, the angle is 23.4 degrees. In the case of the planet Uranus, this angle is much larger.

occultation: a 'hiding' of a selected astronomical object, specifically, the passage of an apparently larger celestial object, such as the Moon, in front of an apparently smaller celestial object, such as a star or planet, so that the apparently smaller object is hidden from our view for a period of time. The precise timing of the beginning and the end of such an occultation event can enable astronomers to refine their knowledge of certain facts, such as the precise size and shape of the Moon.

Oort Cloud: a very large and spherical region of comets surrounding our Solar System, far out beyond the orbit of Pluto. It is named after the astronomer who proposed its existence.

opposition: the position of a planet, or other Solar System object, when it is located in that part of the sky which is opposite to where the Sun is.

parsec: a unit of distance employed by astronomers when they measure enormously large distances. One parsec is about 3.26 light years. (See **light year**.) A *kiloparsec* is 1000 parsecs, which is about 3260 light years. A *megaparsec* is 1 000 000 parsecs, which is about 3 260 000 light years.

penumbra: (1) in describing features visible on the solar disk: the outer, lighter-coloured parts of a sunspot, the central, darker region of which is called the umbra.

(2) in describing a solar eclipse: the lighter, outer shadow of the Moon, from within which an observer may see a partial eclipse. From within the darker, central part of the Moon's shadow, an observer may see a total solar eclipse.

(3) in describing a lunar eclipse: the lighter, outer shadow of the Earth. If the Full Moon enters only this part of the shadow, the event is called a Penumbral Lunar Eclipse, but if the Full Moon partially enters the Earth's umbra, while being partially within the penumbra, the event is called a Partial Lunar Eclipse.

perigee: the point in the orbit of the Moon (or other Solar System object) at which the Moon (or other object) comes closest to the Earth.

perihelion: the point in the orbit of the Earth, other planet, comet, or any other Solar System object at which the object comes closest to the Sun.

perturbation: the deviation in a Solar System object's orbit from the path the object would follow if it were unaffected by the gravitational force of any other object other than the Sun. Perturbations have been noticed in the orbits of some planets because of the gravitational pull of other planets and in the orbits of comets when they pass near a planet.

phase: the part of a planet's or of a satellite's surface that appears illuminated, as viewed from Earth at a certain time. Half of the Moon's surface is always illuminated by sunlight (except at the times of a lunar eclipse), but when we see only a small amount of the illuminated half, we say that the Moon is at the "crescent phase," and when we see half of the illuminated half of the Moon, we say that the Moon is at the "quarter phase." In chronological order, the principal lunar phases are: new, waxing crescent, first quarter, waxing gibbous, full, waning gibbous, last quarter, and waning crescent. The "inner planets" or "inferior planets," that is, Mercury and Venus, show us a variety of phases, similar to those of the Moon. The "outer planets" or "superior planets" show us some "change of phase," but it is never more than a slight variation from "the full phase."

photosphere: the name given to the visible surface of the Sun.

planet: an object that orbits a star and is of a certain size and mass. Major planets are less massive than any star. In our Solar System, the planets are more massive than comets, asteroids, and the objects in the Kuiper Belt, which is beyond the orbit of Neptune. Some astronomers have expressed doubt about classifying Pluto as a planet, saying that it should be regarded as the foremost of the Kuiper Belt Objects.

planetarium: a mechanical projection device that is used to project an image of the night sky on a domed ceiling. The term is also used for the building or theatre that contains such a projection device.

Pluto: an icy object at the outer edge of our Solar System with an orbit that carries it around the Sun in about 248 years. It was discovered in 1930 by Clyde Tombaugh.

power: astronomically, the amount of magnification of an image obtained by using certain binoculars or by using a certain telescope with a certain eyepiece. For all telescopes, there is an ideal range of powers (or magnification), with the maximum possible powers often producing poor images of the targeted object, for several reasons. "Power" (or more properly "magnification") in a telescope is determined by (1) focal length of the objective (that is, the main lens or the main mirror) and (2) the focal length of the eyepiece used. The number representing the amount of magnification may be calculated by dividing (1) by (2), assuming that the two are expressed in the same units.

primary (or primary mirror): the main mirror of a telescope, the one that gathers the light and reflects it to a focal point.

prominence: an ejection of hot gas from the surface of the Sun, when such an event occurs at the limb or edge of the Sun's disk. When such events are seen *on* the Sun's disk, they are known as *filaments*.

pulsar: a rapidly rotating neutron star that emits rapid pulses of radio energy.

quasar (literally: "*quasi-stellar object*"): a bright object at the core of a very distant galaxy. The great energy produced by a quasar is probably derived from the gravitational pull of a black hole. Most quasars appear faint because of their extremely great distance.

red giant: a very large, low-density, "cooler-than-average" star, at a late stage in its evolution, after the outer shell has expanded to its enormous size.

refraction: the bending of light, an event that occurs when light passes through a lens. This is what makes the refracting telescope possible.

resolution: the ability of certain binoculars or telescopes to give detail to objects that are being viewed, and cleanly to separate objects that appear very close to each other.

resolving power (or **resolution**): the least angular distance between two objects that can be clearly distinguished in certain binoculars or a certain telescope with a given eyepiece. To obtain the greatest resolving power (or resolution), a telescope should have clean, good quality optical parts, and be used under clear, unpolluted skies, with good "**seeing**" conditions.

retrograde motion: in regard to the apparent movement of a planet in the sky: moving backwards or moving in the opposite to "the usual and normal direction of movement." Normally, the apparent path of the superior planets around the sky is from right to left, that is, from west to east along the ecliptic, but for a while, both before and after the time of the planet's opposition, the planet appears to have *retrograde motion*, moving from east to west, before again beginning its normal motion.

Right Ascension (R.A.): a measurement of distance in the sky, similar to longitude on Earth. Right Ascension, or R.A., is measured eastward in the sky from the point known as the **Vernal Equinox**, with the unit of measurement being the *hour*, each of which may be divided into 60 *minutes*, each of which may be again divided into 60 seconds. There are 24 *hours* of Right Ascension in a complete circle around the whole celestial sphere.

Saturn: the sixth major planet in the Solar System. Saturn has numerous Moons and a spectacular ring system that may be seen in binoculars and amateur telescopes. Being smaller than Jupiter, it is the second largest planet of the Solar System.

secondary mirror: in a reflecting telescope: a mirror, smaller than the primary (or main mirror), used to redirect the light from the primary. In a Newtonian telescope, the secondary mirror is a flat mirror mounted in the light path at a 45 degree angle to the direction of the light path, in order to direct the light through a hole in the side of the tube, where an eyepiece can be inserted to magnify the light that has come to a focus. In a Schmidt-Cassegrain telescope, a slightly convex secondary mirror is mounted perpendicular to the direction of the light path, in order to reflect the light back through a hole in the primary to a point where an eyepiece can be inserted to magnify the light that has come to a focus.

seeing: an estimate of the steadiness of the air above an observing site. In some cases, astronomers use a rough scale (with the numbers 1 to 10) to estimate steadiness of images and lack of turbulence or twinkling. In other cases, astronomers list the closest binary stars that can be clearly resolved at a certain time. For instance, "2-arc second seeing" means that conditions allowed the two components of a binary system whose stars were 2 arc seconds apart to be clearly resolved into two stars. Besides some factors relating to personal ability and equipment used, the quality of an image in a telescope depends on *the seeing and the transparency at the observing site.* (See **transparency**.)

Solar System: the Sun and all the objects within its gravitational influence, including major and minor planets (asteroids), comets, Kuiper Belt objects, and Oort Cloud objects. Within the last decade, we have learned that other stars also have planets, and probably many stars have "complete systems" like our Solar System.

solar wind: gases, mainly ionized hydrogen and helium, hurled outward from the Sun. It is those particles brought from the Sun that affect the Earth's radiation belt and upper atmosphere, and eventually cause the Aurora. Rather than travelling at light speed (300 000 kilometres per second) and arriving from the Sun in 8.3 minutes, the solar wind particles, in fact, travel at a speed in the range of about 300 to 800 kilometres per second, with the particles arriving in the vicinity of Earth within a couple of days after their leaving the Sun.

solstice: (1) one of the two celestial points along the ecliptic at which the Sun is located when it is farthest from the celestial equator. The Summer Solstice (SS) is at Right Ascension 6 hours 0 minutes, Declination + 23.4 degrees. It is near the border between the constellations Gemini and Taurus. The Winter Solstice

(WS) is at Right Ascension 18 hours 0 minutes, Declination - 23.4 degrees. It is in the constellation Sagittarius. WS and SS are marked on the Star Maps in this book.

(2) one of the two times in the year at which the Sun, in its annual apparent path around the sky, is farthest north or farthest south of the celestial equator. (The word "solstice" derives from the two Latin words referring to "the Sun" and "standing still," a reference to the change at these times in the north-south direction of the Sun's movement on the celestial sphere.) The first solstice in the year, the one traditionally called "the summer solstice" (though it is not summer in the southern hemisphere), occurs on, or about, June 21. That date is traditionally associated with "the longest day of the year" in the northern hemisphere, and at that time, for observers in the northern hemisphere, the Sun, when it crosses the **meridian** at local noon, appears highest in the sky of any time in the year. The second solstice in the year, the one traditionally called "the winter solstice" (although it is not winter in the southern hemisphere), occurs on, or about, December 21. That is the date traditionally associated with "the shortest day of the year" in the northern hemisphere, and at that time, for observers in the northern hemisphere, the Sun, when it crosses the **meridian** at local noon, appears lowest in the sky of any time in the year.

star: a very hot sphere of gas gravitationally bound together, with a mass that is sufficient to ignite nuclear fusion in the core of the sphere. Certain types of so-called stars may not precisely fit the definition: neutron stars, which are extremely condensed spheres made up of atomic nuclei; white dwarfs, which are very condensed objects; and brown dwarfs, which probably have too little mass to sustain full nuclear fusion.

sunspot: a relatively dark and relatively cooler area on the Sun's surface or photosphere, caused by local magnetic fields. Sunspots appear in an 11-year cycle, through which they range from being very numerous to being very scarce or absent, and they are studied and recorded by amateur astronomers who observe them on every day when it is possible to see the Sun.

supernova: a star that has had a cataclysmic explosion. Supernovae become at least a hundred times brighter than novae, and often rival, or exceed, the brightness of the distant galaxies within which they are found.

synchronous rotation: words used to describe the fact that the Moon rotates once on its axis over the same period of time that it takes to orbit the Earth.

synodic period: (1) in regard to the Moon: the time between the Moon's twice showing the same phase, that is, the time between one New Moon and the next New Moon, or between one Full Moon and the next Full Moon. At about 29.53 days, it is over two days longer than the Moon's sidereal period, which is the interval of time for the Moon to pass twice in front of the same fixed stars.

(2) in regard to the superior planets of the Solar System (that is, those with orbits larger than that of Earth): the period of time between a planet's being twice at opposition (in the opposite direction of the sky from the direction of the Sun) *or* being twice in conjunction with the Sun, that is, in the same direction in the sky as the direction of the Sun. (This information provides a close approximation to the precise synodic period of a planet, which is calculated from a mathematical formula using the actual sidereal periods of the planets and of the Earth.) For Mars the synodic period of 780 days is more than its actual sidereal period of 687 days, whereas Neptune's synodic period of 367 days is far less than its actual sidereal period of about 164 years.

(3) in regard to the inferior planets (that is, those with orbits smaller than that of Earth, namely Mercury and Venus): the period of time between the planet's being twice at the *same* conjunction with the Sun. An inferior conjunction of Mercury or Venus, as viewed from the Earth, occurs when the planet is in the same direction in the sky as the Sun, and is on the near side of the Sun. A superior conjunction of Mercury or Venus, as viewed from the Earth, occurs when the planet is in the same direction in the sky as the Sun and is on the far side of the Sun. For Mercury the synodic period of 116 days is more than its actual sidereal period of about 88 days, and for Venus, the synodic period of 584 days is more than the actual sidereal period of about 225 days.

tail: in regard to a comet: the long streamers of gas and dust that are hurled off the nucleus, as it travels in the inner part of the Solar System.

telescope: an instrument used to gather light and focus it, so that a distant object, which was the source of the light, may be studied.

telescope types: (a) *reflecting telescope* (or *reflector*): the type of telescope that uses a mirror to gather and focus the light from a distant source.

(b) *refracting telescope* (or *refractor*): the type of telescope that uses a lens (also called an objective lens or objective) to gather and focus the light from a distant source.

telescope designs: (a) *Cassegrain*: a reflecting telescope in which the light from a distant object is reflected from a primary or main mirror and is again reflected by a secondary mirror placed within the light path so that the light returns and passes through a hole in the primary mirror, and then comes to a focus. The lens of an eyepiece can then magnify the light at the focal point, and so the distant object can be studied. The design is named after a French scientist, N. Cassegrain, who proposed the design in 1672.

(b) *Dobsonian*: (See also **mount**.) a Newtonian reflecting telescope that has a simple mount, allowing the telescope easily to rotate to any direction of the compass (azimuth) and up to any elevation above the horizon (altitude). In short, the mount is often called 'an alt-azimuth' mount. This design was made popular by the American amateur, John Dobson, in the 1980s when he often set up his telescope on the sidewalks and street corners in San Francisco.

(c) *Equatorial*: (See also **mount**.) a type of telescope whose mount allows it to keep a celestial object in the field of view for a prolonged period of time. With one axis of this type of mount aligned to the celestial pole, the telescope can rotate along lines parallel to the celestial equator or can follow any object in the sky, as the Earth rotates.

(d) *Maksutov*: a reflecting telescope with some of the characteristics of a Cassegrain telescope. The incoming light passes through a spherically-figured corrector lens near the 'top' of the telescope's tube, is reflected from a spherically-figured main mirror, then is secondarily reflected back from a slightly convex mirror, or reflective spot, on the back of the corrector lens, and finally comes to a focus after passing through a hole in the main mirror. The lens of an eyepiece can then magnify the light at the focal point, and so the distant object can be studied in a way that is similar to the Cassegrain telescope. Like the Cassegrain, the Maksutov design allows for a telescope of relatively long focal length to be contained in a relatively short, compact, and portable tube.

(e) *Newtonian*: a reflecting telescope in which the incoming light is reflected from a concave parabolic mirror, and before the returning light cone reaches its focal point it is again reflected to the side by a flat secondary mirror placed at a 45-degree angle to the axis of the light path, enabling the light to come to a focus at one side of the tube. At this focal point, the lens of an eyepiece can magnify the image, and so the distant object can be studied. This design was the invention of Sir Isaac Newton (1642-1727), an English astronomer, physicist, and mathematician.

(f) *Ritchey-Chrétien*: a reflecting telescope used primarily for photographing the heavens. Such a telescope may have a spherically-figured mirror, and may incorporate other features in order to produce a sharp image over a wide field . This design is named after George Willis Ritchey and Henri Chrétien.

(g) *Schmidt-Cassegrain* (sometimes called "SCT"): a reflecting telescope in which the Cassegrain design (See above.) has an additional feature, namely a corrector lens at the 'top' end of the telescope. Though this lens may appear to be plane and flat, it is actually figured in a slightly curved and exotic fashion. This modern adaptation of Cassegrain's design is named after Bernhard Schmidt, a German optical worker at Hamburg Observatory, who first used it. His name is given also to the Schmidt Camera which is of similar design and employed exclusively for photographing areas of the sky.

terminator: on the surface of a planet or of a Moon of the Solar System: the line between the sunlit side and the dark side.

terrestrial: earthlike or pertaining to planet Earth.

tide: the periodic rising and falling (or change in elevation) of the Earth's oceans, caused by the gravitational pull of the Moon, and also, to a lesser extent by the gravitational pull of the Sun.

transit: the visible passage of an apparently smaller celestial object across the disk of an apparently larger celestial object, such as the transit of Mercury or Venus across the disk of the Sun at the time of the planet's **inferior conjunction**, or the passage of a Jovian satellite, such as Io or Europa, across the disk of Jupiter.

transparency: the clarity of the atmosphere over an observing site, shown by the absence of clouds, dust, water vapour, and atmospheric particles of any kind. Amateur astronomers often rate the transparency of a particular site during an observing session on a scale of 1 to 10, with 1 being very poor and 10 being spectacularly clear. Note that both *seeing and transparency* are rated, in order completely to describe observing conditions at a particular time and location. (See also **seeing**.)

umbra: (1) in describing a solar or a lunar eclipse: the inner and darker shadow (as opposed to the **penumbra**) of the Moon or of the Earth. In the case of a solar eclipse, from within the Moon's umbra, an observer on Earth is able to see a total solar eclipse (as opposed to a partial solar eclipse seen by those who are within the Moon's penumbra). In the case of a lunar eclipse, if the Full Moon moves completely within the Earth's umbra, the situation is called a Total Lunar Eclipse (as opposed to the situation with the Moon partly within the umbra and partly within the penumbra at mid-eclipse, in which case the situation is called a Partial Lunar Eclipse).

(2) in describing solar observing: the darker, central core of a sunspot. This core is surrounded by a lighter region, which is called the **penumbra**.

Universal Time (UT): the standard solar time at the prime meridian (0 degrees longitude), which passes through the Old Observatory at Greenwich, England. Astronomers usually prefer to use **UT** in order to avoid repeatedly converting to local time at various locations around the world.

Uranus: the seventh major planet in our Solar System. Like Jupiter and Saturn, it is a large, gaseous planet.

Venus: the second major planet in our Solar System. Like Earth, it is a solid, "rocky" planet with an atmosphere. In fact, it has a much denser and hotter atmosphere than has Earth. In size and mass, Venus is quite similar to Earth.

white dwarf: a hot, though somewhat dim, star, with a mass similar to the Sun, but smaller than the Sun, and having a much greater density.

year: the precisely defined time for one orbit of the Earth around the Sun. The so-called sidereal year, by which is meant the interval between the Sun twice appearing in precisely the same position in the sky, as viewed among background stars, is 365.256363 days.

zenith: the point in the sky that is directly overhead.

zodiac (literally, "the circle of animals," because of the "animal constellations" involved): a band around the sky, 8 degrees in width on either side of the ecliptic (See **ecliptic**.). This 16-degree wide band is inclined 23 $^1/_2$ degrees to the celestial equator (See **celestial equator**.), which it intersects at the points known as the **Vernal Equinox** and the **Autumnal Equinox**. Within this band are found the Sun, the Moon, all of the major planets with the occasional exceptions of Pluto and Venus, and a large number of the asteroids or minor planets. Traditionally, and in the pseudo-science of astrology, there are 12 constellations (Aries, Taurus, Gemini, Cancer, Leo, Virgo, Libra, Scorpius, Sagittarius, Capricornus, Aquarius, and Pisces) listed as part of the zodiac. However, on checking a modern star atlas, we can easily see that the ecliptic passes through a 13th constellation, Ophiuchus, and the zodiac passes through at least a small portion of an additional 7 constellations, namely, Cetus, Orion, Auriga, Hydra, Sextans, Crater, and Corvus.

Zodiacal Light: an inverted cone of light seen on clear, Moonless nights in the western sky, beginning at the end of astronomical twilight in late winter and spring evenings. The light extends upward, sometimes 30 or 40 degrees or more, along the ecliptic. Similarly, it is to be seen, as an inverted cone or narrow pyramid, before the beginning of morning astronomical twilight in late summer and autumn in clear, dark, moonless skies, low in the east, and extending upward along the ecliptic. The Zodiacal Light, which is occasionally as bright as, and rarely brighter than, the Milky Way, is caused by the reflection of sunlight from the countless billions of tiny dust particles that are present as a disk in the inner Solar System and extend out as far as the orbit of Mars. Under very transparent, moonless skies, the glow of the Zodiacal Light can sometimes be observed across the entire sky. On such occasions, this glow widens at the spot that is directly opposite the Sun, and it becomes a large elliptical concentration of light about 10 degrees, or more, in diameter. This concentration of light at the anti-solar point on the ecliptic is called the *Gegenschein* or *Counterglow*. It is seen much less frequently than the more usual "inverted cone above the horizon."

26

An Appendix of Useful Information

The Constellations

Constellations are areas or regions of the sky that have precisely defined boundaries. There are 88 constellations. As shown in Chapter 2, certain constellations can never be seen from mid-northern latitudes. These are in the areas of the sky above the region of the South Pole. Other constellations are in areas of the sky that never set. This chart names all of the constellations and gives information about finding them on the star maps.

Name	Where Found	Name	Where Found	Name	Where Found
Andromeda	1	Crux	S	Octans	S
Antlia	2	Cygnus	3	Ophiuchus	3
Apus	S	Delphinus	4	Orion	1
Aquarius	5	Dorado	S	Pavo	S
Aquila	4	Draco	C	Pegasus	4
Ara	S	Equuleus	4	Perseus	5
Aries	1	Eridanus	6	Phoenix	S
Auriga	1	Fornax	6	Pictor	S
Bootes	2	Gemini	1	Pisces	5
Caelum	1,S	Grus	5,S	Piscis Austrinus	5
Camelopardalis	1	Hercules	3	Puppis	1,S
Cancer	1	Horologium	S	Pyxis	2
Canis Major	1	Hydra	2	Reticulum	S
Canis Minor	1	Hydrus	S	Sagitta	4
Capricornus	4	Indus	S	Sagittarius	4
Carina	S	Lacerta	4	Scorpius	4
Cassiopeia	C	Leo	1	Serpens	3
Centaurus	3	Leo Minor	(1)	Sextans	2
Cepheus	C	Lepus	1	Taurus	6
Cetus	5	Libra	3	Triangulum	5
Chamaeleon	S	Lupus	3	Triangulum Australe	S
Circinus	S	Lynx	1	Tucana	S
Columba	1	Lyra	3	Ursa Major	C
Coma Berenices	2	Mensa	S	Ursa Minor	C
Corona Australis	4	Microscopium	S	Vela	2,S
Corona Borealis	2	Monoceros	1	Virgo	2
Corvus	2	Musca	S	Volans	S
Crater	2	Norma	S	Vulpecula	4

Notes:

- The number after the name of the constellation is the number of *one of the star maps* on which that constellation may be found. *Most* of the constellations may be found on *several* star maps. The number 1, for example, may mean that this constellation is found on star maps 1, 2, and 3.
- The letter S indicates that this is a constellation in the southern sky and is not well seen from the mid-northern latitudes.
- A number *and* the letter S, such as found after the constellations Puppis and Vela, indicates that *part* of the constellation is shown on one of the star maps, but that this southern constellation is *not completely* seen from mid-northern latitudes.
- The letter C after several of the constellations indicates that these are circumpolar constellations. When observed from mid-northern latitudes, they do not set. They will be found on *all six* star maps.
- The number (1) after Leo Minor indicates that this constellation is not marked on any of the star maps, but its area is shown on Map 1 and other star maps. It is located between Leo and Ursa Major, but it has no bright stars.

Basic Solar System Data

Object	Diameter (km)	Rotation Period (days)	Distance from Sun[2] (millions of km.)	AU[3]	Period of Revolution around Sun	Number of Satellites[4]
Sun	1392000	25-35[1]				
Mercury	4879	58.60	57.9	0.39	87.97 days	0
Venus	12104	243.00	108.2	0.72	224.70 days	0
Earth	12756	1.00	149.6	1.00	365.26 days	1
Mars	6794	1.03	227.9	1.52	686.98 days	2
Jupiter	142980	0.41	778.4	5.20	11.86 years	61
Saturn	120540	0.44	1423.8	9.52	29.46 years	31
Uranus	51200	0.72	2868.7	19.18	84.01 years	21
Neptune	49530	0.67	4492.1	30.03	164.79 years	11
Pluto	2300	6.39	5926.5	39.62	247.69 years	1

Notes:
1. The rotation period of the Sun varies with its latitude. The shortest rotation period occurs at the equator; the longest occurs at high latitudes. The rotation period of Jupiter, also, varies slightly depending on latitude.
2. The distances given are the mean (or "average") distances.
3. AU means Astronomical Unit(s). 1 Astronomical Unit is the mean (or "average") distance between Sun and Earth, 149.6 million kilometres.
4. These numbers represent satellites discovered as of July, 2003.

Building a Realistic Model of the Solar System

Many models of the Solar System that have been constructed in the past are very incorrect and unrealistic because they do not follow the *same* scale for the *size of*, and the *distance between*, the objects representing the Sun and the planets. (For example, a model using a beach ball to represent the Sun would have to be at least 3 kilometres from end to end, or about the diameter of a small town, in order properly to represent the distance between the Sun and Pluto. A model using a baseball to represent the Earth would have to be at least 30 kilometres wide, or the diameter of a large city to represent the radius of Pluto's orbit.)

A proper model must incorporate the SAME SCALE FOR BOTH THE SIZE AND THE DISTANCE BETWEEN THE OBJECTS. By reducing (1) the numbers given for the equatorial diameters of the Solar System objects, and (2) the numbers given for the mean distances of the planets from the Sun, both by a factor of 20 billion (20 000 000 000), we can produce a model that will fit, or almost fit, within one or two buildings (extremely large buildings!) in Canada (with perhaps a little "cheating," in so far as we will assume that the planets are all on the same side of the Sun at one time, a fact that is almost never true).

Object	Size	→	Reduced	Distance from Sun	→	Reduced
Sun	1 392 000 km		69.6 mm	—		—
Mercury	4 879 km		0.24 mm	57.9 X 10[6] km		2.90 m
Venus	12 104 km		0.61 mm	108.2		5.41 m
Earth	12 756 km		0.64 mm	149.6		7.48 m
Mars	6 794 km		0.34 mm	227.9		11.40 m
Jupiter	142 980 km		7.15 mm	778.3		38.92 m
Saturn	120 540 km		6.03 mm	1 429.4		71.47 m
Uranus	51 120 km		2.56 mm	2 875.0		143.75 m
Neptune	49 530 km		2.48 mm	4 504.4		225.22 m
Pluto	2 300 km		0.12 mm	5 915.8		295.79 m

SETTING UP THE MODEL:

LOCATION: Two of the largest buildings in Canada, buildings that contain a Canadian Football League field, namely Skydome in Toronto and B.C. Place Stadium in Vancouver, are ideal settings for this model, but

> **By reducing the size of the Sun and planets, and the distances of the planets from the Sun, by a factor of 20 billion, we can produce a Solar System model that would fit in two of the country's largest buildings.**

a Canadian university football field, as found in the outdoor football stadia of many Canadian cities, can also provide an equally suitable site for this model of the Solar System. (Remember that, in Canadian football, the archaic unit known as the "yard" (0.914 m) is still used, that there are 110 of them between the goal lines, and that each goal area, or "end zone," is an additional 20 yards long.)

SUN: The Sun may be represented by a good-quality, **average-size orange** chosen from a supermarket. Place it **on the goal-line** at one end of the football field.

MERCURY: Mercury may be a **"micro-ball" from a ball-point pen**, and it should be placed **2/3 of the distance** from the orange (which was on the goal-line) **to the 5-yard line**.

VENUS: Venus may be a **"ball from a standard BIC ball-point pen,"** and it should be placed **one pace beyond the 5-yard line** (that is, about 1/5 of the distance between the 5-yard line and the 10-yard line).

EARTH: Earth may also be a **"ball from a standard BIC ball-point pen,"** and it should be placed **2/3 of the distance between the 5-yard line and the 10-yard line.**

MARS: Mars may be a **"micro-ball" from a ball-point pen**, and it should be placed **half-way between the 10-yard line and the 15-yard line.**

JUPITER: Jupiter may be an **average-size peanut**, and it should be placed **half-way between the 40-yard line and the 45-yard line.**

SATURN: Saturn may be a **small pea** from the end of the pod (from the "peas and beans section" of the garden), and it should be placed **2/3 of the distance between the 35-yard line and the 30-yard line** on the **other side of the field**. (Remember that we have crossed the 55-yard line, which is mid-field, and are now in the other half of the field.)

URANUS: Uranus may be **a seed from a tomato**, and it should be placed **on a seat in Row 10 of the "end-zone bleachers"** at the far end of the field.

NEPTUNE: Neptune may also be **a tomato seed**, and it should be placed **at the near perimeter of the fence that surrounds the parking lot just beyond the "end-zone bleachers."**

PLUTO: Pluto may be a **microscopic ("almost invisible") speck of dust**, and it should be placed **at the far perimeter of the fence that surrounds the parking lot just beyond the stadium.**

Notes: (1) This model may be called the "20-billion-to-1," "football-stadium" model. Remember that the objects were aligned in a row in one direction from "the Sun," a situation that almost never occurs. A much more realistic model would have the objects scattered around the region to represent their proper positions at a specific date. Such a model would, of course, occupy an area with twice the diameter of this one.

(2) Note that Neptune and Pluto are actually in the parking lot, not in the stadium. Neptune could have been within the stadium only if the orange representing the Sun had been placed behind the bleachers at one end of the stadium, and then the objects representing the planets (out to Neptune) had been spread out to the far end of the bleachers at the other end. It is preferable, however, to place the object representing the Sun on the goal line, in order that the relative distances between the objects representing the Sun and the planets may be more accurately represented and more easily appreciated.

List of the 30 Brightest Stars

This is the list of the 30 stars that have the greatest apparent brightness as seen from the Earth. (Actually, the list includes 31 stars since it begins with our Sun.) Many of these stars are marked on the star maps.

The number after each star is the apparent magnitude. The letter "v" indicates that the star varies in brightness. The letter "S" indicates that it is a star in the southern part of the sky and cannot be seen from the mid-northern latitudes.

Star	Apparent Mag.
Sun	-26.70
Sirius	-1.46
Canopus	-0.72 (S)
α Centauri	-0.29 (S)
Arcturus	-0.06
Vega	0.04
Capella	0.08
Rigel	0.14
Procyon	0.37
Achernar	0.45 (S)
Betelgeuse	0.45 (v)
β Centauri	0.60 (S)
Altair	0.76
α Crucis	0.77 (S)
Aldebaran	0.85
Spica	0.96
Antares	1.00 (v)
Pollux	1.15
Fomalhaut	1.16
Deneb	1.25
β Crucis	1.26 (S)
Regulus	1.35
Adhara (ε CMa)	1.50
Castor	1.58
γ Crucis	1.59 (S)
Shaula (λ Sco)	1.62
Bellatrix (γ Ori)	1.63
El Nath (β Tau)	1.65
Miaplacidus (β Car)	1.68 (S)
Alnilam (ε Ori)	1.70
Alnair (α Gru)	1.74 (S)

List of "Naked-Eye" Variable Stars

Below is a list of 10 variable stars that can be observed with the unaided eye. All except Mira are bright enough to be observed in this way throughout their cycles; Mira at its faintest is much too faint to be seen in this way, but for part of its cycle it can easily be seen "naked-eye."

All of these stars are marked on the star maps. Locate them with certainty by using a star atlas. Then label them on the star maps just as Mira has already been labelled on Maps 1, 5, and 6. Detailed maps of the areas of the four marked by an asterisk (*) are given in Chapter 15. The columns headed "Max." and "Min." list the magnitude of the stars when at maximum magnitude or greatest brightness and when at minimum magnitude or least brightness. The column headed "Period" gives the length in days (unless otherwise stated) of the star's cycle or period of variability. Two of the stars have a second, much longer period, which is in addition to the shorter one. This second period may not be noticeable to the observer. The column headed "RADec#" gives the coordinates (right ascension and declination) of the star, so that it may be easily located in a star atlas. In the RADec# column, the first two numbers indicate the hour of right ascension; the second two numbers indicate the minutes of right ascension; "+" indicates its declination is north and "–" indicates it is south; the final two numbers indicate the degrees of declination.

Star	Magnitude Max.	Min.	Period	RADec#
Mira (o Ceti) *	3.4	9.5	332 d.	0214-03
Rho Per	3.3	4.0	33-5, 1100	0258+38
Beta Per *	2.1	3.3	2.86731	0301+40
Lambda Tau	3.5	4.0	3.952952	0355+12
Eta Gem	3.1	3.9	233.4	0608+22
Zeta Gem	3.6	4.2	10.15073	0658+20
Alpha Her	3.0	4.0	50-130, 6yrs.	1710+14
Beta Lyrae *	3.4	4.3	12.93702	1846+33
Eta Aql	3.5	4.3	7.176641	1947+00
Delta Cep *	3.5	4.4	5.366341	2225+57

A List of the 10 Nearest "Naked Eye" Stars

The nearest star of all, of course, is our Sun. It is approximately 150 000 000 kilometres from the Earth. Light from the Sun, travelling at 300 000 kilometres per second, takes only about 8 minutes to reach the Earth. We can, therefore, say that the Sun is 8 light-minutes from the Earth. All the other stars are much, much farther away. Their distance is measured in light years, which is the distance light travels in a year.

The list of the 50 stars nearest to our Sun (published in the *Observer's Handbook* of the Royal Astronomical Society of Canada) includes many stars that are much too faint to be seen with the naked eye or with binoculars.

The list of ten stars presented here includes *only* the stars that are bright enough to be seen with the unaided eye (brighter than magnitude 6). The first number after the star indicates that star's distance in light-years from our Sun. The second number indicates approximately its position on most standard lists of nearest stars. The letter "S" indicates that the star is in the southern part of the sky and cannot be seen from mid-northern latitudes.

The *nearest star of all to our Sun* is a companion to the Alpha Centauri system called Proxima Centauri. It is much too faint to be seen with the unaided eye. Its distance is 4.22 light-years.

Star	Distance (ly)	Listed Order	
α Centauri	4.3	2	(S)
Sirius	8.6	7	
ε Eridani	10.8	10	
61 Cygni	11.1	12	
ε Indi	11.2	13	(S)
Procyon	11.4	16	
τ Ceti	11.8	20	
0² Eridani	15.7	43	
70 Ophiuchi	16.1	46	
Altair	16.5	48	

The Greek Alphabet

The Greek alphabet is used in the Bayer System of naming stars, as noted in Chapter 5.

α alpha	ι iota	ρ rho
β beta	κ kappa	σ sigma
γ gamma	λ lambda	τ tau
δ delta	μ mu	υ upsilon
ε epsilon	ν nu	φ phi
ζ zeta	ξ xi	χ chi
η eta	o omicron	ψ psi
θ theta	π pi	ω omega